THE
LANSDOWNE
ERA

The Lansdowne Era

Victoria College, 1946–1963

Edited by Edward B. Harvey

Published for the UNIVERSITY OF VICTORIA by
McGILL-QUEEN'S UNIVERSITY PRESS
Montreal & Kingston • London • Ithaca

ISBN 978-0-7735-3436-0

Legal deposit third quarter 2008
Bibliothèque nationale du Québec

Printed in Canada

McGill-Queen's University Press acknowledges the support of the Canada Council for the Arts for our publishing program. We also acknowledge the financial support of the Government of Canada through the Book Publishing Industry Development Program (BPIDP) for our publishing activities.

Library and Archives Canada Cataloguing in Publication

The Lansdowne era : Victoria College, 1946–1963 / edited by Edward B. Harvey.

ISBN 978-0-7735-3436-0

1. Victoria College (B.C.)–History. 2. Victoria College (B.C.)–Alumni and alumnae–Biography. 3. Victoria College (B.C.)–Faculty–Biography. I. Harvey, Edward B., 1939– II. University of Victoria (B.C.)

LE3.B88L36 2008   378.711'28   C2008-903197-0

This book was designed and typeset by studio oneonone in Sabon 10.6/14

This book is dedicated to Peter Smith (1933–2006), teacher, colleague, and friend, and all the students who attended Victoria College during the Lansdowne era (1946–1963)

CONTENTS

PART THREE | CONCLUSION

ix

A MESSAGE FROM THE PREMIER

9 July 2008

I am pleased to congratulate the University of Victoria on their publication of the history book, *The Lansdowne Era*.

This special book records the 1946 to 1963 period when Victoria College was at the Lansdowne campus – a beautiful and quintessentially southern Vancouver Island setting with its green lawns and distinctive Garry Oaks. It commemorates the experiences and thoughts of former students of Victoria College in the Lansdowne years, and highlights the economic, social and demographic changes that led to the creation of the University of Victoria.

The contents of this publication will give readers a wonderful opportunity to reflect on the challenges and successes the Lansdowne generation experienced during the post war era. Their inspiring stories will surely touch the hearts and minds of people of all ages.

As we celebrate our province's 150th anniversary, I want to thank everyone involved in this publication for recording an important part of British Columbia's history.

Sincerely,

Gordon Campbell
Premier

FOREWORD

DAVID H. TURPIN

The University of Victoria benefits from a proud history of academic excellence and dedication to post-secondary education. This commitment has existed in our community for more than a century, beginning in 1903 with the opening of Victoria College, proceeding through the establishment of the University of Victoria in 1963, and culminating with a university that today is consistently recognized as one of the finest in Canada.

The existence of the University of Victoria is in large part because of the vision of Victoria College faculty, staff, and students and of many leading members of our community. Each of those who campaigned for the creation of the University of Victoria knew that a full-fledged post-secondary institution, founded on the standards of excellence by which the college had become known, would have enormous benefits locally, across the country, and anywhere its alumni shared their knowledge and skills. Over the years, their dream has been realized in innumerable ways.

This book concerns the time period immediately prior to the opening of the University of Victoria. The Lansdowne era of Victoria College, between 1946 and 1963, also coincided with an incredible period in Canadian life. Canadians had emerged from the shadow of the Second World War optimistic and ready to embrace a new abundance of opportunities. The postwar era brought rapid economic expansion, a booming population, and an unprecedented demand for post-secondary education. The collected memories and insights of former students and faculty included in this book provide first-hand accounts of what it was like to be young, Canadian, and fully immersed in one of the most dynamic times in our history.

As the changes that swept the country reached the Lansdowne campus, evidence of exceptional academic achievement abounded: three Victoria College graduates were named Rhodes Scholars for British Columbia between 1953 and 1956. In the same decade, seven alumni earned Governor General's Gold Medals for highest graduating averages upon completing their studies at the University of British Columbia. In the full spectrum of professions and disciplines, the accomplishments of college graduates have been widely recognized and admired. Clearly, there was something truly special about the education offered by Victoria College.

Within the context of sweeping social and economic transformations, our editor and Victoria College alumnus, Dr Edward Harvey, and his team of contributors have woven a deeper understanding of what it meant to be immersed in the Lansdowne era. Their contributions go beyond the academic realm to incorporate recollections of the social and athletic elements of a well-rounded undergraduate experience. On behalf of the University of Victoria, the alumni of Victoria College, and its former faculty and staff members, I would like to express my personal congratulations to Dr Harvey and a sincere thank you to each of the writers who shared in the creation of this wonderful book of history and personal experience.

The Lansdowne Era stands as a fitting tribute to Dr Peter Smith (1933–2006). Peter was a much-admired colleague who, as a graduate of Victoria College and as an influential member of the University of Victoria community, embodied the finest qualities of scholarship, collegiality, and academic leadership. It is in honour of his memory that *The Lansdowne Era* has been produced. Net proceeds from the sale of each copy of this book will support student awards in Peter Smith's name.

I hope you enjoy your reading of *The Lansdowne Era*.

David H. Turpin, PHD, FRSC
President and Vice-Chancellor
University of Victoria
March 2008

ACKNOWLEDGMENTS

While over the years I have authored or co-authored other books, I have previously edited only one, and that dealt with issues of economic and social-institutional modernization, not a history of an important period in the life of an academic institution. Fairly, then, any defects in the present work may be laid at my intellectual doorstep. Happily, a number of people have done much to support the realization of *The Lansdowne Era* project and helped to ensure its veracity as a portrait of the period. I thank them all.

In particular, I would like to acknowledge a number of people at the University of Victoria who have assisted me in innumerable ways. David Turpin, president and vice-chancellor of the University of Victoria, and his executive and staff have been steadfast supporters of the project. Don Jones, director of Alumni Affairs at UVic, was given the responsibility of acting as project coordinator, and he has discharged that responsibility with quiet, consistent competence. I would also like to mention two other members of the Alumni Affairs office. Lynn Wilson cheerfully and capably dealt with my many questions and requests for information, and one of her colleagues in Alumni Affairs, Mike McNeney, provided helpful comments and invaluable information on UVic's Distinguished Alumni Awards. Throughout this project, the university archivist, Lara J. Wilson, and her staff have time and again helped with the answering of questions, the location of materials, and the scanning of photographs. They are the reason why the University of Victoria Archives are such an outstanding and researcher-friendly place.

This book would not have been possible without the many contributions of former Lansdowne students and faculty, which enabled a compelling portrait of the period to emerge, captured from a diversity of perspectives. The vast majority of those asked to participate accepted. These contributors then proceeded to deliver the sort of insightful, well-written pieces that make editorial work a pleasure, not a trial. In short, people really "stepped up to the plate" for the Lansdowne era, and that says something about the values and qualities inherent in that time. Many thanks to all of them.

Several people at McGill-Queen's University Press (MQUP), the publishers of the book, have done much to make this a better volume. I first want to thank Philip Cercone, executive director and senior editor of the Press, who from our first meeting in December 2006 has been a source of strong support and wise guidance. Joan McGilvray, coordinating editor at MQUP, and Elizabeth Hulse, the copy editor, have been patiently supportive and creatively insightful in bringing this book to publication.

Finally, I would like to express my thanks to a number of other people. Mary Jean Smith, Peter's widow, has been a source of kindness and support throughout the project. I hope she finds the book a worthy memorial to Peter and the large intellectual and leadership contributions he made over his distinguished career, first to Victoria College and then to the University of Victoria. Ivor Alexander, a loyal friend and a Lansdowne era contemporary, is one of the people with whom I discuss writing projects. His comments have always been insightful and a source of intellectual support. This book includes two drawings by Edward Goodall. Permission to use these has most kindly been provided to me by his son, Richard Goodall, a Lansdowne era contemporary. As she has on countless other occasions, my wife, Lorna Marsden, took time from her own demanding responsibilities and projects to listen, read, and comment and in this case – since she was also a member of the Lansdowne era – write a contribution for the book and a memorial for our friend, the Honourable Justice James (Jim) D. Taylor. I am also pleased to acknowledge the fine research assistance provided to the project by Karen Chester and Richard Liu. Jan Given-King, who has helped me with many writing projects over the past twenty years, did a consummate job of pulling together disparate materials to produce a viable manuscript.

Edward B. Harvey
Toronto 2008

THE
LANSDOWNE
ERA

THE LANSDOWNE ERA:

A TIME OF CHANGE

EDWARD B. HARVEY

This book is about the years between 1946 and 1963, when Victoria College was at the Lansdowne campus, a beautiful and quintessentially southern Vancouver Island setting, with its green lawns and distinctive Garry oaks. In some respects, this verdant and pacific environment was deceptive. In fact, the Lansdowne era was a time of dynamic change. It was a time when the steps were taken that would lead to the establishment, in 1963, of the University of Victoria as a fully autonomous, degree-granting institution embodying the unique spirit rooted in its founding years. The achievement of full autonomy was important because from its birth in 1902 until 1963, Victoria College had always operated with the sponsorship of an established university – initially McGill and subsequently the University of British Columbia.

In short, the Lansdowne period was a major precursor to the University of Victoria. This evolution was fostered by major economic, demographic, and social changes that exerted a transformative effect on the people and institutions of Canada. Later in this introduction, I examine these changes and how they affected Victoria College during the Lansdowne era.

This book is dedicated to Peter Smith and the students of the Lansdowne years. I first met Peter in 1960 when I was a student at Victoria College and he, a freshly minted Yale PhD, had just been appointed to the faculty. During his long and distinguished career at Victoria College and the University of Victoria, Peter served in many capacities, including chair of the Classics Department, associate dean of Arts, and dean of Fine Arts.

In more recent years, my wife and I saw Peter and his wife, Mary Jean, with increasing frequency. We last enjoyed his company in early August 2006 when he and Mary Jean were our guests in Toronto during the International Tennis Championships hosted by York University. Tragically, Peter died suddenly and unexpectedly shortly after his return to Victoria. He was seventy-three years of age. Peter and I would often talk about the Lansdowne era of Victoria College. During these conversations, he almost invariably focused on the individuals who were part of that time. He had exceptional powers

The Lansdowne campus of Victoria College (c. mid-1950s)
enjoyed an idyllic setting. The clock tower of the Young Building
is seen in the background. A magnificent Garry oak graces
the foreground.

of recollection, and his observations were characterized by insight, generosity, and a gentle sense of humour. After these discussions, I came away with the conviction that, if one were to do a book about the Lansdowne era, the best approach would be to build it around the lives and experiences of the people who were part of it. That is the path this book has followed.

It is important to make clear what this book does and does not do. In his 1993 history, *A Multitude of the Wise*, Peter Smith dedicates pages 98 to 132 – about 16 per cent of the book – to an account of the Lansdowne period. He did so with his usual insightful thoroughness, and I do not propose to replicate what he has already done so well. Instead, I have built *The Lansdowne Era* on three broad thematic pillars. First, the era (1946–63) coincided with a time when Canada experienced transformative changes of an economic, demographic, and social nature. This chapter will examine some of these changes and how they profoundly affected our lives and institutions, including, of course, Victoria College.

Second, in planning this book, I felt it was important to give voice to the experiences and thoughts of some of those individuals who had been students at Victoria College in the Lansdowne years. I was convinced that there was no better way of doing so than to invite a number of these former students to prepare written contributions. The vast majority of those invited to do so enthusiastically agreed, and they are to be thanked for making Part Two of the book possible. I will return to the written contributions later in this chapter.

Third, as I have already observed, the dynamic and change-filled Lansdowne period forged the foundations for what was to become the University of Victoria, an autonomous, degree-granting institution. The nationwide processes of economic, demographic, and social change which I alluded to earlier, and which I will address in greater detail shortly, unquestionably posed large problems, but they also presented even larger possibilities. Wise leadership during the Lansdowne era captured the spirit of this new postwar generation, and that leadership has had lasting consequences. For although the University of Victoria is a much larger and more complex institution than Victoria College, it continues to embody qualities that made Victoria College such a fine place. I explore this theme in Part Three, the final section of the book, "The Lansdowne Era: An Enduring Tradition."

POSTWAR CANADA: A SOCIETY IN TRANSFORMATION

Although many Canadians and Americans served in the military during the Second World War – and many were casualties – both countries escaped the physical devastation that afflicted large areas of Europe and Asia (with the obvious exception of Pearl Harbor, although Hawaii was not an American state at the time). The postwar reconstruction challenges in many other nations were on a huge scale, but Canada had the good fortune to be richly endowed with resources critical to reconstruction. In addition, postwar decolonization, which would present Canada with many new competitors, was yet to come. Accordingly, our exports expanded, and the country experienced rapid economic growth characterized by strong employment gains and low inflation. This was the "external demand" side of Canada's postwar economic situation.

The nation's internal, or domestic, demand contributed to economic growth in two main ways. First, the war years had been characterized by many privations. The economy was overwhelmingly geared toward the war effort. Consumer goods, such as cars, took a distinctly second place or were even non-existent. With the end of war, the factories that had been producing war goods quickly shifted to the production of consumer items. This was good business because, to use an economist's term, the nation's population was suffering from an extreme case of pent-up demand. As new consumer goods once again became available, they were snapped up in the marketplace, providing further impetus to employment and income growth.

But there was another important factor in the economic growth arising from increased domestic demand. I mentioned above that many types of consumption had been put "on hold" during the war years. This, to a large extent, was also the case with marriage and the raising of children. Despite the early onset of the Cold War, Canada's postwar situation was characterized by considerable optimism. It seemed like a good world in which to form a family and have children.

The age at marriage was young. As Census of Canada data show, in 1951 the median age at marriage was 24.8 years for men and 22.0 for women. These figures had decreased slightly by 1956 to 24.5 for men and 21.6 for women. Further declines had occurred by 1961, when the median age at marriage reached 24.0 for men and 21.1 for women. The earliest comparable data is for 1940, when the median age at marriage was 26.4 for men and 23.2 for women.[1] The most recent data (2004) shows median age at marriage of 27.0 for men and 24.0 for women.[2] The birth rate (live births per 1,000 women) was high in the postwar years. In 1951 it was 3.503; by 1956, it had risen to 3.858, though by 1961 a very slight decline to 3.840 had occurred. By way of comparison, the birth rate in 1936 was 2.696, a reflection of the effects of the great economic depression of the 1930s.[3] The most recent data (2005) shows a birth rate of 1.61.[4]

This pattern of high fertility, which lasted until about 1964, was the cause of the demographic explosion commonly referred to as the baby boom. It was a phenomenon with huge consequences, starting in the 1950s and carrying on into the twenty-first century. The initial impact was seen in a dramatic increase in school enrolments and growing demand for teachers. These would affect post-secondary institutions across Canada and were certainly felt at the Normal School and at Victoria College after its merger in 1956 with the Normal School. By the 1970s, youth unemployment became an issue in Canada as increasing numbers of boomers entered the labour market. That was an era which saw a proliferation of government "make-work" programs, including Opportunities For Youth (OFY) and the Local Initiatives Program (LIP). The subsequent Federal Labour Intensive Program suffered the unhappy acronym FLIP. As the twentieth century neared its end and the twenty-first century dawned, boomer issues began to centre around such matters as pressures on the health care system and our various public pension initiatives.

But in the immediate postwar period, the high rate of family formation was a major source of stimulus to the domestic economy in such areas as housing and consumables of all kinds. Victoria was no exception to this trend.

The bottom line of all this economic growth was that between 1945 and 1970 the real after-tax incomes of Canadians doubled, something that has never happened since. With growing prosperity, Canadians increasingly consumed not only goods but services, including education of all types. This demand presented great new opportunities for universities, including Victoria College. The large gains in employment and income meant that governments, even with politically popular rates of taxation, had far more scope for spending on both physical and social infrastructure.

In the realm of social infrastructure, there were several reasons why increased investment in education became an important priority. A key factor was that Canada was becoming much more urban and industrial. The occupational structure of employment was changing. A more educated and skilled labour force was needed. Many immigrants from war-ravaged Europe came to Canada in the immediate postwar period and brought important skills with them. However, policy thinkers recognized the risks inherent in an over-dependence on immigration as a source of labour force skills. Although immigrants would continue to be welcome, greater domestic self-sufficiency was essential. Investment in education was a critical path to achieving that self-sufficiency.

Policy thinkers also recognized that the great demographic changes emanating from the postwar baby boom would mean, in the years to come, a massive increase in the numbers of young people who would have to be educated. It became increasingly urgent to train the future teachers in even greater numbers. Public policy also reflected a concern with managing the rate at which baby boomers entered the labour force in order to avoid politically unpopular and economically wasteful developments such as rising unemployment and underemployment. Extending formal education, lowering dropout rates, and diversifying educational options would all prove to be useful policy instruments.

Public-sector investment in education, including post-secondary education, was a particularly popular policy. The parents of the baby boomers could remember the "dirty thirties" and the privations of the war years. They wanted more – much more – for their children. As the decade of the 1950s progressed, many of the pre–baby boom young people of that era became increasingly aware of just how the times were changing and that, increasingly, post-secondary education would be an important key to success in life. Correspondingly, governments exhibited increased interest in supporting the development of such opportunities.

All of this shifted into high gear when, in 1957, the USSR launched its earth-orbiting Sputnik satellite. The shock waves from this event, given the prevailing Cold War environment, permeated virtually every aspect of life in the United States. Public officials were galvanized into urgent action by the event itself and the pressures of an increasingly anxious population. Money poured into education, science, and technology. Inevitably, Canada followed.

How did the economic and demographic forces just described affect Victoria College in the Lansdowne years? Between 1921 and 1946 the college had made its home at Craigdarroch Castle. In *A Multitude of the Wise*, Peter Smith describes this building as "perched on a conspicuous rise above Victoria's old Rockland residential district, not far from Government House." He goes on to describe Craigdarroch as "an honest-to-goodness-castle, of spectacular Scottish baronial design, with walls of rough-hewn granite and sandstone, soaring turret and chimneys; and angular red-slate roofs."[5] It had at one time been the private residence of Robert Dunsmuir and his family. Dunsmuir, a talented entrepreneur, had immigrated to Vancouver Island in 1850 and proceeded to make a fortune in coal mining.

Craigdarroch Castle was adequately suited to house about two hundred students a year. This situation, however, came to an abrupt end in 1946 as returned Second Word War veterans took up government subsidies designed to assist them in securing a post-secondary education. As can be seen in the neighbouring table, Victoria College's regular-session enrolment in the 1946–47 academic year soared to 717 students, 380 of whom were veterans. The overcrowding created a dangerous situation. As one faculty member observed, "At least 50 students would lose their lives in the event of a fire. The staff members would undoubtedly stay to try and get the young people out and we'd all perish – God help us!"[6] The disgruntled students marched on Victoria's Legislative Buildings in the fall of 1946, and a petition bearing 14,243 signatures was presented to the premier.

Change followed quickly. On the weekend of 15 November 1946, the entire paraphernalia of post-secondary education was moved from Craigdarroch to the much more spacious Lansdowne campus. Lansdowne, which had served as a military hospital during the Second World War, was home to the Provincial Normal School at the time of the move. Victoria College and the Normal School would exist in relative harmony as independent institutions for nearly a decade. Then, effective 1 September 1956, the Normal School would be merged with Victoria College, to become the Faculty of Education.

Managing Victoria College during the Lansdowne period was not an easy task, particularly during the 1950s, as enrolment (and therefore space) pressures became increasingly pronounced. Harry Hickman was appointed principal of Victoria College in 1952. Born in Wataskiwin, Alberta, in 1909, Hickman had obtained a bachelor's degree in honours French in 1930 from the University of British Columbia, receiving the Governor General's Gold Medal for standing first in his graduating class. He then served as a sessional lecturer at the University of British Columbia and a schoolteacher at Victoria High until 1938, when a French government scholarship enabled him to attend the Université de Paris to pursue doctoral studies. War intervened and Hickman returned to Victoria, where he joined the faculty of Victoria College, serving as head of the Department of Modern Languages from 1939 to 1963. Between 1947 and 1948 he completed his doctoral studies at the Université de Paris and then returned to Victoria College and rapidly rose in the administration, serving as vice-principal in 1951 and a year later attaining full professorship and becoming principal of the college.

Harry Hickman had visionary qualities. He saw clearly the need to expand course offerings and infrastructure at Victoria College in order to move the institution beyond being a two-year college. In his "Principal's Message" in the 1957–58 edition of the *Tower*, Victoria College's yearbook, he observed:

After one or two years at Victoria College, three-fourths of the students will be leaving, either to continue University studies elsewhere or to commence teaching in the schools of British Columbia. The remainder will be welcomed back in September to Second Year Arts or Education. This points up the fact that most of our students pass quickly through our halls. However, it is inevitable that in the near future our students will be able to spend three of four years on the campus, preparing for a degree in Arts, Science, or Education. That happy day, for which many plans are being made in campus extension building projects, faculty growth and library facilities, will give the College a greater maturity and an even more deeply seated tradition than it already enjoys. Professors will cease to be the only non-evanescent personalities.

Craigdarroch Castle (also known as Dunsmuir House) was home
to Victoria College before the move to the Lansdowne campus.
Drawing by Edward Goodall; c. 1950s.

The situation became more complex as enrolments continued to increase, often in an unpredictable manner. As Hickman observed in his 1958–59 "Principal's Message,"

> Every year at Victoria College is a good year, but some, like this year, are more hectic than others. Enrolment for the 1958–59 session was much higher than anticipated with a 50.9 percent increase in the College of Education and a 14.5 percent increase in Arts and Sciences. This unexpected registration resulted in serious overcrowding and taxing of facilities. The good spirit of the Faculty and students showed in their willingness to accept larger classes, and in their patience and co-operation when the Cafeteria, Chemistry and Student Activity huts were not ready.

But despite these complexities, Victoria College continued to make solid progress in the expansion of its facilities and in achieving the goal of becoming a full, four-year institution. This is reflected in Hickman's "Principal's Message" of 1959–60, where he observes:

Regular session enrolment at Victoria College, 1946–63*

Year	Men		Women		Total	Proportion of veterans	
	N	%	N	%	(N=100%)	N	%
1946–47	529	73.8	188	26.2	717	380	53.0
1947–48	319	66.7	159	33.3	478	126	26.4
1948–49	265	63.7	151	36.3	416	45	10.8
1949–50	256	66.1	131	33.9	387	12	3.1
1950–51	211	66.1	108	33.9	319	7	2.2
1951–52	222	70.3	94	29.7	316	3	0.9
1952–53	235	72.5	89	27.5	324	9	2.8
1953–54	196	67.6	94	32.4	290	2	0.7
1954–55	227	67.4	110	32.6	337	4	1.2
1955–56	266	67.3	129	32.7	395	2	0.5
1956–57	303	52.7	272	47.3	575**		
1957–58	364	54.2	308	45.8	672		
1958–59	453	52.1	416	47.9	869		
1959–60	577	54.4	484	45.6	1061		
1960–61	787	55.6	628	44.4	1415		
1961–62	968	55.6	773	44.4	1741		
1962–63	1067	57.7	782	42.3	1849		

Source: Data compiled by the Office of the University Archivist, University of Victoria, from Victoria College calendars.
*The regular session is September to April. These figures do not include enrolments in summer sessions, the evening program, or non-credit offerings.
**The increase in enrolment in this year is a reflection of the merger of the Normal School with Victoria College, effective 1 September 1956.

W. Harry Hickman, principal of Victoria College, 1952–63. Photo by Ken.

Each year at Victoria College is stimulating and different, because each year new students face the challenge of higher education. However, for many reasons 1960 is a year of particular historic significant on the campus. Now enrolled is the first Third Year class, composed of 72 members who will become the first students to complete a full degree course at Victoria College in May, 1961. This year is memorable, too, for the opening of the Gordon Head campus where a gymnasium and playing field are filling an important need in College life.

Harry Hickman had a clear set of goals for Victoria College. He pursued these goals in a reserved but effective fashion with government officials, business leaders, and other constituencies. His style of quiet but focused leadership was right for the times, and he deserves much credit for steering a steady course for the college through the challenging and changeful Lansdowne years and creating the foundations for an autonomous, degree-granting university. In the modern sense of university leadership, Hickman was not a "career administrator." Rather, he was an intellectual with a deep commitment to his field but also a powerful sense of institutional duty. Victoria College benefited greatly from these qualities. He was one of the most significant figures in establishing the foundation for what has become a highly successful university.

Apart from this introduction, *The Lansdowne Era* contains three sections. Part One consists of nine chapters. The first of these, the piece by Gordon Shrimpton, reflects on the life and work of Peter Smith. The remaining chapters comprising the first part deal with areas important to understanding the Lansdowne era.

The second, by Reginald Roy, examines the early years, including the influx of veterans and the impacts they had upon the college. In the following chapter, Norma Mickelson reflects on events and patterns of change at the Normal School during the Lansdowne period. The next two chapters, by Martin Segger, explore two important dimensions of the Lansdowne era: the buildings and the founding of the University of Victoria Art Collection. In her chapter, Anne Saddlemyer presents her recollections and analysis of what it was like to be a new, young English instructor at Lansdowne beginning in 1956. As Dr Saddlemyer documents, Professor Roger J. Bishop, head of the English Department during the Lansdowne period, played a key role in building up both the department and the library. It therefore seemed appropriate, in the following chapter, to reprint his piece entitled "Lansdowne Days, 1947–1963," which he first published in 1976, in "On the Way to the Ring," a special supplement of *The Ring*, a University of Victoria publication. The two final chapters deal with men's and women's athletics during the Lansdowne years. Kenneth McCulloch is the author of the chapter devoted to men's, while Susan Yates has taken responsibility for the chapter focused on women's.

Part Two contains nineteen contributions by former Lansdowne students. During the year 1946–63, over 12,000 students enrolled in the Victoria College regular session (see the table above). In consultation with other members of the University of Victoria community, an initial list of possible contributors was prepared. Most of these received a written invitation to contribute from David Turpin, the University of Victoria's president and vice-chancellor. Three considerations shaped this process. First, we wanted to obtain contributions from persons who represented different years of the Lansdowne era, and second, we were interested in ensuring that both women and men were properly represented.

The latter concern proved a challenge at times. Between the 1946–47 and 1955–56 academic years, women on average represented 32 per cent of the total Victoria College enrolment. Between the 1956–57 academic year and the final year of the Lansdowne period, 1962–63, the average enrolment of women increased to 45 per cent. This rise was largely a consequence of the change in 1956 by which the Normal School became a part of Victoria College. In that era, educational and occupational sex stereotyping was prevalent, and one of the ways in which it was reflected was in the large proportion of young women training to be elementary school teachers. At the end of the day, 37 per cent of the written contributions in Part Two were authored by women.

The third consideration shaping the identification and invitation of contributors was a desire to ensure that these writers would reflect many different fields of accomplishment. This goal proved quite successful. The contributors include people who have pursued their lives in a wide range of careers, including as artists and writers, health care professionals, and librarians; through political activity at the federal level, school teaching and administration, senior public service, work in the private sector, and the judiciary and the practice of law; as university presidents and at other levels of university administration; and as university professors in many fields of the arts and sciences.

Each contributor received a short document that set out the general philosophy behind the approach and organization of the book. They also received some brief and quite flexible editorial guidelines on the kinds of topics they could explore in their contributions. These included, first, what the Victoria College experience was like during the Lansdowne era. Did it help to shape your life and, if so, in what way(s)? What motivated you to study at the college? Second, did you have the sense that "the times were changing" – both in Canada generally and in the local community? What was your sense of what those changes were, and did they affect your desire to pursue post-secondary education? Third, could you comment on any particular college-related events or activities that were particularly memorable? These could include (but were not necessarily limited to) particular aspects of the educational experience (courses, professors, working with other students, etc.), social or sports events related to the many clubs and teams that were part of college life, or anything else on which the contributor might like to comment. Finally, looking back, how do you feel about your Victoria College experience during the Lansdowne era? How would you sum it all up?

Part Two also includes brief tributes to five Lansdowne-era students who have died. In addition, between Parts One and Two, there is a section that focuses on those Lansdowne-era students who have been honoured with the University of Victoria's Distinguished Alumni Award. Part Three of the book consists of a single concluding section, which I have written. In this final chapter I bring together themes expressed in the contributions and explore the extraordinary influence that Victoria College had on the Lansdowne generation.

Two years of my post-secondary education, between 1959 and 1961, took place at Victoria College. It was a good time for me. The college intensified and confirmed my interest in learning. It was small enough that it was possible to know and seriously dialogue with some of the professors – in my case, John Carson, who taught classics, and Allan Cairns, who taught English. I made a number of friends, some of whom I have kept up with over the years. Of particular significance, I also met Lorna Marsden, who was to become my wife.

Although I live and work in Toronto, I have maintained my links with Victoria College, now the University of Victoria, over the years. Partly, this is because of the relationship I have with UVic's Maltwood Gallery as a donor of Canadian works of art. It is also because my spouse, like our friend and colleague David Turpin, a steadfast supporter of this project, has worked for many years as a university president.

In early September 2006, Don Jones, UVic's director of Alumni Affairs, telephoned me. One of the matters we discussed was an idea that had engaged my interest for a few years – a book on the Lansdowne era of Victoria College. Perhaps the idea had gained in intensity because of the recent, untimely, and unexpected death of my friend Peter Smith, a distinguished citizen of the UVic community and author of the definitive history of the University of Victoria, *A Multitude of the Wise*. Perhaps, also, the idea had increased intensity because Peter's death – which would have been difficult to bear under any circumstances – occurred less than a month after he and his wife, Mary Jean, had been our guests in Toronto at the World Championship Tennis Games held at York University.

When I spoke with Don Jones, I was scheduled to travel to Japan and China later in September. After some further discussions, I arranged to break my return journey to Toronto in Victoria and meet with senior UVic officials and selected Lansdowne alumni on 10 October 2006. Later that day David Turpin and I met at the Union Club in Victoria, and a decision was made that, for all practical purposes, the project would go forward.

All that I have described above happened over two years ago. A book such as *The Lansdowne Era*, with multiple contributors, necessarily takes time. But that is a small price to pay for the richness and diversity of views our authors have brought to this volume. *The Lansdowne Era* is a celebration of a dynamic and change-filled time in the University of Victoria's history. It is a recognition that, although most of us attended for only a year or two during the Lansdowne years, the time was important in the formation of our lives. The book is also an opportunity to honour a selfless citizen of the college, the university it subsequently became, and the larger community of Victoria – Dr Peter Lawson Smith.

Victoria College's historic first graduating class of 1961: (standing left to right) Prof. R.T. Wallace (honorary class president), Barry Gelling, David Leeming, David Alexander, Patrick (Bud) White, Brian Sabiston, Brian Carr-Harris, Robin Hutchinson, Philip Punt, Leslie Ferriday, Douglas Kirk, Arthur Affleck, Ian Smith, Phillip MacNeill, Milton Calder, Charles Whisker, Kenneth Walters, Frank Mitchell, Ronald Smith, William Maconachie, Robert Smith, Robert Hunt, Allan MacLeod, Glenn Shipton, Gerald Bowes, Allen Fatt, Dr G. Reid Elliott (honorary vice-president), and George Maggs; (seated, left to right) Cora Browne, Elaine Marr, Alice-Mae Tomlinson, Linda Redden, Roseann Millin, Lillian Easton, Edith Schaeffer, Dianne Whitehead, Kathleen Thornbery, Wendy Etheridge, Rona Haddon, Olive Fairholm, and Anne Mayhew. Missing from photograph: Ralph Burgess, William Emery, Helen Hunter, Marilyn McElmoyle, and Tony Robertson.

EDWARD B. HARVEY, PHD, studied at
Victoria College, the University of British
Columbia, and Princeton University, where
he was a Wilson Fellow. His current teaching
specialization at the University of Toronto is the
effect of demographic change on various areas
of Canadian public policy. In addition to his
academic activities, he is president of UDG Inc.,
a Toronto-based policy and HR management
consulting firm. He is the author or co-author
of eighteen books and over 120 articles.

NOTES

1 Daniel Kubat and David Thornton, *A Statistical Profile of Canadian Society* (Toronto: McGraw Hill Ryerson, 1977), 104.

2 Statistics Canada, CANSIM tables, table 101–6502.

3 F. H. Leacy, ed., *Historical Statistics of Canada* (Statistics Canada in joint sponsorship with the Social Sciences Federation of Canada, 1974), tables B1 to B14.

4 Statistics Canada, CANSIM tables, table 102–4505.

5 Peter L. Smith, *A Multitude of the Wise: UVic Remembered* (Victoria: University of Victoria Alumni Association, 1993), 62.

6 "Preparing for a New Age," *Colonist*, 25 July 1965; reprinted in "On the Way to the Way to *The Ring*," a special supplement to *The Ring* (Victoria: University of Victoria, 22 September 1976), 8A.

PART ONE

PERSPECTIVES ON THE LANSDOWNE ERA

REMEMBERING PETER SMITH

GORDON SHRIMPTON

It was an insular place – Victoria College in the late 1950s – situated on the southern tip of a large, sparsely populated island and in a community of less than a hundred thousand. The students came mostly from the nearby high schools in Victoria. For many, the adjustment must have been minimal, especially if they came from Victoria High School, the largest and most urban. Oak Bay High produced its own phalanx, and a few trickled in from Mount View and, like myself, from Mount Douglas, more rural than urban in those days. The students numbered in the hundreds, and most of them already knew each other. Our conversation tried to be as elevated as possible, but that did not stop many of us from quoting copiously from *Mad* magazine, and when excerpts from the London review *Beyond the Fringe* appeared on vinyl, we howled with laughter at parties.

Some came to college to train as teachers. They entered the Normal School, soon to be incorporated into the college and then the university as the Faculty of Education. Others, like myself, came to continue an education in arts and science. The two streams, teacher training and arts and science, gave rise to attitudes of suspicion, even contempt, among some of us. In arts and science, we tended to look down on the education students. Mickey Mouse stuff, we called their curriculum. The insularity, the arrogance, the juvenile passions of college life (we saw no problem with campus queen contests – nor, seemingly, did the competitors, who lined up in shorts to be photographed and included in the student yearbook, the *Tower*) all speak of an age before we became politically correct. It is easy to forget the energy, the raw enthusiasm, of that time. Perhaps it came at a cost that none of us would pay today, but it was something to experience nevertheless.

Much of the energy came from the faculty, of course. They must have felt special. They were not just filling faculty slots in a department; they were part of history – they were making history. After all, it was hardly a secret that the college was moving forward toward degree-granting status. In 1960 the *Tower* trumpeted a new beginning: the college

Peter L. Smith, 1933–2003.

had indeed become a degree-granting institution. It was also getting larger, too large to include photographs of all faculty members in the *Tower*. Instead of the photographs as before, the teaching staff were simply listed by name, but not just by name, by name and department! The college now had departments. Lest this sound too grand for a fledgling university, there were only fourteen "departments" listed in the yearbook, five of which were staffed by one person: Anthropology; Classics (the department to which Peter Smith would be named); Commerce, Economics, and Political Science; Philosophy; and Sociology. John Carson was Classics; Reid Elliot bore the heavy burden of Commerce, Economics, and Political Science. But pity poor Roy Watson, who in one person was the departments of Anthropology, Philosophy, and Sociology.

The year 1961 was a momentous one. It brought some relief to Roy Watson, who ceased to be the department of Philosophy, thanks to the arrival of Edward Bond, who became that department. Roy was now only one department, but with a double-barrelled name: Anthropology and Sociology. Classics was now peopled by three men: John Carson, Frederick Kriegel, an Austrian whose name also appears in the Department of Modern Languages, and Peter Smith, who doubled as a member of the English Department.

Peter had completed his PhD in 1958 at Yale University, where he stayed for a year and taught. These were the McCarthy years in the United States, and many intellectuals who had options chose to leave the country. Peter, with his wife, Mary-Jean, and his daughter, Cindy, moved to Carleton in Ottawa, where he taught for the academic year 1959–60. But Victoria beckoned. Some people never take to the city, finding it insular – claustrophobic, even – but most people find it gets into the blood. Peter was Victoria born and bred, already part of the city's history. The principal of Victoria College, Harry Hickman, had his eye on Peter and decided to attract him to Victoria to help build the new university.

Harry Hickman was just the right sort of man to be principal of the college. He embodied the aspirations of many young Canadians. We saw in him, born an Albertan farmer (I remember him telling us his students that he was a real "hick man" in origin), a man of elegance and polish, someone who possessed all the grace of a cultured European. He had been educated at the Sorbonne, and his French was as effortlessly correct as his bridge game was masterfully subtle. The English we heard coming from him bore no trace of his farming background. His decision to go after Peter was a stroke of genius, more than even he probably knew.

Peter came to Victoria at both a critical and an opportune time. It was critical for the new university and for Classics to have the inspired leadership he could offer, opportune for the performing arts. Peter was known as an actor, but some knew him also from his choral singing. He was a superb basso profundo. Peter brought his many talents to bear on the developing university. He loved people but was especially fond of their quirks and eccentricities, which he recorded with all the zeal of a committed archivist. In addition, the university had to deal with some growing pains, and Peter came with credentials and a boundless energy that was exactly what the college needed.

At the time, Victoria College was an affiliate of the University of British Columbia. This meant that its curriculum was that of the parent institution. So one of the first challenges of the new university would be to develop its own curriculum. It would also have to carve out an identity for itself. To be a university in North America, it needed to develop a reputation for scholarly integrity and for graduating students who could hold their own anywhere in the academic world. So a continent-wide, if not a global, perspective was needed, but there was always the danger of aiming at a level of instruction that would be of little use or interest to the high school graduate of British Columbia.

Peter had deep roots in the educational culture of the city. His mother, Alice Corry, and his father, Henry (Harry) Lawson Smith, both taught at Victoria High School, and Harry served as principal from 1934 to 1955. Peter's pedagogical inclinations revealed themselves early in life, as a story told by his daughter, Cindy, reveals. Peter's mother, truer to British school fashion than the local trends, sent him, at nine years of age, to school in a "dress shirt, grey flannel shorts, and grey knee socks":

> He was small for his age, and now two years ahead of his peer group, and some
> of the tough Esquimalt boys targeted the smart little ... student and regularly
> chased little Peter home from school every day. Dad escaped his pursuers on most
> occasions, but it soon became apparent that a new approach was necessary unless
> he wanted to spend his year on the run. Boxing lessons were out of the question
> (even at that young age, violence wasn't in his nature), and he decided instead to
> negotiate with his tormentors. Dad claimed that the ringleader accepted an offer
> of regular homework assistance in exchange for amnesty and that the two of them
> eventually became friends. The fact that this young man went on to become a
> respected Victoria police officer always greatly amused Dad, who had a keen

appreciation of irony. This incident was typical of how Dad handled problems or conflict his entire life: he had no desire to conquer an adversary. Instead, he preferred to use his intelligence, creativity, and infectious personality to win over even the toughest opponent.

Cindy describes this as a "Smith story" and therefore subject to embellishment. Nonetheless, anyone who knew Peter knows that it has a ring of authenticity. It may not preserve all the pure facts, but it certainly captures the man.

Those bullies from Peter's youth cannot have known how lucky they were in their tutor. Peter would go on to be an outstanding scholarship student, even winning the Governor General's Gold Medal for highest marks in the province. In high school he had the unenviable distinction of being the "golden boy" son of the principal of the school. According to another story told by daughter Cindy, on the way to work, Principal Harry Smith would often stop his car to reprimand misbehaving students through the turned-down window of the car. Peter reported that he always felt obliged to duck down out of sight in the back of the car to avoid detection by his fellow students. I doubt that this experience should be used to explain Peter's ambivalent attitude to authority – despite his admiration for his father, he knew that there were times when it was politic to distance himself from him – but it must have reinforced an existing inclination. From the college years until Peter's very last at the university, he participated in and helped to organize and run the public ceremonies, especially at graduation, but despite his passion for ceremony, he never lost his ability to laugh at the foibles of the people who took it too seriously.

In 1961, when the surviving records begin, the Principal's Committee on Ceremonies and Special Events was in charge of all matters to do with ceremonial openings, inaugurations, and graduations and award presentations. At a meeting of 3 November 1961, Peter was nominated chair of the committee but begged to be excused because of a heavy commitment to Faculty Association work. He was secretary-treasurer of the association at the time. He remained on the Ceremonies Committee nevertheless. One of his regular contributions was the preparation of "The Book of Words," not unlike a church book of prayer. It laid out in precise detail what would be said by whom and when in the course of the graduation ceremony. In November of 1962 he was unanimously elected to chair the committee, and one of the first things he did was to issue a notice to faculty in the matter of dress at convocation and other ceremonies. I quote from the minutes of 6 December: "The Chairman presented a suggested notice to Faculty with reference to correct academic dress for College ceremonials. The committee approved Dr. Smith's directive and recommended that it be distributed to Faculty when the instructions for the next academic ceremony are circulated."

For the next year, the committee again elected Peter chair "unanimously." This would be a historic year: Peter would oversee the public events having to do with the transition from college to university. The committee had to deal with a legion of matters large and small. The previous year, for example, four gallons of sherry had to be ordered for the reception. As the historic approach to university status loomed, Professor Beattie MacLean

Peter Smith (fourth from left) with friends
at a beach party in Victoria, BC, in 1953.

was charged with finding appropriate decanters for the sherry. He found four suitable
ones at a cost of $14.10. Peter was very active through this and previous years organiz-
ing open houses to which the public would be invited to take in all the activities in which
the college or university-to-be was engaged. It was a vital public relations exercise,
meticulously organized, as one would expect. Through this year the committee addressed itself to the installation of the president of the fledgling university, Dr Taylor.
Beattie MacLean and Peter were charged with putting together "The Book of Words,"
only now the key word would not be "installation" but, at Dr Taylor's request, "inau-
guration." In December of 1964, Peter gave up the chairmanship of the committee amid
enthusiastic expressions of gratitude. Beattie MacLean took his place.

Peter cut a striking figure in his blue Yale PhD regalia. Despite his evident passion for
the colour, pageantry, and solemnity of these events, he was never what you would call
a pure establishment man. When a member of a certain royal family, visiting the campus
once amid elaborate, even painful ceremony, had to visit the bathroom, the dignitaries
and a platoon of Mounties all waited in the hallway outside until a rush of water came
from within. Peter nearly destroyed the solemnity of the whole occasion by quipping,
"That would be the royal flush." He loved the trappings and heraldry of circumstance.
Few professors on campus knew the UVic coat of arms as well as he did. The title of his
history of UVic, *A Multitude of the Wise*, is taken from it: *Multitudo sapientium sanitas
orbis* (A multitude of the wise is the health of the world).

Peter explained how he came to write this history in the introduction. Harry Hickman had anointed him to the task, asking him to "watch the unfolding events [of the metamorphosis of the college into a university] with particular care, so as to be able some day to record this historic event for posterity." As usual, Harry's judgment was sound, Peter would probably have written the book anyway. But he could not resist one of his famous quips even while fulfilling his promise to the paternal Harry: "To any of my friends who may be hoping to read the secret, scandalous history of UVic, this book is bound to be a disappointment. Even though it doesn't carry the official seal of institutional approval, it has been commissioned by the Alumni Association, and should maintain some decorum. When I retire from UVic, I may celebrate the occasion by bringing out a privately published, unexpurgated, no-holds barred second edition. I already have the title, an updated translation of our motto: *Lots of Wise Guys*." He did retire, of course, but alas, that book never appeared.

In fact, Peter took that task of writing the book very seriously. He collected extensive notes going well back into the 1940s. As each building was prepared and opened, he started a file card in which he recorded the name of the architect and other details, such as the square footage, whether he would need them or not. An aspect of life for people like Peter in the Lansdowne years emerges from those notes and from his *Multitude of the Wise*. The Gordon Head campus formally came into existence in 1959, and in the following years building activity on both the Lansdowne and Gordon Head locations proceeded at an accelerating pace. Apart from the regular convocations for the granting of degrees, there were plenty of other formal occasions in which dignitaries came together in muddy fields dressed in resplendent regalia to celebrate the opening of one new building after another.

When I arrived at Victoria College in 1959 to begin my life as an academic, I had not investigated the people who would teach me and was too preoccupied with survival and drinking Mrs Norris's coffee in the smoke-filled cafeteria to take time to find out much about them after I arrived. When Peter came the following year, however, I was immediately aware of something special. He was not what I thought a professor would be. The pipe-smoking, quietly muttering John Carson was closer to the image. Carson had been the Department of Classics for some time before I came. There was a blackboard on wheels, which he had filled by writing out every form of the vastly complex Greek verb for any who might be interested. On one side he added, "Hold, hold, stay, stay, erase not. Thou standest before the garnishings of millennia," instead of the PLO that most other professors would have used. For years I tried to protect that blackboard, but eventually it got in the way, and too few people at UVic shared, or even understood, my sentimental attachment to it. I do not know what happened to it.

Carson was shy; you have to look through many issues of the *Tower* to find a picture of him. His image is regularly replaced by the comment "Not available." Peter was not brash, but shyness was not in his nature either. Carson was romantically passionate about the classics; Peter just enjoyed them. That unexpected (by me at least) joy was infectious. It kept us students going through what could have been depressing times in the classroom. We came to college with some training in grammar, if we had paid attention in high school (and some of us had not). Somehow, we could handle basic grammar and the parts of speech, like subject, predicate, transitive verbs, indirect objects, and such things as that, but Latin had some unexpected surprises for us. I shall never forget the day that Peter had to teach us the construction called the "passive periphrastic with the dative of the agent." Rather than worry about the name of the construction at first, he concentrated on the jingle that one hears in it. The movie *The Court Jester,* starring Danny Kaye, was still fresh in our minds, and Peter evoked the scene in which Danny, hopelessly unprepared, is about to duel a formidable knight. There was to be a ceremonial drink of wine before the beginning of the combat, and conspirators, trying to rig the duel in Danny's favour, had arranged for one of the goblets to be poisoned. They taught Kaye a jingle to help him remember which goblet to avoid: "The vessel with the pestle has the pellet with the poison, but the flagon with the dragon has the brew that is true." We spent a few moments chuckling over the jingle and the hilarious scene in the movie and then moved from one jingle to the next and almost imperceptibly into the lesson. It was masterful, effortless.

In 1962 Geoffrey Archbold joined the department, and Frederick Kriegel left Classics to devote all his time to teaching German. I did not see anything of the behind-the-scenes operations, but Peter emerged logically as the chair of the department in 1963. I would guess that, in some ways, he had once more to employ skills similar to those he had displayed as a nine-year-old schoolboy. He was rising past people like John Carson, who might have had a claim to the leadership of the department on the basis of local experience and seniority. Not that Carson was like those bullies of Peter's school days, but he was a deeply emotional man, and some found him a little unpredictable. Peter had the skills and vision that the department and the university needed, and he would have needed all of his diplomacy to make the situation work. It is not easy in a few sentences to capture his administrative talents, which were formidable, but his own words surely reveal the frame of mind that made him so exceptional. I take them from his introduction to his history of UVic, *A Multitude of the Wise*:

> Much as I have enjoyed watching and recording the development of UVic, I have never felt comfortable about actually publishing an institutional history. It is a genre hag-ridden by three awful demons: Dullness, Smugness, and Hyperbole. It causes the most detached and incorruptible scholars to lose all sense of proportion. Any writer who goes near it is infected with a raging and incurable case of parochialitis. I know I am not immune.
>
> Although I have an obsession with accuracy, I felt that the book mustn't seem too academic in tone and style ... Who needs another President's Report?

The same mind that had absolute control over the minutiae of Latin grammar could set all of life's challenges into perspective and smile at folly, whether another's or his own.

Of course, the leadership the emerging university needed was not restricted to administration or even good teaching. In the next few years, its struggle – sometimes heart-rending – was to find the way from a small-town teaching college to a university. That meant scholarship, publications, but particularly faculty with doctoral degrees. With new faculty arriving each year, the task of establishing the ground rules for promotion and the awarding of tenure, not to mention scores of other procedural questions that affected faculty life, became increasingly urgent. From 1959 the Victoria College Faculty Association began to organize itself formally and address procedural questions in what it would call the "Tenure Document."

Besides the "Tenure Document," the association needed to draft a formal constitution, which was adopted in October of 1963. The records are skimpy, but Peter was evidently involved in its preparation in some way. Again, by February of 1965, Peter, as vice-president of the association, besides sitting on the membership committee (and continuing with the chairmanship of the Department of Classics), was chairing a committee to draft the "Tenure Document" with G.R. (Reid) Elliott and A.D. (Sandy) Kirk. On the ninth of that month, the committee brought to a meeting of the association the first draft of what it called a "proposed statement of University policy on appointments, promotions, and tenure" – a good beginning, but there was still a long way to go.

From the vice-presidency, Peter became president of the Faculty Association for the academic year 1965–66. It was expected, no doubt, that this would be the year for completion of the "Tenure Document," but unforeseen events originating in the Victoria community, the country at large, and from within the university itself conspired to delay its completion at the very time when it was most needed. Hiring of faculty was accelerating through the 1960s as entire departments came into existence and needed to be staffed. On 16 January 1961 the association listed 79 names of paying members, names that included R.T. Wallace, who was the acting principal at the time. By October of 1963 the number had grown to 131 members, out of a total eligible faculty of 144. The rapid growth came with a cost. Young teachers were hired from graduate schools, sometimes on one-year revolving contracts, while still working on their doctoral degrees. When some of them did not complete their degrees in a timely way, they were not granted tenure – fired, in effect. Some of them were well liked by their students, who objected strenuously to the dismissal of their favourite young teachers.

One of the first announcements that came from Peter, as new president of the association on September of 1965, was that he had agreed to be the "campus Community Chest [United Way] representative." Despite the extra work associated with the Community Chest, development of the "Tenure Document" moved forward, parts of it were already being accepted "in principle" by the association. At the same time, the question of pensions arose and became a topic for study by the already very active association. Things were busy but manageable. Next came three emergencies. One was scarcely threatening. On 17 February 1966 the association was called together hastily to discuss "the desirability of the property at 2282 Arbutus Rd. for the establishment of a Faculty Club." This was the Ker property, a fabulous waterfront estate that seemed about to come as a windfall into the possession of the university. All that was needed was for Premier W.A.C. Bennett to give his approval, thereby giving up his claim on the estate taxes. The approval never came, and the property slipped from the university's hands.

The next "emergency" was the publication of the Duff-Berdahl report on university governance. This report outlined a structure of governance for Canadian universities, a structure that was widely adopted and was to remain until the present day. Clearly, it

Peter led many successful tours of the Mediterranean. He is pictured here relaxing in Sicily in 1999.

would impact upon the development of the "Tenure Document." The association struck a committee to study the report: Professor Ron Cheffins, Dr David Chabassol, Mr Tony Emery, Dr Franklin T. Algard, and Dean Ron Jeffels. At the same time a more ominous development caught the association and the university off guard.

It came to public attention as the result of an article written by Dr Charles Tarlton, "newly appointed assistant professor of political science" (MW 161). The article attacked what it called antiquated modes of governance at UVic. Tarlton's essay seemed to have removed the last finger from the dam of concern in the minds of younger faculty. The older faculty, who had run the small college like a country club, were now having to deal with younger colleagues who saw no reason why they should have to accept the judgments of their "elders" without even an explanation, as they saw things. They wanted to be heard. Some made that fact clear by open resignations. There were firings, a sit-in outside the president's office, and complaints about an alleged "dictatorial manifesto" in the English Department, which was the main focus of many but not all of the complaints. The outcome of the ensuing turmoil was a new push to complete the much-needed "Tenure Document" in a form that would address the concerns that had at least crystallized the issues in people's minds. Others, such as Roy Watson, Bill Gordon, James Hendrickson, and Richard Powers, would bring the document to completion, but Peter, who is modest about his foundational contribution, deserves credit as well (MW 161–4). The document gained final acceptance by both the Board of Governors and the Faculty Association in the autumn of 1968.

At the end of April 1966, Peter distributed his report to the membership. It was certainly not the report that he had expected to write when he took office in September of the previous year. He begins: "In approaching the end of this stormy year, one of unprecedented anguish and activity for the Faculty Association, I am able to feel little more than relief for survival. There have been some accomplishments which give rise to cautious hope; but there is no problem that has been finally resolved, and I am afraid that we are leaving to our successors a mass of unfinished business." The anguish he mentions was felt personally. The crisis had taken on a dimension that called for responses uncharacteristic of Peter. About five weeks previously he had circulated the following statement, written from the eye of the very storm: "It is my opinion that the Faculty Association is faced with the necessity of making a public statement, if it is possible to explain to students and the public the complexity of the problems. The dignified course might be one of silence; but dignity seems unimportant if our professional integrity is in question."

The year 1968 was significant to this story for a reason that had little to do with the completion of the "Tenure Document" – at first, at any rate. That was the year that a new president, necessary because of the resignation of Malcolm Taylor the year before, was brought onto the campus from Johns Hopkins University in Baltimore. Bruce Partridge was to be the president, many hoped, who would take the fledgling university from its Lansdowne years into the new age as an institute of higher learning with international credentials. The full story of the turmoil that ensued is beyond the scope of this essay. It has been told already by Peter himself in his *Multitude of the Wise*. It suffices simply to say that the foundation laid by the hard work of Peter's Lansdowne generation in working out due process and codifying the procedures in a clear, systematic document did much to stabilize a volatile situation. There were some ferocious struggles in which the principle of due process seemed to be disregarded by administrators who wanted to exercise dictatorial powers, as many faculty saw things, at least, but eventually, not without scars and some metaphorical bloodshed, due process prevailed. Partridge's presidency lasted a scant two years.

I have a peculiar perspective on these events. I was president of the Faculty Association in the early eighties, when faculty numbers were already in the hundreds. For better or worse, there seemed no question in my mind that the role of the association with regard to the administration had to be of an adversarial nature, though polite as far as possible. Above, I spoke of those early Lansdowne years as a sort of country club, perhaps unfairly. I certainly see a kind of Edenic simplicity in the way things operated. I see the acting principal enrolled as a dues-paying member of the association, deans actively participating on association committees. Committees of the association address the development of the "Tenure Document" and the furnishing of the faculty lounge apparently with near-equal earnestness. Peter was made for a world like that. He flourished in it without really belonging to it, and he possessed the diplomatic skills to influence it positively. He was dean of Fine Arts when, in 1977, the association began its first move toward unionization (a drive that was cut off by an amendment to the University Act by the Social Credit government). In preparation for an expected application for union certification, the association decided that it had to organize itself appropriately. To do so, it determined, it had to remove administrators from membership, and that included deans. Peter was struck from the list of members. From that day forth, even after he stepped down from the deanship in 1980 (after serving for eight years), Peter never again involved himself in Faculty Association business.

No doubt he felt the need for a break, a new direction. In 1981 he took three department colleagues on a heroic hike along the West Coast Trail: Professors John Fitch, John Oleson, and David Campbell. At about the same time he linked up with Ian Baird, and the two of them hiked every known railway right of way in southern Vancouver Island. Peter always loved trains. Unable to leave any part of his life undocumented, he and Ian in 2001 produced *Ghosts on the Grade: Hiking and Biking Abandoned Railways on Southern Vancouver Island*. Through Ian, Peter encountered Elwood White, who was collecting material on Victoria's aviation history. His problem was that he had a great deal of information but needed help putting it together in written form. The result was another collaborative effort: *Wings across the Water: Victoria's Flying Heritage 1871–1971*. It turns out Peter loved planes as well.

He also loved dogs, and this predilection brings me to one of two somewhat sensitive moments in Peter's life. I remember him coming to work and talking about the dog-training shows he had been watching on PBS. Even then I wondered whether he watched the shows in order to learn how to train his dogs or to study and mimic the woman on the show. Peter was an accomplished actor. With his impish sense of humour, he would take her off saying, "Walkies, walkies." I found out later what that was all about. This incredible teacher, who could get students through the intricacies of the Greek optative without breaking their spirits, was incapable of training the family dog. The lowest marks he ever got were from dog-training school. Peter's dogs were never small. Bedtime in the Smith house in later years had become a competition between Peter and Velvet, the family dog, for limited space in the same bed.

And now I come to my second "sensitive moment." Very soon after joining Victoria College, Peter and Mary Jean, his wife, took up tennis. Tall, dark, and handsome, Peter must have cut quite a figure on the tennis courts with his Pancho Gonzales tennis racquet. I had not heard of a Pancho Gonzales tennis racquet. So I phoned a local expert, Helen Kempster. "What can you tell me about a Pancho Gonzales tennis racquet?" I asked. "Oh," said Helen, "well, that would go back at least to the 1940s." "Peter was a closet archivist," said Helen a little later in our conversation. I myself saw a bag with every cork he had removed from every wine bottle in the history of the Smith family. Even his tennis racquet was preserved from the past. No one would come out and say it, but Peter did not shine at tennis. One day, son Dan delivered an overhand smash that caught Peter and not the racquet. Pancho had let Peter down for the last time. The racquet was returned to the archives.

In spite of disappointments, Peter did not change in all the years I knew him. As a consequence, I have no hesitation in quoting from some of his writings produced long after the Lansdowne years to give just a taste of the lively wit and irrepressible energy that we all knew from those years. He never lost his attachment to his high school, Victoria High. So in 1976, the year of its centennial, his *Come, Give a Cheer*, a history of Victoria High School, was published. At the same time, an elaborate review with the

Peter Smith with Iona Campagnolo, lieutenant-governor of British Columbia, in 2003, on the occasion of the fortieth anniversary of the founding of the University of Victoria and the centenary of its opening as an institution of higher education.

same title, *Come, Give a Cheer*, was staged with the multi-talented Sylvia Hosie directing and the personable and hard-working Tommy Mayne serving as producer.

Peter had been brought in as a consultant, but it was not long before he became an active contributor. Apart from the advice and infectious energy he had to give, he was soon contributing to the writing. According to Tom Mayne, Peter wrote two hilarious musical pieces. I quote from one of them (to the tune of "Anything Goes"):

> In old Vic High a glimpse of stocking
> Was looked on as something shocking.
>   Now, heaven knows:
>   Anything goes!
>
> Miss Jessie Roberts once taught better words.
> Now they can use four letter words
>   Writing prose:
>   Anything goes.
>
> They look dumb today,
> They chew gum today,
> In their teens today

They wear jeans today
But no ties today,
'Cause all guys today
Are just long haired Romeos!

We used to grind at math and history.
What they do now's a mystery –
    Heaven knows:
    Anything goes.

"People everywhere are convinced that the high school they attended was unique and special. They are all absolutely right, of course: a school is a dynamic human institution, its character defined by the values and personalities of all who live and work within it, and by the haunting memory of all who have come and gone." These too are Peter's words, taken from the introduction of his *Come, Give a Cheer*. They illustrate the way he moved through all phases of his life as a keen observer, one who had a deep affection for human nature.

Peter's scholarship focused on the great poetry of the ancient Greek and Roman world. He excelled as a translator. His delight in comedy and consummate skill in Latin drew him inexorably to Plautus. He began translating *Miles gloriosus* (*The Braggart Soldier*) in the Lansdowne years and completed it in 1966, just after his year as president of the Faculty Association (one wonders if there could be a connection). He published this translation many years later along with two others. His comments on his own approach to scholarship, particularly the staggering difficulties involved in rendering ancient humour into modern English, reveal the same critical sensitivity visible in other aspects of his life.

Miles Gloriosus was my first experience in translating Plautine comedy for stage production: in the main, this version dates from 1966. Although I believe I would do things rather differently today, I have decided to make only minor corrections and revisions, thus avoiding obvious inconsistencies of style.

The would-be translator of Plautus faces many challenges. These early Latin masterpieces are not mere comedies of situation, for all their frantic pace and occasional slapstick … In trying to cope with Plautus' verbal humor, my goal has been to find the best compromise between linguistic accuracy and dramatic effect.

"Whom the god loves dies young," said the comic poet Menander. He might have been thinking of Peter Smith. Peter did not age. His joy and energy remained with him up to the moment he slipped way at the age of seventy-three, the result of a massive stroke. He was still young.

Special thanks to Ian Baird, Sylvia Hosie, Helen Kempster, Betty Kennedy, Tommy Mayne, Howard Petch, the Smith family, especially Mary-Jean and Sarah, and UVic Archives librarians and staff.

GORDON SHRIMPTON, PHD, studied
at Victoria College, the University of British
Columbia, and Stanford University. All his
degrees are in classics. He returned to the
University of Victoria, where he taught from
1967 to 2007 and was also active in the faculty
association, both locally and provincially. As
well, he has been involved in the Canadian
Association of University Teachers. He is the
author of several articles and reviews and has
written two books: *Theopompus the Historian*
(McGill-Queen's University Press, 1991) and
History and Memory in Ancient Greece
(McGill-Queen's University Press, 1997).

BIBLIOGRAPHY

MW= Smith, *A Multitude of the Wise.*

Baird, Ian, and Peter Smith. *Ghosts on the Grade*:
Hiking and Biking Abandoned Railways on
Southern Vancouver Island. Victoria, BC, 2001.

Smith, Peter L. *Come, Give a Cheer! One*
Hundred years of Victoria High School,
1876–1976. Victoria, BC: Victoria High School
Centennial Celebrations Committee, 1976.

– *A Multitude of the Wise: UVic Remembered.*
Victoria, BC: University of Victoria Alumni
Association, 1993.

– *Three Comedies: Miles gloriosus, Pseudolus,*
Rudens / Plautus. Translated and with an
introduction. Ithaca: Cornell University Press,
1991.

Tunstall, Patricia A. "A History of the University
of Victoria." Unpublished essay, Victoria, 1971.

White, Elwood, and Peter L. Smith. *Wings*
across the Water: Victoria's Flying Heritage,
1871–1971. Madeira Park, BC: Harbour Pub.,
2005.

THE EARLY YEARS

REGINALD ROY

It was an amazing year – 1944. At Christmas time the Americans were fighting desperately in what was to be called the "Battle of the Bulge." On the left the British army was clawing its way toward Germany, and left of that again, the Canadian army, about to be reinforced by the Canadian Corps in Italy, was biting its way into Holland. Further east the Soviet armies were steadily advancing into Europe. The end could not be far. In the spring, advances were being made on all fronts against a desperate enemy. Slowly but surely Germany was crumbling. Finally, on 8 May 1945, Germany surrendered, and for the first time Europe was at peace, Hitler was dead, and most of his cabinet was jailed.

In Canada the end of the war in Europe was celebrated from Halifax to Victoria. Those who would have been conscripted into the army heaved a sigh of relief. The navy and air force were both volunteer services, but all young males at Victoria College had military training during the year, and for years it had been a matter of time before they completed their third and fourth year of academics and received their BA or BCom. at the University of British Columbia in Vancouver.

In Victoria there were two institutes of higher learning. One was Victoria College, which for the past twenty years had been at Craigdorroch Castle. The other was the smaller Normal School, used for the training and education of those intent on following a teaching career. The former was in Victoria. It was really a large house built to accommodate James Dunsmuir and his family. Dunsmuir, of course, was the "coal baron" of Vancouver Island and one of the richest men in the province. His son built Hatley Park on some six hundred acres next to the sea. It was a stately mansion, set in acres of gardens, lawn, and other things, which resembled an English estate at its prime.

The war years had a profound effect on Canada. For the decade prior to the war, the country had wallowed in one of the longest depressions it had ever experienced. Prices were amazingly low, but so too were wages. Despite the war, the population was growing even though the country fielded over a million men and women in the service. What was more important was that the province of British Columbia had begun to feel the impact of the war almost from the outset. As the number of ships in Esquimalt were brought up to full strength, the local infantry regiments on Vancouver Island and elsewhere were brought up to war establishment, and aerodromes were enlarged to accommodate the air training scheme. The call for construction teams grew by the month.

With the defeat of France and, later, the declaration of war with Japan, more troops were moved into the province and new coastal batteries, searchlights, and harbour defences constructed to house the people on the job and the new battalions that moved to British Columbia to defend its shores. Ship construction and repair became a noticeable feature in employment, and slowly but surely the population of the province began to rise. An interesting feature of the wartime growth was that the population did not start to decline when the war was over. It rose steadily as more and more people came to appreciate the benefit of the warm winter in the Victoria-Vancouver area. One must keep in mind that to most Canadians, British Columbia was a bit of a mystery. It was the end of the railway, beyond the mountains, and seemed quite cut off from everything. During the war two divisions were stationed there, and brigades in the divisions were moved periodically, so that they had some considerable experience in the province. Victoria and Vancouver, the two major cities, were well-known. At Esquimalt, the naval base, there were some thirty large and small ships that operated out of the harbour. In both cities and elsewhere, large air force bases were established. Before the war, the population of British Columbia had been fairly modest, but after the war many were determined to move to the Pacific Coast and start a new life there.

The province had originated with the fur trade, developed with the gold rush, and begun to expand with the railway. It was the last that brought in people and established towns and cities, which, of course, created a demand for schools, colleges, and later universities. In Victoria what was to become a college was established at Craigdarroch Castle, as it was called. During the Great War it had been a place where the hospitalized soldiers could recover from their wounds. After the war the mansion was taken over by Victoria College, and for over twenty years it catered to the academics. The general rule was that one could do the first years at the college; then it was necessary to complete one's studies at the University of British Columbia to obtain a degree. At the Normal School, another institution for higher learning in the city, students completed their training as future teachers.

Craigdarroch Castle was the grandest home in the city, including Government House, the residence of the lieutenant-governor. However, it was not prepared for the increasing number of students who wanted to enrol after the war. The veterans had been promised many things after the war was over. One was the opportunity to attend a university, provided they maintained an average of 65 per cent in their exams, were competent, and obeyed the general regulations. If the veteran was married, the couple were given a marriage allowance of $90.00 per month during the time the veteran attended college. During the summer, when the college was not in operation, the veteran had to find work. For example, this was the time when the city's streetcars were being replaced by buses, and many students got summer jobs helping to dig up the rails.

But the conditions inside Craigdarroch Castle were not good, and it was decided to hold a protest march favouring a change in venue to the Normal School. There was plenty of room there for both the teachers and the college students. There was room for a larger library, a canteen, offices, store rooms, and recreation facilities. In the fall of 1946 the students marched through the city to the Legislative Building demanding a change. There were no professors on the protest march, but we knew, from their friendly waves as we left the campus, that they were as much in favour of the protest march as we were. It was probably the first and only such march put on by the college, with the students marching in step and the piper having a silver plate in his head caused by a war wound! In any event, the provincial government approved the move, and for the next two decades the college operated from the Lansdowne Campus, not far from where the city's old Lansdowne airport used to be.

This was one of the most immediate results of the war on Victoria. No shells or bombs had landed on the city. A Japanese submarine lobbed a few shells on the island, which resulted in the formation of the Pacific Coast Rangers, but one could say that the result was negligible. The war did, however, have a considerable impact on the province and the growth of the college into a university.

It took a little while to get accustomed to the new campus. The main building was a three-storey brick-and-mortar structure, while behind that was a separate two-storey wooden annex. It contained a cafeteria presided over by a Mrs Norris, a lady who provided the students with coffee, tea, sandwiches, light lunches, and all the things they lacked at the old castle. Upstairs were tables and benches and places where one could eat in peace, talk about innumerable subjects, compare notes, or engage in any activity that didn't disturb others. The professors had a table where they could go, or if they wished, they could eat with the students.

But before we get too involved with the new campus, let us take a look backward and see what had been happening to Victoria and the island and province in general. It is difficult today to think that during the Depression, which lasted from 1929 to 1939, Saskatchewan had more people in it than British Columbia. In 1939 British Columbia had a population of about 800,000 all told. A year after the war ended, there were about 1 million according to *B.C. Facts and Statistics*, a yearly pamphlet produced by the Bureau of Economic Survey of the government of the Province of British Columbia. Twelve years later the government told us we now had a population of 1,350,000, and in 1963, when we were about to move to the new campus, we had grown to 1,700,000. In a little over two decades, our population had doubled! In the same period, the student population of Victoria had just about quadrupled.

A look at the makeup of the population on the verge of the change in status from a college to a university is revealing. About 9.8 per cent were classified as managerial, 9.8 per cent were professional-technical, 12.8 per cent were clerical, some 7.3 per cent were in sales, 13.5 per cent were in services and recreation, 6.5 per cent were in transportation and communication, 4.3 per cent were farmers or farm workers, 2.2 per cent were loggers or related works, under 1 per cent were fishermen and trappers, about 0.9 per cent were miners or quarrymen, some 24.1 per cent were craftsmen or working in the production process, and the remainder were labourers or not stated. Enrolment at the University of British Columbia at this time (1963) was 14,714.

The climax of the great 1946 protest march.
The student-veterans arrive at the BC Legislature.

During the war years retail trade had jumped significantly. In 1939 it had been $242,349,000. In 1946 it had risen to $593,547,000. Seven years later it was $1,228,373,000, and in 1963 it totalled $1,888,560,000. Farm income had jumped from $20,000,000 to $60,800,000 during the war years, and it more than doubled by 1963. Forest production, which in 1939 was $90,000,000 had more than doubled by 1946 to $200,000,000, and by 1963 it had zoomed up to $850,000,000. Manufacturing had gone from $250,000,000 in 1939 to $560,000,000 in 1946, and by 1963 it had reached $2,225,000,000. It was one of the most significant increases in the provincial economy and, like the other elements, provided a golden stream into the provincial coffers. These figures give the background of what was happening to the province, but they also provide a reason why there was a demand in the capital city for better educational facilities.

But let us go back to the end of the war and its effect on the college. The end of hostilities meant the beginning of the mass release of some 1 million men and women into civilian life. The veterans had been promised many things – help to build their homes, to purchase machines (taxis, for example) to start them in business, small farms for those who wanted to get into agriculture, and so forth. Veterans were also promised a university education, even though they had not yet attained university entrance. This offer attracted a great deal of attention. It should be kept in mind that fewer than 5 per cent of the army officers, for example, had a university degree. A number of these men had become battalion, brigade, and divisional commanders. The opportunity for a university education was open to all – men and women – but the difficulty was that several years of war, six at the most, had left studies neglected while men honed their skills on killing.

It was decided, therefore, that these people, if they wished, would have refresher courses for about six months before attending a college. In Victoria the barracks of a former anti-aircraft battery was taken over, the buildings were easily converted into classrooms, and veterans were invited to attend. The rooms were soon filled. Some of the veterans had a few years of college, but even they welcomed the time to get back into being students. The "school" was located in Victoria, and some of the teachers would later teach at the college.

It should be remembered that the students, if married, were paid $90.00 a month living allowance. This covered rent, food, light, heat, clothing, transportation, entertainment – in fact, everything. If the spouse had a job, it was easier on the budget. If not, the veteran had to make do. Some managed to get a part-time job. Some had some small savings left in the military on discharge. Others had parental help. Generally, it was up to the veteran to sink or swim.

It was also up to the veteran to maintain a decent mark in courses taken. An overall average of 65 per cent in exam marks was the dividing line. Generally, this meant that 65 per cent was the lowest mark one could make in a course, but of course there were exceptions. Work at the college was scarce, normally because it took a senior student to mark a paper and make comments on it. As a result, most of the students were quite serious about their marks and their courses. Unlike the former years, when many students went to college because their parents wanted them to, the drive now came from within, and there was a noticeable difference in the classes.

It should be noted, too, that many of the veterans were widely travelled. It kept the professors on their toes. The army had fought in Italy, France, Belgium, Holland, and parts of Germany, not just on the the Western Front. The veterans knew Britain well. The RCAF had flown all over the world, and the navy, which hardly existed in the Great War, was familiar with the Atlantic and the Pacific. Someone in the history class might mention the Duke of Montefeltro in Italy; a student that his company had liberated the duke's castle in 1944. That clued the professor to the fact that he was speaking to a group of students who had been around, and he would lift the lecture to a higher plane. It wasn't that the student wanted to be "one up" on the professor, but rather, that the student felt his experience might be interesting.

Student veterans made up over half the classes in the college, and in the following year the percentage was somewhat similar. Non-military students benefited from their presence. They questioned and queried much, and professors became accustomed to students who challenged facts and assumptions which, in earlier years, would have been swallowed wholesale. There was a need for more room on the campus and in the classroom. The library was in the basement but was inadequate for the ever-increasing number of students. If there was a class of fifty students taking a course, the library had hitherto been geared to provide only one book on Marx, for example, and there was a surge in demand for the book at the Victoria Public Library. This was true of all courses, and soon it was realized that the more students in a class, the heavier demand there was for books that dealt with the topic.

The same held true of the chemistry and physics laboratories, of maps for the historians and the economists, and so forth. There was also a demand for more prizes and scholarships as the student body grew, just as more space was needed for the college athletic and boating teams. And there was a demand for more lecture rooms, labs, and offices as well. One thing that was maintained at the college, even though the war was over, was the training of officer cadets for the services. It was not on the same scale, however. During the war all able-bodied students were compelled to join the college cadet corps of their choice and take some military training. After the war the cadets were continued on a much-reduced scale and on a voluntary basis. Professors who had been in the forces were the instructors, and the cadets were paid a modest sum of money for their services. The Cold War had started even before the veterans had outgrown their uniforms.

With the growth of the student body in the forties and fifties, it followed that there should be an increase in staff. Percy H. Elliott died at sixty-five during the war. He had been principal of the college for sixteen years, and naturally there was considerable discussion as to who should succeed him. Eventually, Dr John Ewing was selected from the Vancouver Normal School. There was a considerable amount of controversy, but he was installed in May 1944. It should be added that, at the time, he was one of the few professors who had a PhD. There were others close to earning the degree, but of some two dozen on the teaching staff, including the Normal School, he alone had completed one. Some years later it became mandatory that all teaching staff should have their doctorates if they wished to be promoted or even hired.

Ewing was faced with a number of problems when he assumed the principalship of the college. He was new to the campus, whereas his predecessor had had sixteen years as head and knew his staff well. On Ewing's staff were such people as Roger Bishop, who became head of the English department, Phoebe Noble in Mathematics, Lewis J. Clark in Chemistry, William H. Hughes in Physics, Phillis Baxendale in German, H. Aitchison in Economics, Rodney Poisson in English, W.H. Gaddes in Psychology, and G.G. McOrmond, also in English. There were others, of course, but almost all became familiar to the students whether they were in their class or not.

Additional staff members were added as students came not only from the forces but from the high schools in lower Vancouver Island, the Cowichan Valley, and the Gulf Islands in 1947 and 1948. Charles Howatson was taken on in Geography, Fred Kriegel came to teach German, Reid Elliott joined the Economics staff, John Climenhaga taught Physics, Gladys Downes joined Hickman in the French Department, and John Carson assisted those teaching Classics. Some of the new staff members had been in the services. It quickly became apparent, however, that Canada had not produced enough professors during the war to ensure that Canadian university students would be taught by Canadian professors. As time went on and as the search for staff became more desperate, the college, on the brink of becoming a university, had roughly one-third of its professors Canadian, one-third American, and one-third British.

In 1946 the staff had considerable influence on the students. For example, college formal dances were dry. They were held at the Crystal Gardens Pool across the street from the Empress Hotel. Naturally, the male escorts devised various ways of smuggling in drinks and mixtures and hiding them under the table. This was not easy, as a considerable number of the teaching staff were on hand to make sure the dances were held with decorum. They sat at a different table, but the dances were sober affairs on the floor.

There was a dress code to be followed as well. Women wore dresses or skirts, for example, and the only time they wore trousers was when they were writing examinations, when they would wrap their legs around their chairs for greater concentration. Men usually wore sweaters or jackets, except at dances, when they wore a suit. The civilian clothes were generally purchased when veterans had to replace their uniforms. For many of the students, money was tight. Civilian cars were still in short supply. Gas was cheap, but few had a car. So it really did not matter.

The newly formed Victoria College Council played a major role in the college in these years. Each department had a head who did the hiring and firing of the staff with the approval of the principal and council. Generally speaking, however, if a professor found someone he wanted to hire, there was a need for the person, and there was a gap in the faculty to be filled, it was the person whom the head chose who was appointed. If the person did not meet the standards expected, then the head would look elsewhere. The head kept a sharp eye on what had to be taught regarding the implications it would have for library and laboratory facilities. Since library or lab money was limited, there was sometimes a quarrel over what should or should not be bought.

The same thing held true of reference books and money spent on rare books. Fortunately, there were a fair number of second-hand books shops in the city, and also, students were allowed access to the Provincial Library in the Legislative Buildings, as well as to the city library. These may seem minor matters to the lay person, but when a book was in high demand, it had a considerable impact on a student's mark.

With each passing year, as the student body grew in number, the demand for more facilities increased. The pressure came in two ways. At the junior level there were more sections in the junior classes – English, Mathematics, Economics, History, and so forth. That meant that one professor could not teach all the students who wanted to take English, for example, and thus could not control the books when assigning essays. In earlier times a professor might be a part-time librarian, but now trained professional librarians were needed. More staff were required in the library, longer hours that the library was open, a closer account of the books taken out and returned, a microfilm reader, and so on. Laboratory work was somewhat similar. Chemicals, for example, and microscopes had to be acquired in greater quantities. Special storage facilities were needed, and their safety ensured.

For a short period, after the bulk of the veterans had gone through and class sizes seemed to drop as the college apparently returned to its "normal" size, things appeared to go well. However, it was very soon apparent the student body had changed for good. From the figures given earlier, it is clear that the college was growing and would continue to grow. There was no longer an economic depression, and it had been demonstrated by the student veterans that higher education was available to persons from any background once the question of money had been overcome. The tuition cost of a college education in 1946 was about $250 per year, or about $50 per course. Of course, there were variations. But a normal school year for a student was five courses, and with the economy rising, one could normally make that much at work during the summer with enough left over for other necessities.

The optimism that victory brought among the veterans, the desire for an education that would lead to a better life, the tremendous demand for labour following years of wartime civilian scarcity – all these factors and more were involved in the difficult question of trying to estimate the size of the student body that would present itself in the following year. This involved not only classrooms and laboratories but also the teaching responsibilities. Should there be more staff? Where would their offices be? Were there enough books to meet the demand? Were there enough maps and charts to go around?

It should be noted that at this time – the early fifties – the main pressure was on space. Thus there began a building cycle that lasted a decade. Two major brick-and-stone buildings were constructed, and a number of buildings taken over and used as offices and classrooms as more professors arrived on the campus. When the author of this article came to the campus from Royal Roads, for example, he had an office in Dunlop House. Other academic offices were located there, but a fairly large space was devoted to a firm that was to raise money to help pay for the new campus, which was now a foregone conclusion.

From the outset there was considerable discussion regarding what form a new institution would take. Would it continue to be a college, something not huge or impersonal like a university, but kept small and personable, much like some of the American colleges. A figure of about 5,000 total students was frequently used.

It was often said that high academic standards were the key to growth, and dedication to good teaching an absolute necessity. Many were in favour of this concept, primarily among those who had tenure and looked forward to continuing their teaching careers without having a get a PhD, writing articles and books, and working from original resources. There was general agreement at the time that a primary emphasis would be on the liberal arts and that the development of graduate studies would be approached slowly and carefully. Teaching in graduate studies, it was agreed, was not something that every faculty member would enjoy. Before one taught at the graduate level, one had to produce graduate-level articles and books.

There was considerable speculation about what the new institution would be called. At one meeting of the faculty the question arose, and all sorts of ideas were presented. The "University of Western Canada," the "University of the Pacific," and the "University of Victoria" were all debated, among others. Finally, one member humorously suggested that whatever we did, we should not follow the suggestion that we be called the "Juan de Fuca University." Think what a graduate would say – graduating from good old Fuca U. That brought the house down, and a different name was suggested.

Another group, which gained more prominence, was all for developing a full-fledged university. It would mean establishing more faculties; there would be a continuous need

Professor Reginald Roy with students, c. mid-1950s.

for more classrooms, labs, a staff room for faculty, parking facilities, student residences, dining halls, a book and stationery store, physical training facilities, including a swimming pool, a theatre –indeed, all sorts of buildings, including an auditorium.

There was no doubt that the institution, as it stood, was underfunded. In fact, some said that the new institution would present a problem for the University of British Columbia in Vancouver and that UBC was not overly fond of the idea of a new university in the province as a rival for money for higher education. This attitude was to change, but it would take some time. UBC had been quite generous to the college, allowing it to set and mark its own exams and accepting college students going on to university. There would be a struggle for recognition, and, the new university was not yet recognized on the mainland, whatever the wishes of the faculty. In a word, there were arguments both for and against developing the college into a university, but the pressure to do so was steadily increasing. In the mid-1950s the province's population was approaching one and half million, and a decade later it was close to two million.

There was also the question of where the new university should be. One faction saw it continuing on at the Normal School grounds. Others saw a new campus based on a former army camp and one or two adjacent farms. In the 1950s, after it was agreed the college and provincial Normal School should merge, it became clear that a larger campus would be needed. The anticipated campus was not far away – a little over a mile from the Lansdowne campus was an army camp. It had been vacant for some time. Nearby were several farms. The location was ideal. It was a flat area, had good road (and thus bus) connections with the city, had ample room for expansion and student residences, and boasted army buildings easily used for or converted to university purposes.

What was equally important was the fact that the local member of Parliament for the area was George R. Pearkes. He was a popular man, a veteran of the First and Second World Wars and winner of the Victoria Cross, the Distinguished Service Order, the Military Cross, and other awards. Moreover, he was the minister of National Defence and had a great deal to say about the disposal of the camp that the college had its eye on. This fortuitous situation was not lost on the Governing Council of the college nor on Judge Joseph Clearihue, a former artillery officer and soon to be chancellor of the University of Victoria.

The official history of the university, *A Multitude of the Wise* by Peter Smith, goes into more detail about the people involved in the college obtaining degree-granting status in 1963, but there were few who regretted the move. It was the first step, but only the first.

REGINALD ROY, CDII, PHD, FRHS, joined the army (Cape Breton Highlanders) in 1939 and saw service in Britain, Italy, France, Belgium, and the Netherlands. After the war, he attended Victoria College and then went on to earn his BA and MA from the University of British Columbia and his PHD from the University of Washington. He has taught at Royal Roads Military College and the University of Victoria. Dr Roy is the author of ten books and over forty-five articles and book chapters.

THE VICTORIA NORMAL SCHOOL
IN THE LANSDOWNE YEARS

NORMA I. MICKELSON

No discussion of the Lansdowne era or, indeed, of the University of Victoria as it exists today would be complete without including the Provincial Normal School. From its location high atop the hill on Lansdowne Road came generations of teachers who moulded the youth of British Columbia in ways too numerous to mention. Many Normal School graduates went on to other careers, distinguishing themselves and owing many of their successes to the foundations laid on the Lansdowne campus.

The history of the Victoria Normal School long before 1946 – in fact, ever since 1915, when it was first established – is the story of one of British Columbia's significant achievements in post-secondary education. The Normal Schools (one in Vancouver and the other in Victoria) were established to prepare elementary teachers for the public schools of British Columbia, and the fact that many of their graduates circled the globe in future years was in no way part of their early mandate.

Housed in its sparkling new building on the beautiful Lansdowne campus, the Normal School continued to fulfill its mandate until the Second World War intervened and in 1942 the buildings were co-opted for use as a military hospital. But teacher training carried on, this time in the Memorial Hall of Christ Church Cathedral. The quarters were cramped, but as many of the young men in British Columbia were overseas, enrolments were low and were largely made up of young women. After V-E Day in 1946, the Normal School returned to the Lansdowne campus. Now, however, it had to share the facilities with Victoria College, which had grown beyond its previous home in Craigdarroch Castle. And so in the Lansdowne years Victoria College and the Provincial Normal School shared the "campus on the hill," albeit as separate entities and not always harmoniously! Both were experiencing growing pains with the return of the veterans, and it was becoming ever clearer that a new home had to be found for Victoria College if not for the Normal School.

In the interim, however, both institutions continued to focus on teaching. Research seems to have played a very minor role in the curriculum, but students who were part of those years uniformly praise the faculty, and unbeknownst to them at the time, they were the beneficiaries of some of the best teaching in Canada. Indeed, what the college lacked in research capabilities, it made up for in the excellence of its teaching. Likewise, what the Normal School lacked in academic rigour, it compensated for in its methodological excellence. Its graduates may not have been scholars, but they knew how to teach!

But teaching was not the only issue for the very young graduates, most of whom had come to Normal School directly from high school. When they arrived in the schools of the province on their final practicum, they discovered they had a myriad of other tasks to perform! They learned quickly that they had to organize themselves in a very focused way in order to survive! There were no computers and no duplicating machines (a home-made jelly pad had to do the job of making multiple copies of "seat-work" for the students). Timetables had to be made with strict adherence to the time allotments prescribed by the provincial government.

Day books were mandatory, and students were told that when they had their own classes, the district superintendent would visit and ensure that all teachers followed the provincial mandate. Sometimes pot-bellied stoves had to be fuelled and even outhouses cleaned! Accommodation was often difficult to find, and when temperatures hovered below freezing, getting to school was not always easy.

Also of importance was the need to keep careful attendance records. The system was unique, in fact. It required a prescribed register which had to be marked twice a day with an oblique line (/) for morning attendance and another for the afternoon (/). Tardiness was recorded with a single dot – one above the "cross" for morning lateness and another below for afternoon tardiness. By the end of the year the record book was a sight to behold!

But such records have been known to be instrumental in legal cases and therefore had to be scrupulously correct. There is no doubt that the Normal School faculty had many challenges in preparing its young charges for "teaching." Mostly they were inspired to do a great job, but at times, perhaps, they could be overly rigorous. For example, in 1946 (the beginning of the focus of this book) the war in Europe had ended, and V-E Day was a cause of exhilarating celebration. Etched in memory is the rebuke many students received for not turning up for classes that day (a teacher is ALWAYS reliable and gets to school no matter what!) But for those who had dear ones returning safely from overseas, celebrating with the rest of the world was reason enough to go to town on whatever streetcar was available and join the happy throngs on the streets of Victoria. Classes that morning seemed irrelevant! But to this day it seems to take an occasion as momentous as the end of the war in Europe not to turn up on time for classes!

It would be impossible, really, to do justice to the fine tutelage of the Normal School faculty. To mention but a few who stand out in memory – There was Wilfrid Johns, who was a living demonstration to everyone of value of art in one's life. His wife, the former Tressie Gilliland, did the same for music. Percy Wicket, though, was the music teacher, and he tried valiantly to get each student to perform in some facet of music – indeed, even to conduct a choir. He realized that many of his students would be teaching all subjects when they got to their schools and would need to have an appreciation of what he called "the finer things of life."

And who can ever forget Dr Henrietta Anderson, a spry, tiny woman whose advice to each graduate was "not to marry the first pebble on the beach." Perhaps she knew better than most how lonely some of these rural situations could be for first-year teachers, many of them girls barely out of their teens trying to cope with so many things all at once. Dr Anderson was far ahead of her time in the belief that women had an important role to play in society, not just in teaching. Dr Vern Storey, in his book *Learning to Teach*, quotes her as saying, "If we are seeking equality we must produce equality. Let us stand by each other and be all for women and for all women" (106). And further, in support of young people, "I don't see any hope for a great Canada until we see more and more of our young people imbued with the ideal that they have a contribution to make to our country" (107). And she tried mightily to train her students in this belief. Significantly, also, Dr Anderson insisted on careful lesson plans, on a detailed "day book," and on exactitude in everything her students did. Her insistence on focused organization was another of her gifts to her students.

Marion James was in charge of primary education and, like her colleague Dr Anderson, was years ahead of current thinking – in Ms James's case a belief in the value of primary (and preschool) education for all children. It was a treat to watch her give demonstration lessons and to observe her uncanny ability to keep twenty-five or thirty young children quiet and attentive while she told them her wonderful stories.

And Mrs Reese-Burns laboured mightily to enhance the public speaking abilities of all prospective teachers. There was no rambling around in her (and in her students') presentations. She always insisted on a strong opening statement, clear objectives, a progressive development of ideas, and a strong conclusion, often with a recapitulation of the important ideas. She always sat in the rear of the room to be sure her students could be heard and was sometimes heard to say, "If you don't have something worthwhile to say, don't say anything!" It is doubtful if any of her students in future years and in many different contexts ever forgot the lessons learned from her about effective presentations.

H.O. English, John Gough, V.L. Denton, and H. Gilliland were other faculty members, each in his own way modelling effective teaching and insisting on the highest levels of performance. There were, of course, other members of the faculty, but because the students were divided into several classes, not all students met every faculty member in class.

Extracurricular activities, too, were part of the Lansdowne experience. The Debating Club was popular, as was the Theatre Group. Basketball and grass hockey occupied many after-school hours, and of course there was a Normal School yearbook – *The Anecho*. In all, these were activities planned (hopefully) to round out the lives of prospective teachers and more adequately prepare them for life in the communities of British Columbia.

In fact, one of the enduring legacies of the Normal School to the Victoria College (and later to the University of Victoria) was in the geographical diversity of its student body. Quite literally, the Victoria Normal School catered to students who lived "beyond Hope" – the city, that is – and in his book *A Multitude of the Wise: UVIC Remembered*, Peter

Faculty and staff of the Victoria Provincial Normal School, 1953–54: (left to right, standing) Henry C. Gilliland (vice-principal), Hugh E. Farquhar, Dr F. Henry Johnson, Harry O. English (principal), George A. Brand, D. Boyce Gaddes, A. Wilfrid Johns; (seated) Grace D. Tuckey (librarian), D.M. Daniels, Kathleen M. Baker, Winnette A. Copeland, Marjorie A. Hoey (secretary).

Smith notes: "When the PNS graduates returned to their small-town communities to teach they maintained their links with Victoria and these reciprocal bonds of loyalty and friendship would pay dividends in future years" (12).

Many of the students who attended Normal School came directly from high school and had no post-secondary academic education as such, but in future years they continued their education, first at Victoria College and later at the University of Victoria. And it was here that the melding of the two institutions took place. Although courses were often taken at night school or in the summer (there were no online courses at that time!), the values of the institutions remained constant – high moral standards, proactive personal interactions, and excellent teaching. But now there was a gradual metamorphosis from being a trained teacher to becoming a scholarly educator. Friendships that had been born at Normal School were rekindled in the classrooms of Victoria College.

Summer school sessions were rewarding experiences, enriched in the early years with returning veterans, many of whom were once again students. Of particular note were the weekly dances held every Friday night, and it seemed as though many of the "mature students" had perfected their ballroom dancing as guests of the English girls whom they had met while overseas! Now perhaps it was time to "marry one of the pebbles on the beach!"

By 1956 it appeared that maintaining the two post-secondary institutions as separate entities would need to be reconsidered, and thus it was that the Victoria Normal School was merged with Victoria College as the Department of Teacher Education. No longer was the emphasis in teacher education so markedly on methodology (and indeed, on surviving in British Columbia's hinterland); rather, it was on ensuring that teachers would have an adequate scholarly background as they began their careers. As with all changes, however, many thought that the pendulum had swung too far, with experienced teachers in the field worried that graduates would not have sufficient methodological expertise to handle twenty-five or thirty young children on a daily basis.

In 1963 all was changed again when Victoria College became the University of Victoria and the Department of Education became the Faculty of Education, the first professional faculty in the new university. Today, the Faculty of Education at the University of Victoria continues to educate teachers for the schools of British Columbia, both elementary and secondary. It enjoys an expanded mandate, however, and includes in its curriculum not only diverse educational endeavours but also a large and dynamic graduate program. It is not only a teaching faculty but also one of world-renowned authors and researchers.

And now, a personal note. In thinking about the Lansdowne years and my experiences both at the Provincial Normal School and Victoria College, I decided to focus my remarks mainly on the Normal School. This is in no way meant to detract from the value of the experiences I had at Victoria College. Indeed, they were the foundation of my academic life as I proceeded to post-graduate work at the University of Washington and to my career as a professor of education and assistant to the president and vice-president at the University of Victoria and as chancellor at the same university. Indeed, it was a foundation well and truly laid and second to none anywhere in the world. To those professors, I and my fellow students of those years owe a huge debt of gratitude.

But it was at the Victoria Normal School that I learned how to teach and where I developed my great love for and belief in education as a means of enriching society. It was there that I knew I had found my true vocation and where I developed my lifelong love of working with children and young people. To those of us who began our post-secondary education at the Victoria Normal School, who completed their academic work at Victoria College, UVic, and other post-secondary institutions during the years from 1946 to 1963, who witnessed the birth of the Department of Education at Victoria College, and who finally participated in the emergence of the Faculty of Education at the University of Victoria, "Lansdowne" will always be remembered fondly and will resonate with historical significance. It was, after all, a place and a time that provided an excellent education for us and was, in large part, instrumental in laying the foundation for our future lives.

NORMA I. MICKLESON, CM, OBC, PHD, LLD (hon.), began her career as a public school teacher in British Columbia. She joined the University of Victoria in 1967, where she held various senior administrative offices, including, between 1975 and 1980, dean of Education. She served as chancellor of the University of Victoria from 1997 to 2002.

BUILDINGS OF THE LANSDOWNE YEARS

MARTIN SEGGER

Students, faculty, staff, and visitors – few of them could not but have been impressed by the magnificent setting of Victoria College's Lansdowne campus. Located on a granite bench, tucked into the rise of Mount Tolmie and skirted by Garry oak meadows, this vantage point commands a vast panoramic view over the entire city of Victoria, the Oak Bay suburbs, vistas far west to Esquimalt harbour, and then over the Juan de Fuca Strait, defining the horizon through a three-quarter compass arc – the majestic jagged line of the Olympics. It might therefore be easy to justify overlooking the fact that the college architecture is itself monumental and marked significant historical currents in Victoria's urban development. Even the three former army huts, acquired in 1947 and relocated behind the Young Building to house teaching laboratories, reference the war years and military encampments at Gordon Head, Pat Bay, and Work Point.

The college inherited the imposing Young Building (named after Henry Esson Young, BC education minister from 1907 to 1915) when it moved from Craigdarroch Castle and joined with the Provincial Normal School to co-inhabit the site in 1946 after its temporary use as a hospital for convalescent soldiers. This magnificently sited building was the product of Victoria's ambitions and efforts to obtain an institutional match to the University of British Columbia in Vancouver. The site was acquired in 1911, seven-and-one-half acres in what was then rural countryside on Mount Tolmie. A revision of the first more elaborate plan by architect W.C.F. Gillam included the replacement of terracotta ornament with sandstone, the results of which were ultimately to prove very costly. The contract was let to a Victoria firm, Luney Bros., and practically all the materials were locally procured, except for slate from a Welsh quarry. The building was to accommodate about 150 student teachers enrolled in a one-year elementary program.

The basic teaching areas around which the layout was designed were two model schools complete with classroom, cloakrooms, washrooms, and furnishings. Apart from these there were nine lecture rooms, two laboratories, a music room, and two complete

The J. Lyle Dunlop house at the Lansdowne campus.

housekeeping suites. A finely detailed Baroque Revival–style auditorium with a seating capacity of four hundred was centrally located in the rear of the building. The clock tower housed a water tank for the fire alarm sprinkler system. The Renaissance Revival style was detailed with quarry-cut sandstone and red-clay brick. The ornament is concentrated on the entrance block, which is defined by the central clock tower. The general massing emphasized a palatial horizontality, which, along with its spacious formal Italian garden landscape scheme, was intended to convey the Victorian idea of a Renaissance Villa. Gillam finished the building with an ornately decorated auditorium, which today remains the high point of the interior. The school served its original function until 1942, when temporary military hospital conversion was carried out.

The Normal School was a symbolic high point in the development of the public education system in British Columbia. Schools such as South Ward (1894) in James Bay and Margaret Jenkins (1913) in Fairfield adopted the red-brick Queen Anne (English Renaissance) style. This was no doubt adapted from the London Education Authority's 260 similarly styled schools built during the 1870s after the passage of the Elementary Education Act. Here was model school design throughout British Columbia and a reflection of a non-denominational curriculum. By 1910 the English Renaissance had evolved to a more robust and fashionable interpretation of the style, Italian Renaissance. So although retaining the economy of red brick walls, gables and bracketed eaves gave way to columned porticos, roofline triangular pediments, and classical entablatures, all still common and easily readable today in the suburban schools of both Vancouver and Victoria. The Normal School was just a grander and more elaborate version, appropriately marking its place at the apex of influence in the education system.

In 1999 a seven-million-dollar full-scale restoration was undertaken which saw the exterior walls completely removed and reconstituted to the original designs. Restoration architect Carl Peterson used matching brick but substituted cast concrete for the friable sandstone, the failure of which was causing the near collapse of the building envelope.

The J. Lyle Dunlop house and its six-acre grounds were acquired by the college shortly after the move to the Normal School. It was one of the last commissions of Victoria's premier early twentieth-century architect, Samuel Maclure. Maclure had literally defined the architectural vocabulary of Rockland, Oak Bay, and the Uplands during the course of his forty-year Victoria practice. The house dominates a bald rock outcrop at the crest of the Lansdowne escarpment and shares the site lines of its neighbour, the Normal School. The rocky natural grade on top of which this imposing neoclassical edifice is perched is totally subsumed within a terraced garden podium for the house itself.

The bold clarity and self-contained sense of scale with which the classical tradition invested its forms allowed Maclure to generate his personal solution in a quiet, dignified, yet powerful design which developed and refined many features of his earlier classically inspired commissions. The Dunlop facade is a symmetrical balance of elements organized in relation to the central projecting entrance bay. The low-rise hipped roof is slightly flared at the eaves. Wall planes rise from a granite podium at the base. Progression into the house is formal and processional, up through lateral terraces, under the classical portico with its free-standing Tuscan columns, then through a constricting vestibule with flanking cloakrooms as entry to the central hall. The hall space is dramatic but illusionary. An arcade opens on to a Georgian staircase entering off-axis from the left. Finely detailed classical mouldings and friezes are hallmarks of the interior carried through in both wood and plaster detailing. The drawing room and dining room open into the hall through sliding doors. In line across the rear are library, breakfast room, and kitchen. On the west side the living room opens into a sunroom, completing visual access to the southern panoramic vistas as one moves through the first-floor rooms.

The Dunlop residence is the end product and successful conclusion to a lineage of similar designs that still dot the Victoria landscape today, starting with a 1912 Oak Bay commission, the J.M. Whitney house, where Maclure turned his attention from the Arts and Crafts Tudor revival to the Edwardian classical revival vocabulary both in form and in detail. Following the purchase by the college, the house served ably as a social and entertainment centre, as well as temporary administration offices. Camosun College now meticulously maintains it as a showcase restaurant for its world-class culinary program.

Two buildings were actually constructed for the expanding college, the Ewing Building in 1952 (extension added in 1959), so named to honour Dr J.M. Ewing (college principal, 1944–52) and the E.B. Paul Building, completed nine years later in 1961. Architectural design work for these projects was undertaken by the Provincial Department of Public Works. Interestingly, these buildings witness Victoria's final break with the architecture of its nineteenth-century historicist past and emergence into the cool light of

Students in front of the Ewing Building, c. mid-1950s.

The E.B. Paul Building, completed 1961. Bill Halkett photo.

contemporary modernism. Yet even so, Public Works was slow on the uptake – slow to abandon the break with the early modern style, with its hints of Deco, and the Whittaker era of the 1940s. For example, the Elliot Building on the campus (1963) was actually designed for Lansdowne by W.R.H. Curtis and Andrew Cochrane (1967).

The Ewing Building, which was to house the library and administration, was certainly evidence of this. While decidedly contemporary in its solid unornamented box-like blocks, generous windows, and flat roofline, it seemed very much a holdover from the severe functional economy of the war years and echoes the pre-war continental European work of Corbusier and others. The Paul Building was, however, a further departure. Two two-storey blocks are pinned together by a three-storey central stair tower with its ground-level entrance foyer opening on axis through the building. Exterior form reveals the interior organization. The two classroom and office wings seem almost suspended above the concrete basement level. The glazed curtain walls are pinned to the building by vertical bars that intersect the window bands and create a strong, abstract undulating rhythm as windows play against the wall surfaces. The central stair tower, in stark vertical contrast to these horizontal planes, is marked by the use of faceted concrete blocks punctured on each side by six rows of small square portholes. These create a remarkable effect on the interior, at once illuminating the space with shots of lights and also providing small framed views outward for the intrepid stair climber within.

At the same time Victoria was reinventing itself with a major modern monument, Centennial Square, completed to mark the city's own one-hundredth birthday in 1963. A pivotal figure in promoting this project was Mayor R.B. Wilson, who not only kickstarted the urban renewal of Victoria but also, as a board member, spearheaded the campaign to relocate Victoria College – the nucleus of what would shortly be the University of Victoria – to Gordon Head. The seminal document of Wilson's mayoralty, *Over All Plan for Victoria* (1965), established the terms and language of the discourse on the region's growth which would carry forward some forty years.

Oddly enough, a third building was planned for Lansdowne. Designed by Public Works architect W.R. Curtis, it was actually built as the Elliott Science Building on the new Gordon Head campus. The adjacent Elliott lecture wing pushed many Paul Building features, such as cantilevered concrete elements, integrated building envelope, and natural-source lighting, further along the road of abstract expressionist modernism.

MARTIN SEGGER, MPHIL, FCMA, FRSA is director, Community Relations, University of Victoria, director of the University Centre Museum and Auditorium Complex, and adjunct professor of Renaissance Studies and Museum Studies. He has been active in municipal and provincial public service, having served two three-year terms as an alderman in Victoria and twelve years on the Provincial Capital Commission. He has written widely in the areas of architectural history and museology.

FOUNDING THE UNIVERSITY

OF VICTORIA ART COLLECTION

AT VICTORIA COLLEGE

MARTIN SEGGER

By 1962 Victoria College was confident enough in its growing art collection to offer it to the public as an exhibition at the Art Gallery of Greater Victoria. Titled *Exhibition of the Victoria College Collection of Original Works of Art*, the exhibit ran from 29 May to 17 June of that year. The accompanying two-page catalogue, not illustrated, listed 45 works and divided them into paintings (29), chalk drawings and graphics (10), and "other works" (9), which were essentially sculptures. The brief introduction highlighted the fact that the collection had been built up over the previous ten years and also pointed out that it was supplemented by an extensive "print" collection. These were in fact reproductions of world art (about 500) that had been acquired for teaching purposes.

In a further typewritten document that no doubt formed part of the planning for the exhibition, art-education professor Wilfrid Johns provided some hints for the viewer – how to experience the exhibition. He noted, for instance, that the two portraits, one of Dr J.M. Ewing and the other of college registrar Mr J.A. Cunningham, were "in two constrasting styles." He further drew attention to fact that Jack Shadbolt's *The Red House* was "an early realistic water-colour, illustrating Shadbolt's fine draughtsmanship as well as ability to evoke mood," while *Wading Birds and Orange Rocks* was "a complete contrast to the preceding. Poetic, lyrical colour, handled freely, and with symbolist overtones in the bird forms." Within this small collection lay the foundation, and direction, for the development of the now considerable University of Victoria art collection, some 8,000 works of western Canadian contemporary art.

Johns knew the collection well, as he had chaired the Victoria College Fine Arts Committee. However, credit for starting the collection and then quietly remaining in the background making sure it was supported is given to Harry Hickman, who became vice-principal in 1951 and was confirmed as principal the following year. A UBC gold medalist with a Sorbonne doctoral degree, Hickman was a linguist but also known for his knowledge of and support for music and the visual arts. The first work to be purchased for the collection was acquired in 1951 directly from the artist, Bruno Bobak, who was then living in Victoria with his artist wife, Molly. It was a watercolour titled *Okanagan Landscape*. Joe Plaskett's *Seated Fencer*, bought in 1958 and obviously painted in the artist's Parisian studio, might have been a personal choice of Hickman. Another early acquisition was the oil-on-paper *Forest Scene*, by Victoria's much-loved Emily Carr.

The collection developed through various means of acquisition. In 1952 William Straith, who had been minister of education, donated a pastel, *Winter Scene of Kitwanga*, by Judith Morgan. Shadbolt's *The Red House* was a 1952 purchase from the Bau-Xi Gallery in Vancouver, while the large brooding oil *Battle Scarred* – in fact a West Coast forest scene – was a donation by the artist, W.P. Weston, in memory of his friend J.M. Ewing, who had died that year. Pavelic's memorial portrait of Ewing was funded by a student donation through the Alma Mater Society. Her portrait of Cunnigham was presented to the college "by his friends." Ina Uhtohoff's *Suburbia* and *Still Life* were presented by the Greater Victoria Teachers' Association.

Prices might surprise us, but not if we compute the purchasing power of the dollar at the time. Donald Jarvis's oil *Beach Forms* was purchased from the artist for $300.00. There was also some specific fundraising with a view to underpinning the collection with "Canadian" works. A Group of Seven piece, Lawren Harris's *Country North of Lake Superior*, was purchased with a Massey grant. Harris's evocative Laurentian forest scene *Algoma* was donated by the Victoria Chapter of the University Women's Club in 1958. In any event, through those early years Hickman kept the money flowing as most works were bought, and many, such as *Dark Painting* by Vancouver artist Donald Jarvis, acquired in 1962 at a price of $500.00, were not cheap.

The Victoria College Art Collection was a functional one. Some works were obviously commemorative gifts or commissions, but all graced the walls of offices and public spaces in the buildings of the Lansdowne campus. However, the selection, as Wilfrid Johns indicated, was carefully crafted for educational purposes. It also provided direction for future development. Myfanwy Pavelic, who was to become one of Canada's foremost contemporary portrait painters, was to apply her interpretive talent to numerous images of university academics and administrators during her long career – Chancellor Clearihue, President Howard Petch, and teachers Robin Skelton and Pat Martin Bates, among others. Then in 1994 she donated her entire personal collection of West Coast art and a personal archive of her own work documenting her development as an artist from early youth. Many acquisitions were prescient. Several acquisitions over those years – the Pavelic works, Max Bates (*Three Vases*, 1957, and *Washerwomen*, 1959), Herbert Siebner (*The Founders of the Castle*, 1957), Richard Ciccimarra (*The Beggar*, 1958, *Camas*, 1959, and *Nude*, 1959), Bob De Castro (*Fossil Men*, 1959), Nita Forrest (*Cow*, 1959), and Elza Mayhew (*Farewell*, 1959) – not only documented the Victoria art scene and supported local artists but looked forward to the formation of the "Limners," a group that self-defined the Victoria artistic establishment of 1970s and 1980s.

Vancouver, however, was not overlooked. Either directly from artists or through the 1st Avenue Bau-Xi Gallery, numerous forward-looking acquisitions were made. Jack Shadbolt, who had taught briefly at the Provincial Normal School, was an obvious choice. So perhaps was Gitsan First Nations artist Judith Morgan (*Winter Scene of Kitwanga*, 1952), who had attended the Normal School. However, works such as Donald Jarvis's *Beach Forms* (1952), *Dark Painting* (1962), and *Procession* (1963), Fred Amess's

Selected works of art from the Victoria College collection:
(clockwise from the upper left-hand corner) Judith Morgan,
Winter in Kitwanga; Myfanwy Pavelic, *Portrait of J.M. Ewing*;
Jack Shadbolt, *The Red House*; Herbert Siebner, *The Founders
of the Castle*.

Yale Church (1956) and *Sand Dunes* (1957), John Koerner's *Coast Glitter* (1958), Charles Scott's *The Red Sail* (1961), Jack Hardman's *Vestigia* (1963), Lionel Thomas's *Chinese Impressions*, 1962, and the highly abstract *Polar No. 35* by Toni Onley might have seemed more of a risk at the time. Gordon Smith's *Woods in Winter, Markers, Spanish Banks*, and *Nocturne* were early acquisitions, and Gordon was a friend of Harry Hickman.

In addition to Myfanwy Pavelic, who received numerous commissions and an honorary doctorate from UVic in 1984, several other artists were to develop relationships with the university. From the artist and friends of Herbert Siebner, it was to develop one of the most comprehensive collections of his work. Californian expat Margaret Peterson (*Gods of Sun Dogs*, 1962) would produce a large mosaic work for the entrance foyer of the McPherson Library. Flemming Jorgensen (*Denmark*, 1961) would receive an honorary degree and donate a large body of work. UVic would receive the papers and a large body of sculptural work from the estate of Bob De Castro. Oak Bay High art teacher Bill West (*Passing Ships*, 1959) would execute the stabile/mobile sculptures for the three-storey stairwells of the UVic Clearhue Building and then join the Theatre Department to teach set design. Two of Elza Mayhew's powerful large-scale bronzes, *Coast Spirit* and *Bronze Priestess*, now dominate the central quad of the UVic campus.

First Nations artist Judith Morgan was trained and worked in the western tradition. However, the collection also included a 42-centimetre Haida argillite pole dated about 1910, purchased from a collector for $500 in 1961 and noted in the catalogue as "school of Edenshaw." There were also two Inuit carvings and a stone-block print, *Man Carried to the Moon*. The college collection was not wholly restricted to western Canadian work. It also included two Japanese woodblock prints: Heroshi Yoshida's *Stone Lantern* and Jurichio Sekino's *Pond of Night*. There was also a small collection of ethnographic items from Africa, New Zealand, and South America.

The end of the Lansdowne years was marked by a very significant event in the development of the University of Victoria. This was the bequest in 1964 by Katharine and John Maltwood of their house and property at Royal Oak in Saanich. The donation included a substantial endowment and a significant 1,200-item art collection. Along with the work of Katherine Maltwood herself, sculptures, drawings, and personal papers, and an extensive decorative arts collection, both eastern and western, came a substantial collection of western Canadian art which she and her husband John had assembled during the war years and the 1950s. This bequest provided the fiscal basis and facilities which, when re-established on campus at the University Centre in 1978, became the Maltwood Art Museum and Gallery.

MEMORIES AND IMPRESSIONS
OF A NEW FACULTY MEMBER
IN THE LANSDOWNE ERA

ANN SADDLEMYER

I arrived in Victoria just in time for the beginning of the 1956 term, an MA from Queen's still smoking in my gloved hand. Every young lady still wore gloves, or so I had been taught. But my first visit to Roger and Ailsa Bishop's home cured me of that and many other similar notions; this was a new world, still courteous and welcoming but without pretension (though Sydney Pettit was distressed that the men refused to stand up when their women colleagues joined them). Victoria College, however, was also recently thrust into a new image of itself, still reeling from a shotgun marriage with the Victoria Provincial Normal School, which had for ten years tolerated academics in the west wing of what would later be known as the Young Building. Now as members of the College of Education, its faculty eagerly adopted their newly created professorships. Victoria College was suddenly much larger, looking forward to a four-year program, rather than its traditional two-year status as a junior branch of the University of British Columbia. Blissfully unaware of all these complications, I revelled in my new career as a junior instructor with a salary of $3,425. The world was my oyster (and I rapidly became very fond of the real thing).

That fall when Carl Hare, Bob Lawrence, and I joined the English department, we doubled its number and considerably lowered the average age of the Victoria College faculty. The change in structure must have been somewhat disorienting for Rodney Poisson and Grant McOrmond, long-term members, and even for Roger Bishop (familiarly known as RJB), in charge of the department. Carl arrived from the University of Alberta with a promise to complete his MA thesis as soon as possible; we both looked with awe at Assistant Professor R.G. Lawrence, who already had a PhD in hand. Though Carl taught one course in Philosophy, all three of us were specialists in drama; in hindsight, one sees that this was probably a deliberate choice by Roger, who had been much involved in the Players' Club. He gained the added bonus of Carl's bride, Clara, a teacher and fine actress herself, and Bob's wife, Joan, a research librarian and avid theatregoer.

Ann Saddlemyer, c. 1993.

The Lansdowne building had been taken over by the federal government as a veterans' hospital during the Second World War, and occasionally a startled figure would appear at the door of my tiny office explaining that it used to hold a bathtub. I was happy and excited with my teaching – three first-year courses (twelve hours a week from Monday through Saturday) – and kept busy with the incessant marking of composition essays. But there still seemed to be time for extracurricular activities with both students and colleagues. The Faculty Association, under the energetic leadership of Phoebe Noble, held numerous parties, games nights (though I resolutely refused to be drawn into bridge), potluck suppers, and "progressive dinners" where groups walked from one house to another and from course to course. In between there were parties at Vantreight Drive, where Roger and Ailsa Bishop were generous hosts. Despite Hugh Farquhar's recently established athletic program on campus, I recall a brief session at the curling club but little else of an athletic nature that year, apart from a strenuous hike on Mount Arrowsmith in the company of newly appointed marine biologist Arthur Fontaine, his wife, Marion, and Anne Gorham (who later married NDP leader Allan Blakeney).

Like the faculty, the student body (numbering 575) was overwhelmingly white Anglo-Saxon Protestant; except for those student teachers from the interior who were compelled to register in Victoria rather than Vancouver and a few other newcomers to the city, most seemed to know one another from high school. Their tight little world was, on the whole, a continuation, not an initiation. The students' choir serenaded the faculty homes at Christmas; there were jazz sessions and dances at the Crystal Garden (where bottles in brown paper bags were routinely but not that discreetly deposited under the tables). Not much older than the students, despite our formal roles as chaperones, the Hares, the Lawrences, and I were willing conspirators.

Occasionally, however, my five or six years' age difference seemed a major obstacle. Once a week the students had a dance session at lunchtime, which unfortunately was followed immediately by my class on poetry. After some weeks of tolerating a large room of flushed, hormone-happy, and excited students who were clearly not interested in any serious attempt to lead them through the poetic mysteries, I objected in no uncertain terms. A polite deputation arrived in my office to explain their point of view, culminating in one student kindly explaining, "But, Miss Saddlemyer, wasn't there something you used to enjoy dancing to when you were a student – like the Charleston?" I gave up and switched poetry to a quieter, more sedate time.

Excited and enthusiastic, I had at last found the role I was happy with, in an environment where teaching was paramount. (We were usually compared to the venerable American Reed College and proud of the quality of students who went on to capture awards at UBC.) But very soon Roger called me into his office for a serious talk – if this was the life I wanted, the writing was on the wall. Besides, it was clear that the college was on its way to becoming a degree-granting institution. I would need to get a doctorate, and soon. Disgruntled, I looked at my options: the only research I was interested in pursuing was the Irish dramatic movement, and the one scholar I admired was at the University of London. Unenthusiastically, I wrote to Professor Una Ellis-Fermor and set about applying for funding; by December I learned that I had won an IODE scholarship, and at the end of a College Council meeting I submitted my resignation to Principal Hickman. Privately I saw no future as a scholar; I wanted to teach.

Meanwhile, RJB was having equally serious discussions with Carl, who was torn between teaching and performing. If he was accepted at RADA, he and Clara would also go to London; if not, he would complete his MA thesis. He eventually finished the thesis, but in the meantime his audition for RADA was successful. Clara decided that her career, too, should be with the theatre, and once they settled in London, she would enter the Central School of Art and Drama. The academic year ended, the Faculty Association gave us a farewell party (I still have their gift of a bead necklace and earrings), and the three of us set off for London, where we continued in close companionship for another three years.

Ties with Victoria College also continued – Bob and Joan Lawrence spent a research year in London, joining us on almost nightly visits to the theatre; the Bishops came over on book-buying tours, Ailsa claiming that Roger's familiarity with Britain was entirely in the basements of second-hand bookstores; I looked forward to completing my thesis (ostensibly from London but I spent most of my time in Dublin) and returning to my chosen career. In the fall of 1960 I was back in Victoria, though it would take another summer in London to complete the doctorate. The Hares returned to Canada also, determined on the professional theatre.

Meanwhile, I discovered a remarkable sea change in Victoria, not only in a further enlarged English department but in a college on the verge of becoming a university. Even more significant, I returned to a faculty that was no longer a cosy, contained group and a little less WASPish. RJB had brought over Bill Benzie from Scotland to replace Bob Lawrence while he was on leave, and like so many others, Bill remained; Peter L. Smith was there on a joint appointment with Classics; Pat Köster, whom I had known in London, had returned to her home town. Anthony Jenkins and Joan Coldwell walked into the first departmental meeting with me (Joan and I were appointed to pour the tea). The following year we were joined by Chet Lambertson, John Peter, David Buchan, Michael Warren, John Hayman, Elizabeth Brewster, and Jean Kennard, and still they continued to come – Margaret Doody, George Forbes, Tony Emery (whose creativity as College Council recorder was truly inspiring), George Cuomo (who brewed his own lethal saki and persuaded John Peter to become a novelist). The women were no longer expected to preside at the tea table. RJB soon had an empire of enthusiastic teachers from Europe, South Africa, and North America. Over the years, he would also send many of them off to get their doctorates; some returned, while others were replaced by yet more young recruits.

It was a voluble, energetic, intense, sometimes unruly, always opinionated group. But we were all enamoured of teaching and full of fresh, new ideas. We visited Royal Roads more frequently when a branch of the Humanities Association was established. Attending one lecture, I was shocked to discover the formal notice "Cadets must polish their own door-knobs." Trying to keep ahead of the students in new courses (my office mate of the Faculty of Education thought I worked too hard), I still seemed to find time for extra projects, the most astonishing perhaps a full-fledged Shakespearean production.

That story deserves a page to itself. Despite the steady advance towards an honours program, English 100 was still the core course, and all of us were expected to teach it. Sitting around the faculty lunchroom in the Ewing Building, a number of us bemoaned the fact that it was unlikely any of our students had actually seen a Shakespearean production. So why not show them *Othello*? Chet Lambertson, who came with considerable experience as a theatre composer, was appointed director; David Buchan's throaty Scottish voice lent strength to the role of the Moor, while Anthony Jenkins and Michael Warren were superbly matched as Iago and Roderigo. John Hayman as Cassio wooed Joan Coldwell's Bianca; Ailsa Bishop was transformed into Iago's wife; Bob Lawrence, John Peter, Peter Smith, and Librarian Dean Halliwell were among the courtiers. The Young Building auditorium was our theatre, the creaking stage surrounded by hastily painted flats. One lasting memory is of Rodney Poisson being prompted by Jean Kennard on a stepladder behind the shaky flats, when he wasn't close enough to the many notes he had thoughtfully pinned to the side curtains. Costumes – not always well-fitting, sometimes too much so – were rented from Malabar's in Winnipeg. I was stage manager, enjoying the opportunity to wander onstage during intermission in blue jeans, hammer in hand, on a platform usually reserved for more lofty ceremonies. Flushed with success – we had actually done it, and made money too! – most of us were distressed by the less than enthusiastic reception by Victoria critic Audrey Johnson. She was not warmly received at the next party on Vantreight Drive.

Two years later Carl Hare was lured back by the promise of a theatre; a willing band of volunteers turned up with paint brushes, brooms, and hammers, and the Campus Players were established in a freshly painted Quonset hut on the new Gordon Head campus. Appropriately, the first productions were two one-act plays featuring David Buchan, Michael Warren, and (directed by Clara) Carl himself. Critical reviews were much more positive. By then I was not only stage manager but in charge of the box office. Those first plays were designed by Clara Hare; soon Biddy Gaddes and Bill West joined the team, which rapidly became far more ambitious.

My own efforts to encourage interest in the arts resulted in a small informal "arts and letters" group that met at the home I shared with my aunt and uncle. I can recall readings from their own work by Robert Foster (who would later work on a new verse translation of *The Bacchae* for Carl Hare's Players' Club) and Michael Stephen (who later became a theatre practitioner in Toronto) and contributions by young artists Michael Morris and Eric Metcalfe. Encouraged by RJB, who provided a small budget, I launched a series of poetry readings by West Coast authors. And then, after meeting Robin Skelton on his first visit to Ireland, I suggested that the poet would be a stellar addition to our expanding department. By March 1965 Robin's energetic enthusiasm resulted in the Yeats Centenary, a week-long celebration of the Irish poet, including productions of two plays, an exhibition in the Art Gallery of Victoria drawn from Robin's and my private collections, enhanced by portraits from as far away as the National Gallery in London, a series of lectures on the CBC, and the first book published by the University of Victoria, which we co-edited. *The World of Yeats* included essays also by Gwladys Downes, Joan Coldwell, and others and, thanks to the University of Washington Press, managed to stay in print for a quarter of a century. Robin and John Peter then followed this achievement with the founding of the *Malahat Review*.

The English department would soon spawn separate departments for Theatre and Creative Writing, but RJB insisted that, despite the emphasis on research as we developed an honours program, teaching must remain paramount. He continued to visit each new recruit's classroom during the first term and was alert to any slackening on the part of the rest of us, no matter how senior. With new courses to prepare, I sometimes found it nerve-racking to face a phalanx of very bright students: Julian Reid sitting throughout the class with arms crossed; Rona Murray, a published poet and dramatist; Robin Jeffrey, a sports journalist for the *Victoria Times*; Michiel Horn, who has never forgotten my chastising him for talking in class; Anne Mayhew, who had returned from UBC to take additional courses before joining us as a colleague.

Stirring times indeed! The spring of 1961 saw our first graduating class parade into the Old Gymnasium – a small, homogenous group of thirty-seven. From my bird's-eye view of the stage, I observed that one of the Education professors was wearing shocking pink high heels below her academic gown, while one of our own departmental instructors sported mismatched socks. Clearly, we did not yet measure up to the sophisticated formality of UBC – if we ever would be. I had been granted tenure a good two years before Acting Principal Bob Wallace pulled out an office drawer and casually informed me of the fact; university though we might aim for, there was still a casual college atmosphere.

As the faculty enlarged and the student body grew, we moved from one building to another. I revelled in my office in the Paul Building, no longer having to share bookshelves or space. Betty Kennedy from mathematics was across the hall, already displaying formidable organizing skills; Gordon Tracy expounded on German literature; Edward Bond tried unsuccessfully to clarify our lessons in logic. Avoiding "Ma" Norris's lethal coffee in the cafeteria building, we elected instead to share the responsibility for providing supplies in the new lounge. But nothing was more challenging – and nothing more divisive ever became public – than the decision in the spring of 1961 to move the entire campus to Gordon Head. Alarmed at the prospect of becoming a large, faceless institution, and doubtless also distressed that the consultants hired were from south of the border, a small group, myself among them, vociferously objected to the proposal. Although I spoke as a very junior member of faculty, I was listened to courteously; but now, looking back on that eventful day, I can see that the auditorium was already too small to contain the entire faculty. Further separation was inevitable; we would never again be able to discuss issues facing each other.

Maturing as an institution took its toll in other ways too. With the gradual move to Gordon Head, the students no longer had a departmental base. Some of us were shifted to temporary quarters in the army huts (where once again the college community would band together, paintbrushes in hand, to create the first Faculty Club), while others remained behind at Lansdowne; lectures took place in different buildings. Long-sighted as RJB's concern for a lively, well-versed department was, sending his most promising instructors away to pursue their doctorates resulted in a constantly shifting group, uncertain of one another and, indeed, of the ground rules. Even those were changing from year to year as the "Californian influence" made itself felt on campus. I recall a student gravely informing me that under the influence of pot (or LSD, perhaps both), he could feel the heart beating in one of the great Lansdowne oaks; a few years later I would encounter another former student on the ferry, who cheerfully admitted that he was a drugs courier. I no longer remember his name.

Often our teaching methodology adapted accordingly: the seminar and tutorial situation took over from formal lectures; where formerly the desk was the great divider, now discussion (sometimes in a circle on the floor) was encouraged. Young instructors demanded the right to set their own exams; one errant colleague actually distributed the questions on the final exam in advance, necessitating a hasty convening of a small Saturday committee to create a new test. On the whole this loosening was a good thing, challenging the brightest in the course to form their own opinions. This was the advent of the "anti-Calendar," when we were assessed not by an avuncular department head but by hard-headed, sometimes disenchanted students. This stronger and openly critical attitude was all to the good in shattering complacency, but I sometimes wondered, as the student body became more heterogeneous, whether the less confident were too frequently blindsided by their outspoken confreres.

Always alert to the needs of the library, RJB soon took advantage of my research summers abroad to commission me to "take a look" at various collections advertised in antiquarian book catalogues. One memorable visit (by appointment) to "The House of LDF" in New York led to an enriching educational experience for me and the beginning of Victoria's collection of modern manuscripts. Lew Feldman, major supplier to the wealthy University of Texas, was intrigued that a small college on the west coast of Canada should be interested in his catalogue; as a trial run, he offered a small collection of Ezra Pound manuscripts for which Roger immediately found the funds. Then an even more exciting offer came our way while I was in London. Lew and his wife, Sally, invited me to join them at a sale in Sotheby's, and afterwards I was taken down to the docks (the taxi was kept waiting), where the caretaker was ordered to break the locks on a large trunk of papers. With a flourish, the old showman displayed the large collection of letters and related manuscripts purchased from the Herbert Read estate: correspondence with Richard Aldington, T.S. Eliot, Barbara Hepworth, Henry Miller, Henry

Moore, Kathleen Raine, Stephen Spender, George Woodcock, and others, notebooks, and worksheets were flashed before my startled eyes. I returned to my flat and immediately phoned RJB; with barely a pause as he shook himself from sleep, he said, "Buy it" – the money would be found. It was, of course, and some months later Howard Gerwing and his staff in Rare Books began the long task of cataloguing. Some time later the *Malahat Review* produced a special issue on the Read collection, and scholars continue to visit it from all over the world. Lew and Sally Feldman even made a special journey themselves to see this brave little college; I suspect some members of my honours seminar never quite recovered from the elegant visitor with his silver-headed cane and New York air of confidence. We also made a special visit to the College Council, but they did not take seriously Lew's offer of a collection of Sir Arthur Conan Doyle papers and some property in England (the details of which I do not recall). Dazzled myself by these adventures in the antiquarian book world, I wondered briefly if I should take up another trade. Here was where the real world of research began.

By the final move to the new campus, I was committed to that research in the field I had reluctantly entered as a young graduate student. Again, RJB was supportive of us all as head of the department, ensuring that we had leave when necessary and always three summer months free, as much as possible, from administrative duties. But with the status of a fully accredited university on a campus that seemed to sprout another building every time one turned around came numerous committee responsibilities and less free time. Though perhaps the Lansdowne years had in some ways been too "cosy and claustrophobic," as a friend has described them, the adventure and flexibility of those times soon faded, and we were embarked on the serious world of the new academia.

ANN SADDLEMYER, OC, FRSC, FRSA, LLD (hon.), DLITT, PHD, started her career at Victoria College, continued there after it became the University of Victoria, and then moved to the University of Toronto. Between 1988 and 1995 she served as master of Massey College at the University of Toronto. She is currently visiting professor of English at the University of Victoria. An internationally recognized scholar, Dr Saddlemeyer has written extensively on Irish theatre, Canadian theatre, and modern poetry and drama. Her award-winning book *Becoming George: The Life of Mrs. W.B. Yeats* (Oxford University Press, 2002) is world-renowned.

LANSDOWNE DAYS

1947–1963

ROGER J. BISHOP

EDITOR'S NOTE
As chapter 7, by Dr Ann Saddlemyer, shows, Professor Roger J. Bishop played a key role in building up both the English Department and the library resources of Victoria College. This article by Professor Bishop originally appeared in *On the Way to the Ring*, a special supplement to *The Ring*, published by the Department of University Relations, University of Victoria, on 22 September 1976. Professor Bishop reflects insightfully on various aspect of the Lansdowne experience. E.B.H.

Whenever I think of the Lansdowne days of Victoria College, I think of Wordsworth's lines:

> Bliss was it in that dawn to be alive
> And to be young was very heaven.

I think both students and faculty had a feeling that they were in at the creation of a new and very good institution. It was a heady time. The six hundred veterans who had swamped the slender facilities of Craigdarroch Castle had, under the generalship of Principal Ewing and Student President Terry Garner, led the battle to get the larger quarters of the underused Normal School at Lansdowne released for college purposes. They had marched on the Legislature with their plea, and John Hart's government had overruled the reluctant educational bureaucrats to divide the Normal (Young) building into two: the college was to occupy the west, while the Normal would be confined to the eastern half.

To make the college opening on the new campus possible in January 1947, every student and every faculty member had to make a maximum effort. The biology lab and the chemistry-physics huts had to be lifted from their Craigdarroch foundations and carried

The approach to Victoria College with the Young Building
in the background. Drawing by Edward Goodall, c. 1959.

to a new site back of the Normal Building. And every piece of equipment had to be taken down, labelled, and packed. I had to supervise the movement of the library, and that was simple by comparison. (There were only some four thousand books in those days!) The main problem was getting the shelving down at Craigdarroch and then up at Lansdowne before the books arrived!

Once established at Lansdowne, we discovered we were not popular with the Normal staff. An iron curtain of suspicion existed. What were the further intentions of those pushy college types? Though gym and auditorium were supposed to be shared, in effect these facilities could be used freely by the college only in the few weeks of the fall and spring terms when the Normal students were out practice teaching. Anything more than that required negotiations worthy of the United Nations. Despite all the difficulties, however, (and a more inadequate stage never can have existed than the apron stage in the Young Building!), the College Players' Club did produce a reasonable *School for Scandal* and a splendid *Night Must Fall* in 1950 and 1951. Disinterestedly, too, they put all of their profits from these and subsequent productions into a trust fund which eventually helped to make the Phoenix Theatre possible.

And all the time the enrolment of the Normal School was rising, the college library was growing, and general pressure on space was increasing. But splendid Dr Ewing had foreseen that new quarters must be provided. Through friends in the government, he had had an amendment attached to the School Act which safeguarded college surplus funds (the federal government had begun to pay special grants to help universities and colleges meet the veterans' educational needs), and he had used these funds to buy six acres from Mr Dunlop, who owned property east of the Young Building. Further than this, he had accumulated enough money to erect a small building so that the library and the college offices could be shifted to make more classroom space available to the Young.

When Dr Ewing died of a heart attack early in 1952, the completed building was named in his memory by a faculty and student body determined that one who had served so well should not be forgotten. I well remember when the building was opened by then education minister Tilly Rolston in late 1952. With pride, she stated that the Ewing would provide space sufficient to meet all college needs to Victoria until 1967. Well, only a few years passed before the roof had to be jackhammered off, and a third storey added. No cloistered quiet that winter! And then the Paul Building was built, Dunlop House bought, and Hudson's Bay Company land acquired on both sides of the extended Foul Bay Road.

Meantime, in the early fifties, when the government brought the Normal Schools into the university system, the problem of separate and conflicting jurisdictions on the Lansdowne Campus was solved. But then the question of the terms of affiliation with UBC. began to emerge. More and more students were questioning why they should have to cross to Vancouver to complete their degrees. Why couldn't they have the courses they needed in Victoria? Though most faculty and students started as UBC loyalists, the constant difficulties encountered in getting authorization from UBC authorities for upper year work in Victoria led to a movement for independence. And when geometric increases in student population in the Vancouver area led to government approval of a separate Simon Fraser University, how could an independent UVic be resisted?

So in a very few years the thirty-five acres which had seemed luxury at Lansdowne were despised as totally inadequate. It was then that the hundreds of acres of ex-army camp and Hudson's Bay land north of Cedar Hill were bought, and plans for a new university improvised.

ROGER J. BISHOP, MA, was born in Vancouver. He received his BA in English from the University of British Columbia in 1938 and his MA in English from the University of Toronto. After two years at the University of Saskatchewan, he joined the faculty of Victoria College as head of the English Department. In this capacity, his scholarship and leadership were crucial to the building up of both the Department of English and the library resources of the college. He remains an admired friend of many colleagues and former students.

MEMORIES, MENTORS, AND A CANADIAN BASKETBALL CHAMPIONSHIP: MEN'S SPORTS AT THE LANSDOWNE CAMPUS

KENNETH McCULLOCH

The proud heritage of athletics at Victoria College on the Lansdowne campus commenced in 1946 and made a relatively flawless move in 1964 to the University of Victoria at Gordon Head. Because I was a member of the 1956–59 men's basketball team, I have been invited to share my youthful experiences at Victoria College and to recap the Canadian Championship run of 1958. As well, I have been requested to briefly review the men's teams and individual male athletes of the Lansdowne years, which and who have so noticeably contributed to Victoria's sports history. Hopefully, I can achieve this end without complete confusion of memory and imagination.

Although I had been a member of the Future Teachers' Club at Victoria High School, the idea had obviously not been deeply rooted, for when I phoned home in the late summer of 1955 from Ucluelet after a summer working on a West Coast trawler, I told my father that I would be staying on and fishing for winter Chinooks. I can clearly remember how shocked I was to hear his regret that I would not be continuing on to Victoria College. Post–high school study was not something I had ever heard my parents discuss as an impending possibility for me, and certainly, school work had never been a part of my serious repertoire. Unusual to declare, but it was a fortunate experience when I fell overboard two days later, with the skipper asleep and the boat on automatic pilot. I spent only thirty minutes in the water before being rescued, but it was more than enough time to formulate a new plan. "There has to be another way," I said to the skipper as he pulled me aboard. My father's few buoyant words a few days earlier and the near drowning had been enough to instill in me a dream of scholarship that has stayed for a lifetime.

Because I had been such an elusive student through most of my public school years, there were several deficits in my education that now had to be filled. However, I was ready for the challenge, something I can partially attribute to an experience during the summer of 1954 while a member of the Air Force Reserve at Sea Island. It was nine years after the war had ended, but they were still teaching Fighter Control Operation and paying us for the privilege. Each Friday we were set an exam of the week's teachings, but little did I know at the end of that first week that the results would be posted for all to see. I recall running my finger from the top to the absolute bottom of the results and agonizing over the humiliation, so painful, in truth, that the crest of the roll became my future intention. Two summers and two fortunate life-shifting experiences proved invaluable for a student commencing serious study.

Victoria College seems now, through challenged memory, to have been a relatively straightforward transition from high school, probably because so many of us were freshmen and we solved the many confusions jointly. Fortunately for all of us, Dorothy Cruikshank, registrar, and Patricia Sullivan, assistant registrar, were patient and knowledgeable, ready to answer a myriad of questions, and always with a smile. I found my new professors enthusiastic, fostering fierce pride in the institution and scholarship. I now know what dedication is required of a leader to develop the caring staff who would become our teachers, mentors, and friends. Harry Hickman, a distinguished scholar and forward-thinking leader, obviously had that proficiency. The 1955–56 college annual, the *Tower*, included the principal's memorable message: "Already you have discovered that there is much to learn; much will be forgotten too. Yet in the lifelong process of learning and remembering and reflecting, you will develop as a thinking being; moreover before the year 2000 you will make a valuable contribution to our extraordinarily promising Canada." Many of my fellow learners and I were inspired by this message, which was often reiterated by our professors, and we bought the dream.

I recall feeling considerable delight with my day-to-day experiences, almost a sense of exhilaration. Life was full with study, club activities, and new responsibilities. New friendships entered our lives, and we challenged and assisted one other. We were positively influenced through close contact with our professors and infused with new beliefs, which we espoused frequently. I can remember Tony Emery stating in a history course some years later that there was nothing worse than "a little knowledge." I had plenty of these "little" bits and pieces, nuggets that were freely shared but often and unfortunately grossly unexamined. The result was, of course, that these gems were regularly challenged and disputed. Little did I know that I was spreading disdain for knowledge among my so-called lesser-educated friends and parents at an alarming rate. This too was learning, in spite of the discomfort.

When I enrolled at Victoria College, there were just over one hundred students in second year. Though the frosh class had exploded to over two hundred and fifty students, this was a huge decline in numbers from what most of us had experienced in high school. The faculty and staff comprised twenty-seven members. There were no playing fields, but there was a downstairs, basement gymnasium in the Young Building about the size of a large classroom. There were many positives to the small student and staff numbers, as they provided the basis for a tightly woven group, and the lack of facilities never seemed a problem. All games were played away, mostly in the adjacent Lansdowne Junior Secondary or on its fields.

G. Grant McOrmond was my English professor in first year, a man of considerable patience whom I found agreeable to giving considerable time to keen students. He was a keen participant in student social activities, and my memories are buoyed when I think of the dazzling couple he and his wife made as they danced together at our school functions. Over the years, as I majored in English, he would become a mentor and friend whom I respected and admired.

Lewis J. Clarke was my chemistry professor; he was a strong supporter of the athletic program and of students generally. He informed us of the wealth of nature at our doorstep and the importance of establishing a strong link with our environment. His knowledge of and passion for plants spilled into the classroom, and he introduced us to the joys of hiking, particularly on the Forbidden Plateau.

Sydney G. Pettit's passion for history was as conspicuous as his portly figure, and we prized both. Enthusiasm spilled from his lectern while he encouraged us to delve for historical bits that would enlighten our unencumbered minds.

German was a new adventure for me. Though Gordon L. Tracy did his best to enrapture us in that guttural language, one thing became clear. Not only did I not have an ear for music, but I also didn't have an ear for language. The written textbook word made more sense than the spoken classroom lessons, and I struggled under the tuition of a fellow student, Joan Sutherland, whom I can thank for a passing grade.

William H. Gaddes introduced me to psychology and proved to be both a persuasive and a motivating scholar in a field of knowledge that I believe should have been mandatory for every young student. I enjoyed him as a professor and later had the pleasure of his further teachings when I entered the College of Education. He was another of those who actively supported the lives of his students.

A couple who would prove to have a significant influence on me were Professors David B. McLay and R. Jean McLay. David was not a practised basketball coach, but he took a group of inspired players in 1955, both the Norsemen and the Vikings, and made them into cohesive groups. He brought joy and purpose to the gym, which was the required combination for a few wins and abundant fun. I think his greatest contribution was the self-worth he instilled in his players. There is no doubt we were the beneficiaries of his strong values. Jean inspired us with simpler things, such as the warmth of their home and social gatherings. Three players from this team – Lance Finch and Douglas Patterson, both graduates of Mount View High School, and myself – would in 1958 have the opportunity to play for a Canadian Championship.

In 1956 the ranks of Victoria College swelled again as the Victoria Normal School came under the jurisdiction of Victoria College and became known as the College of Education. H.C. Gilliland was the director of Education, and he was on top of his job, ever willing to assist while ensuring that the established standards were met. I could not help but develop some favourite new mentors with whom my contact was necessarily limited by courses or club activities. At the top of my list were two men who were energetic, focused on students, and dedicated to quality education. Hugh E. Farquhar and Fred L. Martens, though quite different men, were dedicated professionals. K.M. Christie, W.A. Copeland, the Gaddes brothers, Alfred E. Loft, Robert T. Wallace, and Neil A. Swainson all made memorable and significant contributions to my life.

Hugh Farquhar was very aware in 1956 that a talented group of basketball players were arriving from Victoria High School, and he wanted to provide a worthy challenge.

He hatched the dream of a run for a Canadian Junior Championship, and he was keen to have a knowledgeable coach. He found what he wanted in Bill Garner, a former Viking and all-round athlete who was teaching at Lansdowne Junior High School. Bill brought expertise, but he also had the necessary motivational skills. Fred Martens became the faculty sponsor, and the leadership team was in place. The captain of the team was Tom English from Victoria High School, the smoothest player on the team with natural leadership skills to go with his broad smile. Other former Victoria High School players were Art Chiko, Bob Tomlinson, Waldo Skillings, Terry Lore, and Ed Kowalyk. Doug Flynn came from St Louis College, and Lance Rossington was from Revelstoke. Ken Brousseau was a Belmont product, and I was the only holdover from the previous year's team.

The team won several championships during the 1957–58 year, including City, Lower Vancouver Island, Vancouver Island, and British Columbia, before we travelled to Lethbridge, Saskatoon, and Winnipeg, where we were well tested but successful. With the Western Canadian Trophy tucked safely away, we were off on the final leg of this three-and-a-half-week train trip to Toronto to meet the Toronto YMHA Whites, a better and bigger team, who defeated us in three games to win the Canadian crown. A rather humorous aside is that the college did not have the funds necessary to send all players by train with their own bunk. Terry Lore and Doug Flynn believed that this was a trip not to be missed; so with some well-deserved reluctance, they took on the challenge of sharing. What we do for sport! Another sidelight is that in Saskatoon we met a player named Bob Bell, who would later become a professor in the UVic Physical Education Department.

In an article written under the byline "Viking Views" by Robin Farquhar, son of Hugh, I discovered this bit of forgotten information, which was written after a rough-and-tumble series in Winnipeg where team decorum was tested. Fred Martens sent these heart-warming words by telegram to Hugh: "Sportsmanship exemplary and gentlemanly all-round and morale at peak. Bill and I are bursting with pride." This was such an emblematic message from Fred and plainly demonstrates the sportsmanship he so valued and imbued in the team. We were indeed better because of his presence. It was gratifying to note that the *Tower* of that year called the team the "strongest team ever to play under the College (Vikings) name."

September 1957 brought a renewed desire for a Canadian Championship, together with the knowledge that if we were successful, the Western Canadian and Canadian Championships would be played in Victoria. There were few changes to the team personnel. Doug Flynn, Terry Lore, and Lance Rossington moved on to other educational pursuits, and they were replaced by two players from the 1955–56 Vikings, Lance Finch and Doug Patterson, as well as Jack Showers from Oak Bay High School. Another significant addition to the team was Murray McIntyre, also a graduate of the Oak Bay basketball team, who took on the role of team manager. He became a stalwart supporter of the team, and his contributions were admired and respected. The same teamwork and divided workload that had been successful the previous year was employed with even greater success by coach Bill Garner. The same championships were won as in the previous year, with one new addition, the Bowering Cup. This cup was emblematic of Canadian Junior Mens' Basketball Supremacy and was attained against the Windsor

Eaton's store welcomes the Victoria College Vikings, Western Canada Junior Basketball Champions, to Toronto on 27 March 1957: (back left to right) Ken Brousseau, Waldo Skillings, Bob Tomlinson, Ken McCulloch, Bill Garner (coach); (front) Tom English, Doug Flynn, Lance Rossington, Ed Kowalyk, Art Chiko, Fred Martens (manager).

AKO on the hardwood of Victoria High School in the spring of 1958. It was the first and only Canadian Championship ever won by a college Viking team, but many more would follow as the college became the University of Victoria.

There can be little doubt about the importance of sports in our culture, but the benefits are exponential when the participants are positively active in the societal fabric of Canada. I am admittedly impressed with the academic credentials and career accomplishments of the 1958 team members:

Ken Brousseau – pharmacist
Art Chiko, BSc, MS, PhD – plant pathologist
Tom English, BCom, LLB, LLM – professor, Faculty of Law, UBC; lawyer, corporate and business law
Lance Finch, LLB – chief justice of British Columbia
Bill Garner, BSc, MEd – teacher, principal, assistant superintendent, superintendent
Ed Kowalyk, BA, BEd – secondary teacher in law, history, English, and physical education
Ken McCulloch, BEd, MEd – teacher, principal, educational consultant, Ministry of Education
Murray McIntyre, BSc, BSP – pharmacist

Doug Patterson, BA, BEd – elementary and secondary teacher, counsellor and
  administrator, businessman
Jack Showers, BPE, MEd – secondary school teacher, physical education and
  student services
Waldo Skillings, BCom, MBA – labour and staff relations
Bob Tomlinson, BEd, MEd – teacher, curriculum coordinator, supervisor of
  education, principal

Valerie Parkin was captain of the cheerleaders in 1957–58. The other high-spirited
members were Marilyn Phillips, Joanne Gingel, Kay Rae, Tricia Armstrong, and Carole
Slater. The ensemble's contribution to the team and fans was substantial in informing
team spirit. I am sure that it was also significant in enhancing ticket sales as these lovely young ladies appeared at all home games of the Vikings.

On 2 February 2008 the University of Victoria raised a blue and gold banner in the
gymnasium which will now hang in perpetuity, recalling a championship that happened
fifty years ago. Biased but not blushing, I continue to consider that this was one of the
essential acorns from which the University of Victoria's proud athletic record was ger-
minated. Clint Hamilton, athletic director, and Brent Dobbie, development and alumni
relations officer, were instrumental in the planning of this recognition event, and the
team is thankful for their many efforts.

Cheerleaders, c. mid-1950s: (left to right) D. Landers, J. Hague, M. Malamos, D. Adams, B. Keuhl.

Once I began my review of the eighteen years of the Victoria College annual, the *Tower*, it invoked many memories. Confident vitality sprung from the words of the principals, Dr John Ewing and Dr Harry Hickman, student presidents, the *Tower* staff, the faculty, the students, and the coaches.

In 1945-46 the rugby team is described as an intermediate team, "there not being enough king-size men around interested in playing senior rugby." It did overpower the Oak Bay Wanderers twice, and Ron Dakers, the captain, was singled out as follows: "Ron has played sensational rugby all season and, in doing so, has inspired the rest of the team to similar feats."

Other sports played that year included men's basketball. The team played in the senior C Division and won the title, led by Ron Dakers and Jim Cairnie. Men's soccer was also successful, and they were triumphant in competitions with the high school teams as well as the Saanich Indians and Esquimalt Meat Market. The only other sport of that season was badminton, with Gordie Ballantyne becoming the men's champion. He also figured in the mixed doubles, winning with Jan Flemming, and in the men's doubles, winning with Jim Doran.

The 1946–47 athletic season was successful on a number of fronts. The rugby Vikings collected the Heyland Trophy, emblematic of the city intermediate championship. Ron Dakers (captain) was again singled out for his "sensational" play and for having, "inspired the rest of the team to similar feats." The team also included Jim Burland, John Dobie, Chuck Edwards, Chuck Roberts, Bal Skillings, Jim Stevenson, Bill Thorburn, Ed Estlin, Gerry Byrnes, Roger Anstey, Harry Irwin, Hugh Ferguson, Jim McKellar, Al Barnes, Dan Thompson, Harry McKay, and Rick Rowe. The basketball team won the city and lower island championships in the senior C Division. Coached by Hank Rowe, it comprised Jim Cairnie, Don Hall, Keith Taylor, Stan Cains, Russ Monroe, Reg Barclay, Darrell Popham, and Al Nicolson. Soccer, too, was a success, as the team defeated all the high school teams and played several exhibition games against the Saanich Indians and Esquimalt Meat Market. The men's badminton singles champion was Gordie Ballantyne, who also teamed with Jan Flemming to win the mixed doubles and with Jim Doran to win the men's doubles.

In 1947–48 the senior rugby team did not gain a playoff berth, but Bob Dunlop, Don Smyth, Geoff d'Easum, Roger Ross, and Jack Gibbs were honoured by being selected from the senior rugby team to play for the city's Crimson Tide. Professor Bob Wallace was instrumental in both the senior and intermediate teams, with forty-three students practising on a regular basis. The basketball team competed in the senior B League and lost out in the finals of the playoffs after a very successful season. Other sports that year were swimming and golf. Harold Harris is described as a hopeful for the Canadian Olympic swim team, while Don and Aileen Smythe, Frank Wills, and Margaret Mowbray were also star performers. A golf club was formed, but play was reported as minimal. Mary Richardson and Don Henderson, as women's and men's athletic representatives, were instrumental in encouraging a large number of participants in several forms of recreation.

The yearbook of 1947–48 concludes the athletic section with a poem extolling the virtue of teamwork which was appropriate at the time and is still highly fitting today:

It's all very well to have courage and skill,
And it's fine to be counted a star,
But the single deed with its touch of thrill
Doesn't tell us the man you are.
For there's no lone hand in the game we play,
We must work to a better scheme,
And the thing that counts in the world today
Is, "How do you pull with the team?"

Don Henderson later became a well-known and successful principal in Victoria. Participation, sportsmanship, and teamwork were but a few of his very visible and often-expressed sporting goals. I can't give him credit for the poem, but his contribution to children and sport was second to none.

The year 1948–49 saw the number of college teams reduced somewhat. Meanwhile the men's basketball team won the A League in commercial basketball as well as the Island Championship. This was a first for a Viking team, which was comprised of Des Corry, Don McKinnon, Bob Grundison, Jim Loutit, Don Robinson, John Canova, Keith Lamont, Ken Wright, Bhagat Basi, and Evan Oakley. The coach was Larry Booth, a well-known Victoria athlete. Rugby, too, had a very successful season, with the team winning the Barnard Cup, symbolic of supremacy in the city senior division. Roger Ross, John Stone, Ron Alexander, Fred Choat, Dave Bryn-Jones, Reg Lott, Don Smythe, Peter Paterson, Macgregor Macintosh, Ken Yeomans, Peter Powell, Gerry Main, John Foote, Scott Kerr, John Campbell, Stuart Wismer, Bob Dunlop, John Murray, Des O'Halloran, and Geoff d'Easum were the players. Jack Wallace was the staff sponsor. The only other sport of that year was badminton, in which Derek Aylard was the victor.

The 1949-50 results showed that coach Scott Kerr's rugby team "boasted the tallest and heaviest scrum seen in the city for years, but the big fellows never seemed to get together too well and relied too much on brute force and individual efforts." At the time of publication of the *Tower*, the team "looked well on their way to retaining city supremacy, won by College for the first time last year." Professor Howatson was the staff sponsor. Team members were Dave Jones, Glen Guest, John Goult, Walt McDonald, Jim Loutit, Ray Orchard, Dave Molliett, Murray Saunders, Russ Robertson, Dick Baker, Dick Vogel, Ted Howard, Don Taylor, Stan Heal, Bob Hebbert, John Jeffrey, Denis Levy, Ian Hogarth, and Geoff Craven. Men's basketball received no write-up that year.

There were two men's basketball teams in 1950–51. Both teams had mixed success, but the senior men seemed a much better unit when Elmer Mathews and Bill Garner were in the lineup. The Vikings again captured the First Division rugby title. "Using their weighty scrum and speedy three-line to advantage in every game they met little opposition in their drive for the title." The team, coached by Bob Wallace and managed by Ian Hogarth, had John Shipley, Dave Riddell, Charlie Brumwell, Nigel Scott-Moncrief, Frank Gower, Lewis Knott, Norm Alexander, Doug Bel,l and Ray Orchard in the scrum,

Denis Stead at scrum-half, Bhagat Basi, Bob Shipley, Hugh Burnett, John Campbell, Ken Bridge, and Bob Monaghan on three-line, and Art Bridge at fullback.

The 1951–52 rugby Vikings started "the season with the youngest and lightest squad in the league." They enjoyed a winning season before losing in the semi-finals of the city championship. Two members of the team, Gary Webster and Keith McDonald, were chosen to play on the Crimson Tide representative squad throughout the intercity series. The basketball team of this year was entered in the senior B Division of the city league but went winless. For the first time, the college soccer team entered the city Junior Division. "Playing in more than twenty games, the team was not too successful in league play and lost to Combines in the play-off series." The cross-country team had some successes in the Victoria High Invitational and the Royal Roads Invitational. The team included Bob Elliot, Phil Taylor, Art Hubscher, Hedley Sampson, Dick Hales, and Gord Smith. George Forbes won the men's badminton single championship and teamed with Frances Appleton to win the mixed doubles championship. Ron Birch and Geoff Conway were victorious in the men's doubles.

The 1952–53 season was described as a "rather dismal athletic year at Victoria College." However, the rugby Vikings reached the finals of the Barnard Cup for the first time in three years, and Malcom Anderson, Gary Webster, and Tom Ward were selected to play for the Crimson Tide. The soccer team failed to make the playoffs but enjoyed some successes in exhibition matches. The basketball team, which was entered in the "Inter A competition did not win one game." The team did get to the finals of the Interscholastic Tournament but lost to the Normal School. George Forbes again won the men's singles badminton crown, while Ron Birch and Geoff Conway teamed once more to win the men's doubles. Conway and Sally Pollard were the mixed champions. Geoff Conway also paired with Art Gamble to win the men's table tennis championship.

The rugby team was undefeated in the second division during the 1953–54 year with University School, Oak Bay Wanderers, and College II providing the competition. The team was coached by Mr Carson. The players were M. Anderson, A. Richardson, T. Ward, E. Achtem, M. Kendall, G. Jackson, P. Ney, D. Owen, M. Rose, D.Cox, H. Simpson, P.McMullan, P. Filleul, I. Lochhead, S. Wright, D. Callan, and R. Shearing. Mention was made of new sweaters, shorts, and socks, which gave uniformity to the team. "The soccer team … repeated the dismal ending of previous years." Interest in cross-country was somewhat higher than in previous years, and team members competed against local high schools and Royal Roads. Bill Gelling and Jim Moore led the way with Graham Elliston, John Hill, Ron Wickstrom, and Harold Robinson providing great support. The basketball team competed against local high schools and enjoyed a very successful season with Len Anderson as captain and Lorne Oakley as coach. Christie Smith was the manager. Other team members were Dave Price, George Bowering, Bruce Browne, Gary Corbett, Monty Little, George Plawski, Duncan Smith, Al Snowsell, and Peter Winters. Ron Birch won the badminton singles title and joined with Peter Sharp to win the men's doubles. Ron also paired with Marilyn Bassett to win the mixed doubles.

The 1954–55 year saw a full complement of men's teams, and though none of them had highly successful seasons, there were several athletes who were all-rounders, playing on more than one team. In particular, Merlin Hawes, who was on the swim team, also played basketball and rugby. Several players, including Danny Beaveridge, Noel Boston, Colin Creighton, Harold Robinson, Barry Broome, Barrie Goodwin, Chips Filleul, and Walter McLean, played on two teams. It is probably not so surprising that soccer and rugby players who toil outdoors in the mud seemed most likely to participate in both these sports, while basketballers seem less likely to leave the warmth of the gymnasium. I can easily relate to that. Bob Hunt was men's badminton champion and then partnered with Marilyn Bassett to win the mixed and with Vic Bradley to win the men's doubles. Garth Anderson was a significant swimmer of that year. The cross-country team had a notable year led by Brian Perry-Whittingham and followed by Jim Moore, Harry Stephens, John Hill, and George Laundry.

The 1955–56 Vikings soccer team was very successful in the Inter-collegiate League, winning first place. Members of the team were Ray Bryant, Gary Fletcher, Derry Simpson, Monty Little, Dave Edgar, George Laundry, Dennis Atkinson, Bud Rutherford, Doug Patterson, George McCreadie, Phil Willis, Peter Bousfield, and Murray Little. Peter Bousfield was also prominent on the city tennis courts. Standouts of the season for the rugby squad, which competed in a very tough league, were noted as being Merlin Hawes, Tom Robinson, Ron Hurley, and their ace kicker, Stewart Smith. The basketball Vikings, having perhaps their tallest team ever, played only exhibition games in a season with a modest amount of success. Jon Magwood, at six foot seven, Art Adye, at six foot six, and George McCreadie, at six foot four, were a formidable sight. Dennis Atkinson led the bowling scores, while Merlin Hawes, Ron McKenzie, Ernie Watchorn, Art Adye, and Stan Powell led the men swimmers.

History was made in 1956–57 when the basketball Vikings became the Western Canadian Junior Men's Champions in Winnipeg, but that story has already been told. The rugby Vikings won the Kiwanis Cup and the city's Second Division Championship. Captain of the team was Stewart Smith and vice-captain was Bob McKee. It interesting that a young man, Ian MacDougall, who would become one of Canada's finest trombone players as well as a professor in the Music Department at UVic, was willing to risk his teeth and his fingers as a member of this team. Other members were Mike Sanguinetti, John Booth, Ron McKenzie, Doug Graham, Don Lezetc, Wally Watson, John Greenhouse, John Davies, Mike Kaye, Dave Anderson, Glen Di Georgio, Ed Kenney, Peter Bousfield, Robin Farquhar, Rod Kirkham, Doug Stewart, and Paul Phillips. Hugh Farquhar was the coach. The soccer team played in the inter-scholastic circuit, with wins equalling losses and team spirit flourishing under the coaching of Professor Neil Swainson.

Curling did well under the tutelage of Professor Alf Loft. Now that the college included the Faculty of Education, many of the students who came from the interior of the province brought a culture of winter sports. Dennis Atkinson once again was the leading bowler, while John Gilliland and Gordon Wilkie led the cross-country team, which included Mal Potts, John Green, and Mike Kaye. Warren Bell was men's badminton champion. Water polo, which comprised only practices, was led by Rich Young. On that team was Alf Pettersen, who would become Council president in 1992–93. The swimming team, which was successful in the High School Swim Gala, was comprised of Rich Young, Hamish Redford, Al Smith, Wally Watson, Pete White, and Bob Provan.

History was made again as the Viking basketball team won the Canadian Junior Men's Championship during the BC Centennial Year of 1957–58. The Athletic Council in its second year proved to be a valuable organization in moving the direction of sports successfully forward under the leadership of Professor Hugh Farquhar. The rugby team had a successful year but lost to James Bay in the city final, and the soccer team was second in the Inter-services League. Coaches were Professors Hugh Farquhar and Neil Swainson. Playing for both teams was a young Doug Stewart, who was also Council president that year and would later become a successful lawyer and member of Parliament.

Mike Deane, Jon Stott, and Roland Hawes led the men's swim team with strong support coming from Pete White. A water polo team was organized but was unable to arrange any games. The seventy-member bowling club was led by Barry Gelling and Dave Dawson. The outstanding performance of the year was attained by Barrie Foster. Don Wilson was the men's singles badminton champion and then teamed with Jerry Patrick and Jane Wilson to win the doubles and mixed doubles.

In 1958–59 the soccer Vikings won the city Inter-collegiate League Championship with a 5–3 win over Royal Roads. Professor Swainson coached the squad, consisting of Doug Jordan, Bill Gosling, Bernie Sinclair, John Hicks, Leo Beinder, Pat Mulcahy, Brian Cornall, Tom Bourne, Blair McLean, George Brice, Gerard Prinsenberg, John Whittaker, Gerry Booth, and Stew MacFarland. The rugby Vikings also had a very successful season winning the city second division rugby championship and the Heyland Cup. They vanquished JBAA by a score of 10–0 in the league final. Team members were Lorne Ross, Bryan Price, Denis Fieldwalker, Derek Hood, Jere Mitchell, Ed Kenney, Phil Clark, Adam Ustik, Pat Floyd, Bob McWhirter, Craig Andrews, Russ Chambers, Tom Bourne, Rol Fieldwalker, John Hogg, and Curtis Purden. Hugh Farquhar was staff sponsor, Bob McKee was coach, and Phil Clark was manager. Basketball, for the first time, fielded three teams: the Senior "A" Vikings, the Junior Vikings, and the Norsemen, which has always been the traditional name for the second division squad. None of the teams proved to be particularly strong, but it is encouraging to see the large number of participants. In badminton Barry Saunders won the men's singles and partnered with Vern Smythe to win the men's doubles. Don Wilson and Sue Batterbury won the mixed doubles. Professor Maureen Bray was the staff sponsor, while Don Kirkby, Diana Lawrence, and Don Wilson provided the student leadership. Blair McLean, Bill Matichuk, Rich Newell, and Tom Bourne were the winning bowling team, and curling flourished under the leadership of Professor Alf Loft and Lyle Garraway. The swim team continued to expand, with Mike Deane and Dennis Fieldwalker being given the nod for outstanding performances. Water polo, organized by team captain Roy Innes, gained the city tournament, and it became an established college sport.

The basketball team of 1959–60 was one with considerable potential under the coaching of Lew McCorkall. They played a successful exhibition season and won the Island championship before losing to the Vancouver YMCA in the BC semi-final. Players included Ken Jones, Barry Saddler, Dave Black, Ellery Littleton, Dave Nelson, Darrell Lorimer, Angus Mitchell, Fred Wright, and Tom Wyatt. Volleyball was also a success, with the team winning a twelve-team invitational tournament held at the Gordon Head gymnasium. The soccer team was successful in a league that included Royal Roads, Venture, Army, and Navy. Best of all, they had the pleasure of beating UBC 7–0, a feat that had not been achieved in many years. The rugby team was entered in the First Division and achieved a successful record under the captainship of Tom Fitzsimmons and coach Sam Patterson. Members of the team were Ron McKenzie, Bernie Sinclair, Lorne Priestley, Mike Bassett, Craig Andrews, Bruce Chambers, Bob McWhirter, Larry Lutz, John Hogg, Gerard Princenburg, Gordie Woods, Lyn Christian, Gray Eaton, Larry Rooney, Ian Ogle, and John Wenman. The men's water polo squad, which competed in a league with Crystal, Royal Roads, and the Naval Training School, won both the league and the Victoria City Championship. Roy Innes, Jan Smith, Darrel Lorimer, Mike Muirhead, Doug Gray, Bruce Warburton, Bob Turner, John Kendrew, and Bob Wheaton comprised the team. The annual badminton tournament was won by Diana Lawrence and Cliff Russell, while Dave Fidler and Al McLeod led the men bowlers. Alf Loft's curlers had another busy season and were led by an executive that included Lynn Mather, Sue Bellward, and Bruce Williams.

The 1960–61 year saw the introduction of ice hockey, which immediately captured the interest of fans. John Oster was the coach. Armand Lalonde, Tom Krall, Luziano Luchin, Rolando Cauchione, Barry Hodgkins, George Laundry, Dave Harris, Terry Todd, Graham Rogers, Cliff Russell, Ian Strang, Jim Gailbraith, Ross Grenier, and Mike Todd topped the league and won the Heaney Cup. The water polo team continued to be successful, and rowing was introduced by Tony Robertson, John Carson, George O'Brian, and Les Millin. The basketball team played several exhibition games against colleges in the Pacific Northwest and defeated the UBC Jayvees twice. Curling, bowling, and badminton continued to appeal to a large number of students, and though fencing numbers were small, it was a successful club. The cross-country team was led by Eric Carlsen, Stewart Brown, Brian MacDonald, Bruce Hawkes, and Palle Jensen.

In 1961–62 ice hockey continued to be the best fan-supported sport, with weekly evening games at the Esquimalt Arena that were both boisterous and crammed with drama. Volleyball did not have the player support of previous years. The rugby team was second in the Victoria Rugby Union, with John Wenman and Ian Appleton selected to join the Crimson Tide. "Led by dynamic captain, Barry Menzies, the soccer team" won the city championship and defeated UBC 2–1. Jerry Melissa, Ray Addison, Peter Furstenau, Tom Moore, George Brice, Peter Fralick, Jim Mansley (manager), John Chapman, Al Crawley, Dave Humphries, Ernie Leenheer, and Ron McMicking comprised the team. The basketball Vikings had a successful season playing in the local league. Five-pin bowling had a membership of over seventy, with Bill Atkinson having the highest average and Ed Nicholson attaining the highest single game score. Barry Saunders presided over a new ten-pin club, where Dennis Page had the highest average scores. Don Shannon was the men's singles badminton championship, while Hugh Rothe and Bill Atkinson won the doubles. Barry Saunders teamed with Margot Izard to win the mixed doubles. Tennis was started, and curling continued with its large membership. The cross-country team, with David Rasmussen, Eric Henry, Roy Hamilton, Ron Gunter, Bruce Hawkes, and Carl Gustafson under their manager, Robert Trotter, won the Pacific Northwest Junior Championship and the Admiral Nelles Trophy. The fencing club, sponsored by Dr Anne Saddlemeyer and coached by Mr A. Modos, included Tom Stock-dill, Dave Goodenough, George Acs, Terry Leung, Jennifer Lockyer, Margaret Murray, Johann Simmons, and Gill Fan. In golf John Hadfield won the college championship, and Jim Nesbitt won the low net cup. Water polo continued its high membership and winning ways by capturing the city championship again that year.

The 1962–63 Vikings basketball team played exhibition games with Calgary and other colleges in the Pacific Northwest. Once again Bill Garner was at the helm. Ice hockey was in a rebuilding year, but men's grass hockey was able to field two teams. John Brierley and Chris Murray were credited with "upholding the prestige of the sport." Cross-country was never able to get more than five runners out to a competition and thus minimized their success. Membership in the fencing club increased, and there were plans in place to compete against clubs from Vancouver and Seattle. For the first time the college had enough soccer players for two teams but not enough talented players to repeat as city champions. The badminton program, under the leadership of president Ray McLeod, sported over seventy-five members, while for the first time squash appeared as a campus sport. The rugby Vikings started slow but were led in the scrum by Gray Eaton, Bob Turner, and John Wenman, who were supported by "more than competent backs." Volleyball saw a revival, and the team competed in a league with PPCLI, Naden, and the YMCA. Forty golfers were active at Gorge Vale Golf Course under the leadership of president John Hadfield. Terry Clark and Wayne Hendry led the five-pin bowlers, while Harry Lum, Wilburt Jay, and Bruce Chan led the ten-pin bowlers. The water polo team again won the city championship. Team members were D'Arcy McGee, Keith Newell, Bruce Warburton, Craig Mearns, Doug Patterson, J.J. Camp, and Hubert Williston. A judo club was formed for the first time and met twice a week in one of the huts. Curling was once again a well-attended activity. The tennis club "had a successful year, largely due to efforts of president, Randy Smith, who offered instruction to all learners."

In 1963–64 the athletic system was reorganized, with one of its aims to be "giving fairer representation to the 'minor' sports and intra-murals." Bowling continued to prosper under the presidency of Jim Hay, and gymnastics appeared for the first time and was led by Andrew Wade, Ben Solomon, and Dave McLaughlin. The judo club increased its numbers significantly. There was no basketball team for the first time, but hockey enjoyed a successful season after a slow start. Don Smythe signed on as coach for the first volleyball team to compete in the big leagues of university volleyball, and they finished sixth out of twelve teams at the Canadian Championships in Winnipeg. Team members were Bob Vosburgh, Bob Ireland, Gary Ross, Gary Vigers, Tom Skinner, and Dennis Morris. The soccer team was second in its league, while the rugby team was less successful. Earl Francis won the UVic golf championship at Gorge Vale, with Bob Buffam winning the handicap honours. Terry Clement won the men's singles badminton championship, while Rick Kurtz and Bruce North won the doubles championship. The fencing club continued its success under the tutelage of Mr A. Modas, its members being Melvin Peters, Russ Tyrrell, Vicki Hanland, Wendy Martin, Ann Thompson, Tony Patriarche, Bjorn Simonsen, Stan Raine, and Fred Schemitsch.

This summary is by no means a complete history of athletics at Victoria College, as that would require someone to complete a review of all the local newspaper reports for the eighteen-year period. I offer my apologies to anyone who believes he should have been mentioned in these gleanings from the annual *Tower*s and the more frequent *Martlet*s. For those who were mentioned and would rather not have been included, I offer my apologies as well. Please blame the writers of the time for omissions or errors.

I am pleased to report that my family seem to be doing their share when it comes to the production of Viking athletes. My wife, Nanna Fibiger, was a rowing Viking, my brother-in-law, Chris Fibiger, was a rugby Viking, and my son, Mike McCulloch, as well as his wife, Lara McCulloch (Melville), were both volleyball Vikings. Hopefully, the grandchildren who follow will enroll at UVic, but we will leave that choice to them.

KENNETH McCULLOCH, MED, played for Victoria College's highly successful Vikings basketball team. He has since been a leader in education. His career has included teaching, principalship, working with the Department of Education in accrediting British Columbia schools, and serving as a consultant on education matters.

WOMEN'S SPORTS DURING

THE LANSDOWNE YEARS

SUSAN YATES

I was fortunate to have attended Victoria College from 1960, when I arrived as a young first-year student just graduated from a small girls' school, until 1963. The college opened up a new world of opportunities and friendships for me. My memory of the college, as the first step into adult life, is of a supportive, collegial place with high academic standards. With under two thousand students, primarily in first and second year, Victoria College provided a friendly beginning for first-year students.

In reviewing old Towers and Martlets, I am reminded of the strong leadership provided by Dr Hickman. Both as principal of a young and rapidly growing post-secondary institution and as professor and head of the French Department, he exemplified intellectual rigour, excellence, and commitment. I found his second-year French literature course both demanding and rewarding. Dr Bill Gaddes, head of the Psychology Department, is also particularly memorable; his commitment to the field of psychology, his encouragement of students, his involvement in the sound practice of his field in the community, and his empathy for others were an inspiration.

WOMEN'S TEAM SPORTS, 1946–1963

In regard to team sports for women, primarily basketball and grass hockey, the college provided opportunities for women athletes to continue with sports they had excelled at and enjoyed at school, to make new friendships, and to maintain continuity with other players from high school. The grass hockey players were most likely to be from the southern part of Vancouver Island, particularly the girls' schools, where the sport was often played with fanatical enthusiasm. At that time, basketball was the primary women's team sport played at schools in the interior of the province; as a result, after the Normal School amalgamated with the college, there was strong representation from the interior on the basketball teams. Women's volleyball started up at the college with a first team in 1955–56.

Through the years, a greater variety of sports activities, particularly more coed intramural activities, became available to the students. By 1962 women were participating in a number of different sports, including curling, swimming, badminton, fencing, bowling, golf, table tennis, tennis, and a gym club, as well as the three team sports already mentioned. There was also a cheerleaders' group.

It was a challenge for a relatively small college with regular-session enrolment at 717 in 1946–47 and still only 1,849 in 1962–63 to operate a well-supported athletics program. In the Lansdowne era the college provided the best support it reasonably could. What it lacked in facilities and coaching support, the students and faculty made up for with their enthusiasm and commitment. It is my recollection that in the early 1960s, when I played field hockey, we mostly played for the enjoyment of the game rather than for some higher competitive goal. As I look through the *Tower*, it seems that the women's basketball and grass hockey teams not infrequently lacked faculty sponsors, and some years played without coaches. Women's sports certainly did not have such a high profile as men's sports at the college; nor do they today in our society. Coaching women's sports in those years was an issue, particularly in western Canada, where the introduction of women physical education instructors was slow in the public school and post-secondary systems.

The field of women's sports was challenging during the Lansdowne years. Women's college sports were not well represented at the national level until 1969, when the Canadian Women's Intercollegiate Athletic Union came into being. The 1970s and 1980s saw the introduction of formal national championships for college women in swimming, basketball, field hockey, volleyball, soccer, and track and field. These new championships at the national level clearly provided many more competitive opportunities for keen women athletes at colleges and universities. As well, the development of national women's athletic teams in Canada and the eventual addition of more women's team sports (such as field hockey) to the Olympic Games provided new competitive opportunities for women. Organized and rigorous training programs accompanied this new phase of women's athletics.

THE YEARS FROM 1946 TO 1950

In November 1946 Victoria College moved from Craigdarroch Castle to the Provincial Normal School building at Lansdowne, which it would share with the Victoria Normal School for some years. The college, with over seven hundred students, would have sole use of ten classrooms and would share the gym, auditorium, and science lecture room with the Normal School. Science labs and a cafeteria would be housed in four army huts. Use of the shared facilities would provide some challenges in the years ahead.

With 188 regular-session women students in the academic year 1946–47, the college easily fielded both a women's basketball team and a grass hockey team. The basketball team, captained by Maud Wallace and coached by Jim McKeller, a fellow student, played in the Hamilton Smith series, which was won by the Normal School. The college team travelled to Vancouver, losing to Varsity (UBC) but defeating the Vancouver Normal School. In the Hocking Cup round robin tournament in Victoria later in February, the college was again defeated by the Normal School. The grass hockey team, captained by Gwen Lloyd, played local high schools (members of a new league), Queen Margaret's School in Duncan, and UBC's Varsity team. Roger Bibace, a fellow student, was coach.

In the 1947–48 year the *Tower* notes in regard to women's basketball that "a terrible blow was struck at the women athletes at Victoria College this year when they were excluded from the City High School Leagues, the reason being that they were too old and too big." The college did not feel that this decision was reasonable. Captained by Mary Richardson, the team played local private schools and the Normal School. The grass hockey team played only exhibition games that year. Women also participated in swimming, as well as skiing on a trip to Forbidden Plateau Lodge, a student skiing destination of choice for many years to come.

In 1948 the Student Council noted its concerns regarding the lack of playing fields and the general inadequacy of sports facilities available to the college. In November of that year, to help remedy this situation, about three hundred college students (men and women) volunteered to dig ditches and lay two thousand feet of drain tile (half of what was required) for the new playing field at Lansdowne and Shelbourne; this work was supervised by school board employees. The volunteer work done by the students considerably reduced the cost of developing the new playing field. For the next two years, both basketball and field hockey played exhibition games and participated in tournaments, but they were excluded from league play. The grass hockey team apparently played without a coach.

THE YEARS FROM 1950 TO 1956

During these years, prior to the college's amalgamation with the Normal School, the enrolment of female students in regular session ranged from 131 in 1950 to only 89 in 1953 and back up to 129 in 1956. The more enthusiastic athletes played on more than one college team, which caused some scheduling and other problems. Curling, table tennis, bowling, and badminton all became increasingly popular among the students, both men and women. First-year students were in the great majority, so that the women's teams were mostly made up of new students; this provided challenges in continuity and team building. Coaching support varied.

The *Martlet* of 25 October 1950 notes that there was a particularly large turnout at the first general meeting for girls interested in sports; that year the sports schedule included grass hockey, basketball, and badminton, although swimmers, golfers, and bowlers were also invited to advise Beverley Huff, the girls' sports representative on the Student Council, of their interests. Although the number of regular-session female students continued to drop, to 108 from 131 the previous year, the college managed to field two basketball teams, one playing girls' rules and another playing boys' rules. Archie McIntosh and Bill Garner were the coaches. Mr Clark sponsored both teams.

In the Hocking Cup the girls' rules team tied for third place, losing only to the Normal School, Victoria High School, and Oak Bay High School. The boys' rules team won over McMorran's but lost to Victoria High School and Esquimalt High School. (In regard to rules, it seems that boys' rules were played throughout most of the public schools, where most of the PE instructors were men, and girls' rules were played in the private schools, as the PE instructors there were women; UBC played girls' rules, as the university had trained women coaches.) Six players – Lynn Newton, Annette Cabeldu, Marg Nixon, Betty Yardley, Marg Williams, and Joan Whitten – played on both the college basketball teams; Annette Cabeldu, Lynn Newton, and Margaret Nixon played on both basketball teams and the grass hockey team. In grass hockey, although the team had only one practice, it ranked fourth out of twelve teams in the Bridgman Cup (Island Championship). The team, made up of mostly first-year students, seems to have carried on without coach or sponsor.

Both basketball and grass hockey had few games in 1951–52 and therefore not a very satisfactory year. At the UBC Invasion, college women, including Wave Matcham, Barb Rose, Bernice Jennings, Yvonne Mouat, and Frances Appleton, provided the main strength in badminton, taking nine of fifteen matches against UBC. Table tennis and bowling proved to be popular intramural coed sports.

The *Martlet* of 5 October 1952, in a column on girls' sports, encouraged participation in basketball, grass hockey, and badminton, and it went on to comment that "sports is definitely the very best way to keep that slender College girl figure and to relieve those 'sit-me-down' aches." That year, despite the lowest female enrolment (89 students) in a regular college session for the 1950s, both basketball and grass hockey managed to field good teams. The basketball team, led by Irene Young, was coached by Norrie Paget and Hal Gregg. In the Hocking Cup the college placed fourth in a field of ten squads. The UBC Invasion in Vancouver provided the team with a challenge, as the college players had difficulty adjusting to the floor and to girls' rules; Marion Stevenson dominated scoring for the college. Overall, it was a good year for the basketball team, but the grass hockey team did not have a memorable season, as there were few opportunities to play. Women athletes also participated in the forty-member Badminton Club, which joined the Lower Vancouver Island Badminton League. The college purchased its own table tennis tables that year, and men and women students played in intramural competitions.

The *Martlet* of 6 November 1953 asked students to turn out and support their men's and women's athletic events and spend less time in the cafeteria. The question of a possible booster club was raised. That year the college women's basketball team, consisting of Pam Campbell, Roberta Crombie, Sheila Kingham, Gloria Molofy, Anne Snowsell, Marion Stevenson, Marlene Vance, Pat White, and Louise Heal, captain, won all its games in Victoria with the exception of one loss to the Normal School. It was invited to the Evergreen Conference at UBC, where it played the University of Washington, the University of Western Washington, and UBC, with one win and two losses. The team manager was Jennifer Little, and the coaching was provided by Pete Winter and Christie Smith.

The grass hockey team had an enjoyable year but not many wins, placing fifth in the Bridgman Cup with two wins and two losses. The team's big win of the year was against UBC, 2–0, during the Invasion. Sheila Kingham led as captain, and coaching was provided

Women's basketball, 1954–55: (back row, left to right) Margaret Dobrocky, Dave Price (coach), Beverley Aitken; (front row) Joan Sutherland, Sandra Davis, Anne Snowsell, Ina Corbett, Gloria Molofy, Betty Bratvold.

by Cecil Branson. The team also played hockey against the college rugby team, an event that may have been the beginning of this tradition at the college.

The Student Council write-up in the *Tower* for the year notes that the UBC Invasion was the highlight of the year for many students: "Over half the College spent the weekend in Vancouver and had a wonderful time." The *Tower* continued, "Before leaving on the UBC Invasion tonight, went to the gay 'Invasion Dance' from 8:30–11:00, when we all boarded buses to take us down to the Vancouver boat. Highlights of the trip across were a sing-song and dance held on the after-deck." It was also noted that there were few scandals that year during the trip! (The old CPR midnight boat was the usual mode of transport for student athletes travelling to and from Vancouver well into the fifties, a trip usually enjoyed by the students.) That year the college sent a curling team (lost), grass hockey (won), rugby (tie), badminton (lost), basketball (won).

The women's basketball team won three out of five games against high schools and the Normal School in 1954–55. Anne Snowsell was captain; Jenny Little, manager; and Betty Bratvold vice-captain. The team was coached by Dave Price. In the UBC Invasion game, the team lost. That year the girls' grass hockey team placed third in the Bridgman Cup series. Coached by Hilary Hale, and managed by Tom Hale, it held its practices at Oak Bay High and the Lansdowne grounds. Vivien Sanguinetti served as captain and Gill Scott-Moncrieff as vice-captain.

Women also participated in bowling, with Gloria Molofy taking the lead for women. In college badminton Marilyn Bassett topped the women's singles, and Betty Cummings and Gill Scott-Moncrieff took the women's doubles. In swimming the college coed team placed third in the annual high school swimming gala, with Barbara Westinghouse and

Gael Stott winning firsts and the girls' relay team placing second. Gloria Molofy, active on the Student Council and in athletics, received the President's Award for the year.

Women's basketball, although the team had no league play, did well in exhibition games with city teams in 1955–56. The trip to UBC in February constituted the high point of the season, with the college team winning over the UBC junior team. The grass hockey team won its league play games, as well as all games in the Pacific North West Grass Hockey Conference. Sadly, it lost one game in the Bridgman Cup, to Queen Margaret's School, and consequently did not take the trophy. Donna Burridge was an outstanding player. The team – Ruth Orton, Ina Corbett, Carole Kennedy, Elizabeth Jaggers, Winnie Simpson, Sally Simpson, Pat Jones, Joan Sutherland, Sue Burnett, Gael Stott, Nan Baxter, Hilary Hale, captain, and Jenny Little, manager – was coached by Mr Yeomans and sponsored by Miss Gorham.

Women's volleyball started up with great enthusiasm in 1955–56, playing against UBC, the Normal School, and local high schools. College swimmers Ruth Anne Gordon, Ruth Orton, and Gael Stott excelled in the High School Swimming Gala, along with their male counterparts. In bowling Daphyne Chan took third place in the individual scores at the cross-Canada bowling tournament.

Donna Burridge shared the Martlet Award with Bud Rutherford for greatest contribution to sports and sportsmanship. Mr and Mrs D.B. McLay were presented with an engraved silver tray by the Alma Mater Society at the Awards banquet in appreciation of their support of student activities, including men's and women's athletics. Athletic awards included Big Blocks and Major Athletic Awards (which seem to have been referred to as Small Blocks in some years.)

During this academic year, it was decided by the Student Council to establish an Athletic Council to better represent and manage sports at the college. Ina Corbett, women's sports rep on the Student Council, and Mike Partridge, the men's sports rep, contributed significantly to the planning of the new council for sports.

THE YEARS FROM 1956 TO 1963

These were years of considerable change and growth, beginning with the amalgamation of the college and the Normal School and ending with Victoria College's tranformation into the University of Victoria. With these changes, the increase in student enrolment, and the rapid changes in society during this period came new demands on the institution.

The amalgamation of Victoria College and the Provincial Normal School came into effect in the spring of 1956, increasing the student population of regular-session students to 575, the highest it had been since the 1946–47 academic year. More than 40 per cent of the students were women, a larger proportion than ever before at the college and providing a significantly bigger pool of athletes to participate on women's teams and in various coed sport clubs and initiatives. As well, as a result of the amalgamation, Miss Maureen Bray, associate professor with training in physical education, provided a strong lead in the development of women's sports at the college.

In the fall of 1956 the students now had an Athletic Council with reps from the Student Council, an able and supportive faculty member, Mr Hugh Farquhar, to provide direction on behalf of the College, and individual reps for the major college sports; for women, Donna Finch was the women's basketball rep and Pam Bingham the grass hockey rep. Sue Burnett served as director of Women's Athletics on the Student Council, and on the Athletic Council she was vice-chair initially and then chair.

The 1956–57 women's basketball team – Donna Finch, Sue Burnett, Carole Salonen, Rosalynd Fielder, Linda Hanson, Barb Marshall, Pat Beath, Nan Lyon, Anne Sutton, Marisa Degan, and Norma Calvert – played under the name "Vikettes," wearing new colours: green and gold. Most of the team members were Faculty of Education students. This successful team defeated the high schools and most of the commercial junior and senior competition. The Vikettes also defeated the UBC junior team, as well as the Island Meteors, the island junior champs. Bud Rutherford and Mrs Middleton provided excellent coaching.

The grass hockey team, coached by Miss Bray, had an enthusiastic but not a winning year. In volleyball, also coached by Miss Bray, the college entered two teams in a round robin tournament, placing first and third over local high schools and the UBC team. Miss Bray, a former Victoria badminton champion and runner up in the BC championship, sponsored the Badminton Club. Top woman player Sue Butt was on her way to becoming Canada's first ranked woman tennis player; she would eventually compete at Wimbledon and other international events. On the college swim team, Margaret Duke, Carlie Westinghouse, Jill Denny, and Donna Finch all took first-place awards in the High School Swim Gala.

Women athletes received a number of awards this year, including Donna Finch, who was presented with a special sportsmanship award, and Sue Burnett, chair of the Athletic Council and a member of the Vikettes, the grass hockey team, and the volleyball team, who won the President's Award for outstanding contribution to college life.

The year 1957–58 was a great one, as the Vikettes won the island championship and then took the BC junior basketball championship for the first time. The team was coached by Mel Briggeman; Norma Calvert was captain and Ann Burridge manager; the rest of the team included Pat Beath, Rosalynd Fielder, Val Peden, Bernie Beninger, Doreen Johnston, Sheila Clark, and Julie Beecroft.

Women's grass hockey, coached by Miss Bray and led by Ann Burridge, produced one of the best hockey teams the college had ever assembled, with a strong defence and forward line. The first team included Sally Timmis, Allene Spilsbury, Sally Furneaux, Val Peden, Wendy Sanderson, Norma Calvert, Diana Symons, Sheila Clark, Mary Goward, and Ann Burridge, captain. As well, the college was able to produce a second team. For the first time, the college reached the Bridgman Cup finals, only to lose by one point to Oak Bay High. The first team lost its annual match with the rugby team 0–7.

Volleyball emerged as the winner over eight schools in a tournament. The winning team consisted of Barbara Turnley, Bernie Beninger, Norma Calvert, Elsie Jackson, Rosalynd Fielder, Mary Luchin, and Irene Webb. In badminton two members of the club entered the Canadian Championship; Sharon Whittaker reached the semi-finals, and Jane

Susan Butt (Vic '55) went on to be ranked number one women's tennis player in Canada. Here she is seen (left) at Wimbledon in 1961, about to play Sandra Reynolds (right), ranked number one and number one seed in South Africa. Photograph provided by Dr Susan Butt courtesy of the All England Lawn Tennis Club, Wimbledon.

Lee was defeated in the finals. (Sharon would go on to win the 1965 women's singles Canadian Championship.) Norma Calvert received the Martlet Award for her contribution to sports and sportsmanship. She was the Vikettes captain and volleyball rep on the Athletic Council, as well as playing on the first grass hockey team.

In basketball in 1958–59 the Vikettes were led by Julie Beecroft and coached by Wayne King. Miss Fleming was their sponsor. The team had seven wins and five losses and reached the finals of the Island Championship, losing to Brentwood after some excellent play. Grass hockey, coached by Miss Bray, fielded two teams that year, both teams playing a busy season. The first team had seven wins, five losses, and a tie and placed third in the Bridgman Cup. The college was invited to join the Victoria Grass Hockey Association, which planned to organize league games in the fall of 1959. Volleyball, led by Julie Beecroft and coached by Miss Bray, held a successful invitational tournament in which the team won three straight games before losing the final to UBC.

Julie Beecroft, captain of the Vikettes, director of Minor Sports, and a member of the volleyball team, won the Martlet Award for her outstanding contribution to sports and sportsmanship. The year 1959 was an important one for the college, which was able to take possession of 135 acres at Gordon Head for future development. This acquisition gave the college athletes access to their own playing fields and facilities almost immediately. As well in 1959, the college began enrolling upper-year students, a development that would allow for more continuity and maturity in athletics.

Women's grass hockey, 1960: (back row, left to right) Miss Maureen Bray, Marilyn Ward, Joan Harris, Val Lomax, Sue Dickinson, Pam Genge, Sally Ford; (front row) Alix Henderson, Diana Lawrence, Florence Goward, Barb Emery, Ann Lee.

The Athletic Council was congratulated for its outstanding work organizing the various college teams in the 1959–60 year. The basketball team mainly played exhibition games. In the Bridgman Cup competition, the grass hockey team successfully played the finals against Queen Margaret's School to tie for the trophy. This was an exciting first for the college team, coached by Miss Bray, led by Florence Goward, and including Alix Henderson, Diana Lawrence, Barb Emery, Ann Lee, Marilyn Ward, Joan Harris, Val Lomas, Sue Dickenson, Pam Genge, and Sally Ford. The team also defeated UBC. The second team played well, defeating all comers except the first team. Women's grass hockey lost its annual game with the rugby team; the rugby team presented itself with its own award – the UVic Bullying trophy. Diana Lawrence, director of Women's Athletics and member of the field hockey team and the Badminton Club, was co-winner with Craig Andrews of the Martlet Award for her outstanding contribution to sports and sportsmanship.

Basketball had a very successful year in 1960–61 and placed second in the BC finals. The team was led by Sandra Futcher and included Judy Jerome, Sandra Worboys, Carol Casilio, Sylvia Wedman, and Heather Inglis. (No coach is identified.) Grass hockey fielded two teams. The first team won the Bridgman Cup outright for the first time; it included Alix Henderson (captain), Sara Hughes, Sue Dickinson, Joan Harris, Renee Poisson, Pam Genge, Sue Mearns, Elizabeth Philpot, Jennifer Genge, Lee Husband, and Barbara Emery. Mrs Maureen Hibberson coached the team. The second team also had an active year. As well, the grass hockey team won the Maycook Trophy (donated in 1959 by Anne Mayhew and Ron Cook) for promoting school spirit.

The basketball team, captained by Julie Stone, worked hard in 1961–62 and ended the season with an equal record of wins and losses. Grass hockey again fielded two teams. The first, the Valkyries, captained by Sue Mearns and managed by Wendy Hocking, again won the Bridgman Cup, stayed on top of the Victoria Ladies League, and played well at the Evergreen Conference in Washington (in the snow, with a yellow ball and 25 degrees Fahrenheit weather). At the conference they were ranked with UBC as one of the top two teams. The team included Sue Dickenson, Anthea Fisk, Priscilla Jacobs, Heather Bridgman, Joan Harris, Valerie Hall, Jean Dunbar, Sandra Noble, Ann MacDougall, and Frances Nicholls. The second team defeated UBC's second team and had an active year as well. Sue Dickenson, director of Women's Athletics and top grass hockey player, received the President's Award for the greatest individual contribution to student activities.

The basketball team, coached by Miss Marlene Mitchell, had a challenging year in 1962–63. The team played in the Victoria City Basketball League with mixed success. It did, however, defeat the UBC junior women's team. In field hockey the Valkyries, captained by Frances Nicolls and managed by Sandra Noble, held their own in the city league but lost the Bridgman Cup. At the Intercollegiate Field Hockey Conference in Oregon, the team defeated all American teams but was defeated by UBC. The second team, captained by Judy McKay, played in the Victoria Ladies League and finished the season with more wins than losses. The volleyball team, coached by Miss Archer, had a number of games and a somewhat mixed success. Women continue to be active in a variety of other sports at the college, including fencing, badminton, bowling, curling, and tennis.

THE STATUS OF ATHLETICS IN 1963

During the early 1960s the athletics program at Victoria College was beginning to show stresses and strains. The college was growing rapidly; students were involved in an increasing number of sports, extramural and intramural. However, there was not a fully developed infrastructure in place to support all the new demands. In a report from Mr Fred Martens, coordinator of Athletics, to Dr Hickman, principal of the college, issued early in 1962, a variety of issues are raised. As well, the report gives a statistical picture of athletic activity at that time.

Regular-session enrolment in 1962 was 1,849. At that time, 434 students participated in athletics: women's basketball (8), men's basketball (25), women's grass hockey (22), soccer (20), rugby (39), curling (70), water polo (21), swimming (11), women's volleyball (12), men's volleyball (8), ice hockey (15), rowing (14), badminton (24), fencing (9), bowling (95), golf (10), cheer leader (6), cross-country (8), table tennis (no numbers available), tennis (8), gym club (10), and men's grass hockey (11). Ten of the sports were men's, four were women's, and seven were mixed.

Students managed most aspects of the sports programs, including purchasing, much of the scheduling of games, leadership of programs, selection of award winners, and policy review and development. The Athletic Council was given the responsibility, stated in its constitution, of organizing and controlling college athletics. Mr Martens's report raised a number of issues, including control of equipment, scheduling of games, travel and accident insurance, supervision, program continuity, eligibility rules, and planning for future programs.

In March 1963 the Principal's Committee on Athletics released its report and recommendations, providing a profile of university athletics programs across Canada and noting issues such as administrative control and fees. The recommendations included the creation of a Department of Physical Education and Athletics (with a director) to direct, organize, and coordinate the athletic program at the college. An Athletic Advisory Board was to be established and would include both faculty and student representatives. In relation to Athletic Council, it would assist the director of Athletics in carrying out athletic programs and encourage and promote student participation in athletics. The report also contained clear recommendations for projected sports facility and playing field requirements in the future.

Although this was a time for a new approach in the management of the college athletics program, I do have fond recollections of a more informal, and perhaps more amateur, era in sports. In the Lansdowne years, when the college was challenged by a lack of playing facilities and by limited resources generally, enthusiastic students were given the opportunity to form and substantially manage a successful and enjoyable sports program, with the support of interested and enthusiastic faculty. On 1 July 1963 Victoria College, with a new campus at Gordon Head, became the degree-granting University of Victoria, and another era began, leaving the Lansdowne campus to eventually become the home of Camosun College.

SUSAN YATES, MLS, attended Victoria College from 1960 to 1963. She was active in college life and was an accomplished and very popular athlete. Much of her career was spent at the Vancouver Public Library as a librarian and library administrator. In her own words, she is "currently learning to manage a vineyard in the Cowichan Valley."

THE UNIVERSITY OF VICTORIA DISTINGUISHED ALUMNI AWARDS

THE UNIVERSITY OF VICTORIA

DISTINGUISHED ALUMNI AWARDS

The University of Victoria Alumni Association encourages and supports the tremendous achievements of its members with the annual presentation of the UVic Distinguished Alumni Awards. Since 1993 these awards have become synonymous with the inspiring talent, effort, and influence of the university's graduates, locally and worldwide.

Recipients are selected on the basis of their exceptional achievement, prominence in their field of endeavour, impact on their community, and the example they set for UVic students. A one-time scholarship is awarded to a UVic student in the name of each recipient. Nine alumni of the Lansdowne era have been honoured with University of Victoria Alumni Awards.

NORMA I. MICKELSON
Entered Victoria College, '60
UVic Alumni Association Distinguished
Alumni Award, 1995

Norma Mickelson began her career as
a public school teacher in British Columbia. In 1967 she joined the University
of Victoria, where she became the first
woman at a Canadian university to be
appointed dean (in the Faculty of Education). She went on to hold other senior
administrative responsibilities at the
university and culminated her career by
serving as chancellor of the University
of Victoria between 1997 and 2002.

Norma Mickelson has long been recognized as a leader in the movement to
address issues of gender bias in university
learning, teaching, and research. Her own
research resulted in 140 articles, books,
poems, and educational videos that have
enriched children's verbal learning and
literacy assessment. In recognition of her
ground-breaking work in this area, she
was the inaugural recipient of the Sarah
Shorten Award from the Canadian Association of University Teachers.

Norma Mickelson's outstanding contributions to university life, the province
of British Columbia, and Canada have
been recognized with other honours,
including membership in the Order
of Canada, membership in the Order
of British Columbia, and an honorary
doctor of laws degree.

PETER L. SMITH
Entered Victoria College, '49
UVic Alumni Association Distinguished
Alumni Award, 1996

Classical scholar, author, honorary UVic
historian – Dr Peter Lawson Smith
(d. 2006) was a major contributor to
the development of the University of Victoria. After attending Victoria College
(and serving as *Martlet* editor) at the
Lansdowne campus, he graduated from
UBC and received his master of arts and
his doctorate from Yale.

In 1960 he joined the faculty of UVic,
where he was the founding chair of the
Classics Department and served as dean
of Fine Arts from 1972 to 1980. His
community service included leadership
positions with several arts and historical
societies. On campus he played a prominent role in UVic ceremonies and served
on Senate and as president of the Faculty
Association. With his keen sense of
humour and dramatic flair, Dr Smith
was always an engaging and eloquent
ambassador for UVic. As a teacher, he
truly inspired and instilled in his students
a love of learning.

CAROLE SABISTON
Entered Victoria College, '57
UVic Alumni Association Distinguished
Alumni Award, 1998

Carole Sabiston is an artist who works
with textiles and mixed media, and major
public art galleries, museums, and universities across Canada have featured her
work. Her talents in the fine arts have
been highlighted on CBC TV, the Knowledge Network, and TV Ontario.

She designed a giant Sunburst for the
Expo '86 opening ceremony in Vancouver. Her work *Commonwealth Cape of
Many Hands* was featured in the closing
ceremony of the 1994 Commonwealth
Games in Victoria and was presented to
Kuala Lumpur, Malaysia, the host city
for the 1998 Commonwealth Games.
Carole Sabiston has received the Saidye
Bronfman Award, the highest honour
in applied arts design in Canada. She
was awarded an honorary doctorate in
fine arts from the University of Victoria
in 1995.

TIMOTHY R. PRICE
Entered Victoria College, '59
UVic Alumni Association Distinguished
Alumni Award, 2001

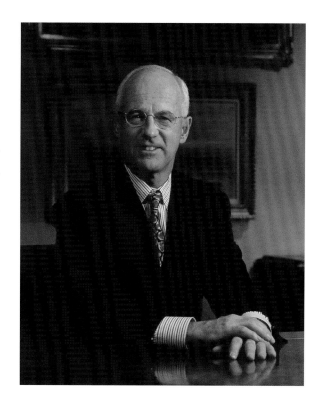

Timothy R. Price received his bachelor of arts degree as a member of the University Victoria's first graduating class in 1964, after completing most of his undergraduate studies at Victoria College.

Tim is chairman of Brookfield Funds in Toronto. He has had a long and distinguished career in business. He serves as a director of numerous private corporations, including HSBC Bank Canada and the Morguard Corporation. Dedicated to community service, he has devoted his time and effort on behalf of organizations such as the Canadian Business and Economic Roundtable on Mental Health and as governor of Roy Thomson/Massey Hall, vice-chair of the Board of Governors of York University, and chair of the Board of Directors of the York University Foundation.

The UVic Alumni Association's Distinguished Alumni Award was presented in honour of Tim Price's tremendous leadership in business and service to his community. All through his career and volunteer efforts, he has tirelessly promoted the University of Victoria across the country.

THE HON. WALTER McLEAN
Entered Victoria College, '53
UVic Alumni Association Distinguished
Alumni Award, 2002

Following his term as manager of the Vikings basketball team, Walter McLean was president of the Student Christian Movement (SCM) at Victoria College, and he continued this involvement while completing a BA at the University of British Columbia. He then began a lifetime of service through the Presbyterian Church, into which he was ordained, and through service to the developing world through NGOs and government.

A co-founder of CUSO, he became the first Nigeria coordinator in 1962. This activity ended with the tragic Biafran war. Walter McLean returned to the Canadian Centennial staff in 1967 and led the Miles for Millions walks. In 1970 he served as executive director of the Manitoba Centennial Corporation. The following year he was called to the ministry of Knox Presbyterian Church in Waterloo, Ontario; he was also twice elected to Waterloo City Council. In 1979 he was elected to Parliament for the riding of Waterloo, and he served as an MP for fourteen years. He also held the cabinet posts of secretary of state of Canada, minister of immigration, and minister responsible for the status of women. Always concerned with international issues, Walter McLean had, across party lines, a great influence on Canadian foreign policy. For eight years he served as the parliamentary delegate to the UN General Assembly and was an activist against both the arms race and apartheid.

Since leaving elected office, Walter McLean has continued his work with the church, universities, and many voluntary associations. His contributions have been recognized with awards and honorary degrees, including doctor of divinity from the University of Toronto/Toronto School of Theology and doctor of laws from Wilfrid Laurier University. He currently serves as honorary consul in Canada for the Republic of Namibia and, with one of his four sons, has formed McLean and Associates.

ALBERT R. COX
Entered Victoria College, '48
UVic Alumni Association Distinguished
Alumni Award, 2003

A former academic vice-president at
Memorial University of Newfoundland,
Albert Cox is a cardiologist who achieved
the highest mark in his graduating class
in medicine at UBC in 1954. His wife,
Margaret, received her medical degree
from UBC one year later.

Albert Cox completed several special
medical programs and held a variety of
academic and professional appointments
provincially and on the national level,
together with an extensive record of
community service. He is a member of
the Order of Canada.

Entered Victoria College, '60
UVic Alumni Association Distinguished
Alumni Award, 2003

Lorna R. Marsden spent one memorable year at the former Victoria College (1960–61) and graduated with a BA from the University of Toronto. She went on to do her doctoral studies at Princeton University and returned to the University of Toronto, where she held various senior administrative positions, including department chair, associate dean of the School of Graduate Studies, and vice-provost. In 1984 she was called to the Senate of Canada by Prime Minister Pierre Trudeau, where she served until she became president and vice-chancellor of Wilfrid Laurier University. In 1997 she moved to the presidency of York University, a position she held for two terms.

She currently serves on various private-sector boards of directors, including Manulife Financial, SNC-Lavalin, Gore Mutual, and GO Transit. She is also active on boards in the voluntary sector, including the Roy Thomson/Massey Hall Corporation and the Gardiner Museum. As well, she serves on the Senior Advisory Panel to the auditor-general of Canada and is a continuing fellow of Massey College. She has also been active as a feminist, including service as president of the National Action Committee on the Status of Women.

Her work has been recognized with the Queen's Silver Jubilee Medal, five honorary degrees, the Arbor Award of the University of Toronto Alumni Association, the Canada 125 Anniversary Medal, the Queen's Golden Jubilee Medal, the Golden Apple Award of the FWTAO, the Women's Executive Network Hall of Fame, membership in the Order of Canada, and the Order of Merit (First Class) of the Federal Republic of Germany.

Lorna Marsden is currently president emerita and professor at York University, where she is active in research and writing. She is the author or co-author of several books and many articles.

IAN McDOUGALL
Entered Victoria College, '56
UVic Alumni Association Distinguished
Alumni Award, 2004

Ian McDougall is considered one of
Canada's great jazz trombonists. His professional career began in Victoria at the
age of twelve when he performed with
local jazz bands in fifties-era venues at
the Union Club, the Sirocco Club, the
Empress Hotel, and the Crystal Gardens
Ballroom. By 1960 he had moved to
Great Britain, joining and touring with
the John Dankworth Band. Two years
later he returned to Canada, where he
became an established performing and
recording artist, bandleader, composer,
arranger, and teacher. Until 1991 he
was the lead and solo trombonist with
Rob McConnell's award-winning Boss
Brass band.

Ian McDougall has released several
solo recordings, and his compositions
have been performed by the Lafayette
String Quartet, the Toronto Symphony
Orchestra, and the CBC Vancouver
Chamber Orchestra. As a teacher, he was
director of the jazz program at UVic until
he retired in 2003, earning praise from
his students for his knowledge, patience,
and understanding. He was honoured
with the Order of Canada, 1 July 2008.

CONSTANCE "CONNIE"
ISHERWOOD
Entered Victoria College, '47
UVic Alumni Association Distinguished
Alumni Award for Lifetime
Achievement, 2006

On completing her studies at Victoria
College in 1949, Constance "Connie"
Isherwood (née Holmes) was one of eight
women admitted to the UBC law school
(in a class of 208). She graduated at the
top of that class, becoming the first
woman to win the school's gold medal.
She returned to Victoria to be among a
very small contingent of women lawyers
in the city. After fifty-five years, Connie
Isherwood continues to offer legal
services in the areas of wills, estates,
mortgages, and family law. She is the
senior practising female lawyer in the
province, commuting each day to her
Fort Street office from the home she
shares in Sooke with her husband, Foster.

A consummate legal professional and
a leading citizen, Connie Isherwood was
the 2006 recipient of the UVic Alumni
Association's Distinguished Alumni
Award for Lifetime Achievement. Colleagues who endorsed her nomination
cited her "quiet self-confidence that
comes from intellectual equality." They
also drew attention to her community involvement. As chancellor of the Anglican
Diocese of British Columbia, Isherwood
provides legal advice. She has served as
president of the Family and Children's
Service of Victoria. She also authored the

original constitution of the UVic Alumni
Association and is a past president of the
association. A remarkable woman, energetic and enthusiastic, Connie Isherwood
is, as a nominator put it, "legendary in
Victoria for her sense of fairness and
integrity."

PART TWO

REFLECTIONS OF THE LANSDOWNE GENERATION

REFLECTIONS OF THE
LANSDOWNE GENERATION

EDITOR'S NOTE
In the following contributions by members of the Lansdowne generation, the year after a contributor's name following "Vic" indicates when he or she entered Victoria College. Authors' biographies are provided after each contribution. E.B.H.

THE HON. JUSTICE
ROBERT B. HUTCHISON
VIC '49

It would be difficult to reminisce about Victoria College and the Lansdowne campus without first taking a look at the different community that it served in those years. The Second World War had just ended, and the small, sleepy-town atmosphere that marked British Columbia's capital city was a far cry from the greater Victoria of over three to four hundred thousand it has grown to be in the twenty-first century. For a generation that grew up on three- and six-cent bus rides and ten-cent movies and milkshakes, the end of war brought great social changes fuelled by the return of hundreds of veterans. They were in a hurry to renew their lives and opportunities. Not the least of such opportunities was government assistance to finance higher education. Summer jobs were plentiful for students at seventy to eighty cents an hour!

Thus it was no surprise when the casual small college, situated at Craigdarroch Castle, no more than a large character home, became overwhelmed with returning veterans. Suddenly a couple of hundred students were confronted with an enrolment of over six hundred, close to half of whom were returning veterans.

My first recollection of collegiate activism was my sister's organization of signs and marchers. She had enrolled at Victoria College in 1946 fresh out of Oak Bay High

School, where I was starting my second year. Of course, I was more interested in making the rugby team than worrying about the college. Nonetheless, I was made fully aware of the students' protest march to the Legislature demanding a move to the old Normal School, recently converted back from its wartime hospital status.

The remarkable story of the protest march of 10 October 1946 demanding the college move was told in detail by the late Professor Peter Smith in his book *A Multitude of the Wise: UVic Remembered*. The book contains a news photo of the marchers, most dressed in jackets and ties (a far cry from today's protesters). It shows the student president, Terry Garner, led by a bass drummer, Doug Main, the student body president of Oak Bay High in 1945–46, with the drum carried by classmate Ed Estlin. Of course, there was the perennial bagpiper. Prominent in the front of the parade is George Cumming, the provincial exams gold medallist of 1945, later to become a judge of the Supreme Court of British Columbia and to be elevated to the Court of Appeal. Among the marchers was Harry McKay, a veteran, later to become MLA for Fernie and a judge of the County Court of Nanaimo. He was subsequently elevated to the Supreme Court in 1971. Justice McKay would be greatly revered by his colleagues and universally acknowledged as one of the province's finest jurists. Victoria's fire chief, only days before the protest march, had conveniently condemned Craigdarroch Castle as a fire trap. His edict made relevant the prominent sign at the head of the parade: "Into the College of Death Filed the 600."

The government of the day, a coalition led by John Hart, quickly (in less than a week) changed its previous refusal to allow the college into the Normal School, so recently returned to its original purpose from a wartime hospital. The student activists had had the media on their side from the beginning, and I am aware that my father, Bruce Hutchison, a long-time member of the press gallery, was not about to turn down the urgings of his only daughter to add weight to the media protests. Of course, the 14,243-name petition delivered to the government and the political pressure articulated in the student sign that read, "The government says nothing is too good for the veterans. Gentlemen, they mean it, we've got nothing," didn't hurt the cause either.

It was with that background that I was to register at Victoria College in 1949, along with many of my high school class. The motive was not so much a thirst for higher education as a lemming reaction. By this time the college had reorganized itself and was at home in the Normal School, though peace between the principal, Dr Ewing, and the principal of the Normal School, H.O. English, was an uneasy one. Peter Smith in his book describes in detail the correspondence between the two protagonists, and it is an enlightening and amusing read. However, as a student, as I suspect for the great majority of us, I was never aware of any friction. I do recall that the warm relationship that most of the Oak Bay High students had had with Hugh Farquhar was never quite as intimate as previously. He had coached a number of Oak Bay Howard Russell Cup championship rugby teams and Oak Bay Wanderers Intermediate teams, before joining the faculty of the Normal School. After reading Peter Smith's book, I conclude that it was Mr English who made it politic for Normal School faculty to keep their distance. Hugh's warmth and congeniality was a big factor later, when he became university president under trying circumstances. His deft hand in keeping the university moving forward with distinction was and is fondly remembered by his colleagues.

I do recall that the college faculty were much more intimate and closer to the student body than had been the case in high school. While this may be the mark of a change to university life, I suspect the many veterans had a hand in creating this culture. After all, it would be hard for a young faculty not to feel they were among equals who may well have returned as a former squadron leader or from the command of a frigate.

By the year 1949, student enrolment was reduced from over six hundred to just over three hundred. The great mainstream was made up of Oak Bay and Victoria High School students. Of course, Mount View, Mount Douglas, and Esquimalt high schools were also part of the mix, along with some "out-of-towners" and a fairly large sprinkling of private school grads, principally from University School and Brentwood College. Victoria High boasted the premier student in British Columbia, Peter Smith, whose high marks established a record. However, Oak Bay High was not too far behind, as the silver medallist, Pat Carstens, was registered in our class as well. Both later joined UVic's faculty.

No more eclectic group of students could be found than composed our city rugby championship team. The Shipley brothers from University School and Peter Powell, Des O'Halloran, and John Campbell from Brentwood College came from these major private schools, where rugby was king. From Vic High, John Newton and Reg Lott were outstanding, and Oak Bay's Gerry Main captained the team, while big, bad John Olson was a powerhouse in the scrum and kicked penalties and goals. Johnny Foote and I also hailed from Oak Bay. Charlie Brumwell, who went on to become a physician, was a mainstay in the scrum from Mount View, along with Tom Ballard. I am not sure from whence the Bridge brothers, Ken and Art, or scrum-half Geoff d'Easum hailed, but they were an integral part of one of the best senior teams ever assembled in Victoria up to that time. Scot Kerr, the team coach and hooker, was an ex–Oak Bay High student who had graduated to join the military a year or two prior to the college moving to Lansdowne.

Of course, the indomitable Bob Wallace was the faculty representative, and while I missed making his math class, I nonetheless was fortunate to be registered with the effervescent and charming Phoebe (Riddle) Noble. In the class was Peter Smith, and while it was hard not to understand Professor Noble's simplification of difficult mathematical theories, if ever I was stumped, Peter was always willing to come to my aid. I was at first shy of such a brilliant student, but he even then showed the signs of a great teacher: patience, politeness, and modesty mixed with an engaging charm. His credentials as the dean of Fine Arts and chair of the Department of Classics are an integral part of the history of the University of Victoria. All of us at the college knew that his dad, H.L. "Harry" Smith, was the principal of Victoria High. That was because he could remember your name even though you were from a different school. His reputation for remembering the name of almost every student he ever taught from 1914 on was renowned.

What really got one's attention on entering Vic College was the number of clubs and societies one could join. Apart from organized athletic teams, the Players', Jazz, and Radio Clubs cut a large swath with students. More intellectual clubs, such as International Relations, Science, Pre-med, Psychology, Music Appreciation, and the Literary Arts Society, attracted a number of more serious students. My recollection of two "big club men on campus" was of Denny Boyd in Jazz, Radio, and the *Martlet* and Gerald Coultas in the Players' Club. Denny, true to his interests, became a sports reporter at the Victoria

Daily Times and was lured to the *Vancouver Sun* by its then publisher, Stuart Keate, who had moved from the *Times* to Vancouver. Denny was to become Vancouver's favourite columnist after the death of Jack Wasserman, when Denny was moved from sports to city side. Gerry Coultas took to the law and was appointed to the Provincial Court, where he was made its chief judge, and then went on to finish his career on the Supreme Court of British Columbia.

Other Victoria College students from the Lansdowne era to become judges of the BC Supreme Court or Court of Appeal, apart from myself and those already mentioned, were Lance Finch, AMS president in 1956, Allan Thackray, and Robert (Bob) Edwards. Justice Finch moved from the Supreme Court to the Court of Appeal and was appointed Chief Justice of British Columbia on 5 June 2001. Allan Thackray recently retired from the Court of Appeal and was a Supreme Court judge prior to his elevation. He was a Vic College student from 1951 to 1953, in the same class as Walter Young, Rhodes scholar in 1956 and later chair of UVic's Political Science Department. Out of Oak Bay High School the following year, and a close associate of both Walt and Allan, was Brian Smith, one-time attorney general and mayor of Oak Bay. Sadly, Robert (Bob) Edwards, who served with distinction on the Supreme Court of British Columbia, died suddenly in November 2007.

The highlight activity in 1950, I recall, was the ski trip to Deer Park Lodge on Hurricane Ridge on the Olympic Peninsula. The trip was a thousand laughs from the time we set sail on the Coho for Port Angeles. Grant McOrmond was the faculty rep. He was a favourite, and I was fortunately registered in his English 101 course. He was particularly kind to me, and at his urging, I took a Minnesota aptitude test, from which results he talked me out of pursuing my first thoughts of pre-med. Professor Gordon Fields's biology class along with Miss Bethune, who had us dissecting frogs, played a role in the decision! Later Professor McOrmond urged me to use a little good old-fashioned nepotism to get a summer job at the Victoria *Times*. To my surprise, it worked. This mentoring had a profound effect on my later college life and career, for which I am ashamed to say I never formally thanked him.

The faculty assembled by Dr Ewing was, I now realize, outstanding. Later to be vice-principal and then principal, Dr Harry Hickman was a patrician gentleman whom I got to know better when serving on the Alumni Board of Directors. Even in retirement, Harry took an abiding interest in the university and its alumni. He taught French, and I opted for German with Miss Baxendale. Mr Lewis Clark and Mr Ed Savannah taught me chemistry and were warm-hearted and delightful gentlemen of the old school. Mr Clark liked to reminisce about sprinting, the sport of his youth, and he knew I was involved in the activity. Mr Jeff Cunningham was vice-principal in my day. His daughter, Gertrude, was in our class and had graduated from Oak Bay High along with the great majority of us who entered the college in 1949. As for Mrs Phoebe Noble, I can only associate her in true affection with the last words of Peter Smith's book: "Even in a multitude, she's very special."

Always a highlight of college life in our days were the dances at the Crystal Gardens. Not forgotten was a coed dance sponsored by the Women's Undergraduate Society. Patricia Sparks, later to dance with the Winnipeg Ballet, and Cory Moore, my girlfriend and wife-to-be, undertook to teach the rugby team ballet. To see six-foot-six John Shipley and six-foot-four John Olson in tutus was a laugh and giggle in itself. I suspect that some of us got through the indignity with courage provided by the proverbial brown paper bags found under most tables at Crystal dances.

Both Cory and Pat played on the women's grass hockey team. As well, the women had a basketball team coached by the "Two Kens" of Oak Bay High, Hill and McKay. Ken McKay was later elected student body president in a tight six-person race. Maybe his coaching got him the feminine vote! The only female candidate among the six, however, was Marion Gibbs, who the following year became the first woman president in the history of the Alma Mater Society.

The Two Kens went on to become chartered accountants. Both played for the Vikings basketball team that included Vic High's Elmer Matthews, Bruce Naylor, and John Newton. Others were Art Olson, Pete Leung, "Sam" Firth, Jim Loutit, and Pat Alair. I recently asked Ken Hill whom they competed against, and he allowed he could not remember but said it was a hit-and-miss proposition. Later in 1957 and 1958 coach Bill Garner started the Vike's basketball dynasty with the Canadian Junior Championships. As the campus had no gym, Lansdowne Junior High provided room to practise. Coach Garner, while not a Vic College alumnus, was a highly successful high school teacher and school board executive. He had graduated from the University of Oregon and was the younger brother of Terry Garner, who led the notorious 1946 march to the Legislature.

That trek was the beginning of the Lansdowne campus, finally to end in the move to Gordon Head and transition to a full degree-granting university. The word "transition" is the nearest I could find to sum up Victoria College if limited to a single word. A wonderful teaching faculty transformed mere youngsters to serious university students in a short, enriching, but painless way. As I drove by the familiar tower on Lansdowne Road recently and observed the campus packed with parked cars and students from Camosun College, I thought of the words of the old song: "Those were the days, my friends."

THE HONOURABLE MR JUSTICE ROBERT B. HUTCHISON, LLB (ret.), was a member of the Canadian Olympic Track Team in 1952 and, in succeeding years, was active at a senior level in organizations such as the British Columbia Track and Field Association, the National Council on Fitness and Amateur Sport, and the Victoria YM/YWCA. After a distinguished career in private practice, he was appointed to the Supreme Court of British Columbia in 1990, where he served until his retirement in 2004. Mr Justice Hutchison was also honorary president of the University of Victoria Alumni Association from 1995 to 1999.

MARGARET GARNER
NORMAL SCHOOL '52, VIC '54

I have a feeling that when I was at the Lansdowne campus at the Normal School and Victoria College in the early 1950s, it was a very traditional era. At that time most of the high schools divided their students into two streams, university or general. If you chose the university, you would go to Normal School (teacher training), nursing, or college or university. I don't remember that I had any sense that times were changing; things were the way they were.

Daily, we wore skirts and sweaters or blouses, belts, ankle socks or stockings, and low shoes (sometimes saddle shoes). The boys wore casual slacks or washable trousers, shirts or sweaters, and oxford-type shoes. We never saw jeans or training shoes in the general wardrobe.

We went to dances on the lower floor of the Ewing Building or the Crystal Gardens or the Crystal Ballroom of the Empress Hotel. The girls wore calf-length party dresses or full-length evening gowns (with long gloves to above the elbow in kid leather if you could afford it), stockings, and high-heeled shoes. The boys wore sports jackets, shirts, ties, and trousers, suits, or tuxedos, whichever was appropriate. Liquor, if you wanted it, was brought in a paper bag and kept on a shelf under the table. Mixer and glasses were bought from the waiter.

When I look back on my Lansdowne experience, I am grateful for the friends and acquaintances made. Below I have included comments about the Provincial Normal School, which was housed in the same building as Victoria College and shared the same campus and cafeteria. It became, after all, part of the University of Victoria when that institution was formed. Some of the teachers went from the Normal School to the Education Department at the university. One of the members from the staff of the Normal School was Hugh Farquhar, who was not only one of our teachers but also a sponsor of such activities as soccer, badminton, men's basketball, cross-country, and the athletic society. As many will know, the large theatre/concert hall on the university campus is named after him.

The reunions held by the Normal School group have been lots of fun. It is amazing to me how easily we pick up our conversations from one reunion to another. We recently held our fiftieth anniversary on the Camosun College campus. It was fun to have our opening reception near the Ewing Building. When I came to the door and paused and looked around, it was hard to believe that it had been fifty years since we had all been students here. Where had it all gone?

My memories of Victoria College have been strengthened by writing for this project. Many of the people I see around Victoria and take for granted are often ones I met at the college. I never think of them in that way. Now that I give it more thought, some of my best friends are from that time.

I have always supported the University of Victoria. Part of that support comes from having been at Victoria College. Part of it comes from my brother having been a student at the university in the sixties because of the strong support of Dr Fields for my brother's tenuous acceptance in the university. Part of it comes from my son having been a student of the university in the eighties. My brother and my son were fortunate to receive encouragement from some of their professors.

The Normal School

My introduction to the Lansdowne campus was the Normal School (teacher training) in the fall after high school graduation. Students came from all over British Columbia. They could choose either Victoria or Vancouver for this training. Some came from communities so small they had to learn how to use the bus system to get to and from school and around the Victoria area.

The Provincial Normal School was based on the concept (as stated in our yearbook) that it was not merely a building of brick and stone mortared by human hands. It was a monument to a philosophy of life, a life dedicated to the service of mankind. The Honourable Mrs Tilly J. Rolston was the minister of education at that time. She wrote that it is the teacher more than anyone else who is entrusted with the task of forming the strongest link between the present and the future. She told as that as young teachers, we must be prepared for disappointments and problems as in any other profession, but a career in education offered as great, if not greater, a challenge than most other callings. She told us our work as teachers would be hard, but we could make a difference in the lives of our pupils, which in turn could make a difference in our country; we were the builders of a better tomorrow.

The principal, Mr English, was considered, even then, a very old-fashioned man. He was so encouraging in his own quiet, stoic way that you could tell he was a dedicated teacher. He told us that whatever else a teacher would do for his pupils, he or she must first of all awaken, arouse, and startle them into thought. Motivation was a word we heard many times in all our classes.

The Normal School was almost an extension of our high school except we were expected to be adults. We numbered less than two hundred. We were all in this place together with the same goal; we wanted to teach school. It was expected that besides our studies and as part of our training, we would participate in many activities. Our teachers often joined us as our sponsors and guides. We appreciated their help, and in many cases we hoped we could emulate them in our own classrooms.

We had a student council, a literary society, drama and debating societies, a social organizing group for dances (the Tinsel Twirl dance at Christmas), picnics and swimming parties, cross-country running, cheerleaders, badminton, inter-house sports, swimming, soccer, tumbling, basketball, volleyball, bowling, and ping pong. We were busy!

In these ten months we also had three practicums, when we became the teacher in the classroom. In October we taught one week in an elementary classroom. In November we taught for two weeks in the classroom. In March we taught somewhere by our choice for one month. October was a nightmare of fright; November was better. By March we had some idea of what to do. The homeroom teacher was very important for help and encouragement. Our teachers came to see us teach and offered advice. We did not see some of our classmates in the New Year. They knew they were not destined to be teachers. I am sure they were disappointed but as least they found out early in their lives that this was not the career for them.

Victoria College

Most of the students at Victoria College came from the area; some also came from up island. The college was a natural progression for them. They could live at home or board for little expense in those days. Money, as with all students, was a factor in our lives. At least we could get Saturday jobs and work in the summer, as there were not many students competing for those jobs.

College was a place to learn, study, and socialize. We were lucky. The classes were small; so there was a close rapport and friendly association with most of the faculty. Most of the time this close rapport motivated us to do better in our studies. After all, in a small class we could discuss or question without drawing too much attention to ourselves. Because the college was so small, it didn't take us long to get acquainted with one another.

Most classes were held in the Young Building and the wartime huts down a path in the woody area. Some classes could be held in the Ewing Building. Part of the lower floor of the Ewing was used as social and drama areas. The cafeteria was a wartime hut directly behind the Young Building.

Classes and studying were important, but so were the other activities. Some of our expressions and named events give a clue as to the unsophisticated fun of a small-town college. Very important in early September was the Howdy Hop, which happened at the end of Frosh Week. Then came hazing, really only fun, never degrading. It was a way for second-year students in our two-year college to show some sort of superiority. No one cared. The first-year students just appreciated the attention. It all ended at a dance-party at the Crystal Gardens. In the afternoon at the end of Frosh Week, a tea party was held by the Women's Undergraduate Society (WUGS) to welcome the first-year girls to the college.

Our dances were an important part of our life. Different groups or clubs held fund-raising dances. One such was held in the Crystal Gardens, hosted by the Men's Undergraduate Society (MUGS). At that time the Crystal was a favourite place to hold a function. The Christmas dance was held in the Union Room of the Ewing Building. We had a real orchestra! The buffet dinner came from the cafeteria. It was great! The February dance was, of course, the annual coed dance. It ended the TWIRP season (The Woman Is Requested to Pay). There were lots of awards, such as the Milk Can Award for the couple most often seen together, or the International Lover, male only.

One of the most important events of the year was the "Invasion" of the University of British Columbia. The ferries at that time went from the inner harbour of Victoria to the harbour of Vancouver. They made only two trips each day from each side. So at midnight on the 10th of March we boarded for Vancouver, We slept on benches or in chairs. There were very few cabins.

We arrived early in the morning, made our way to UBC, and began our events. We played soccer, grass hockey, women's and men's basketball, and badminton. The rugby and bowling were cancelled. We lost every game. We left on the afternoon of the 13th and arrived home in early evening, exhausted but happy. We had been to the big city!

Besides sports, we had many clubs to interest us. Among them were the Inter-Varsity Christian Fellowship Club, the Newman Club, and the Student Christian Movement, all

A Players' Club production,
c. mid-1950s: (left to right)
John Gittins, Margaret Dobrocky,
Pat Gray.

of which studied religion. The International Relations Club focused on people in different parts of the world. The Science Club broadened the students' knowledge in topics such as spectroscopy, forest biology, biochemistry, and even pathology. They had a visit to a hospital pathology lab and speakers with knowledge in all topics. Other groups included the Square Dance Club, Glee Club, Players' Club, and Debating Club.

In late February we had a major Players' Club production. The first theatre in the round was performed in the Union Room of the Ewing Building. Seats all round the stage created a challenge to performers, lighting, technical, and prop organization, all done by students. Flora Nicholson, who was a well-known director in Victoria, was our leader and instructor.

These were wonderful, busy, challenging, and sometimes confusing days. Those of us who survived the Normal School went on to be teachers, some returning to Victoria College later to continue our studies. Some, even later, went on to the University of Victoria or the University of British Columbia or elsewhere to get their degrees.

MARGARET GARNER studied at the Provincial Normal School and Victoria College and subsequently taught at Stride Avenue School in Burnaby, BC, and Lansdowne Junior High School in Victoria. In 1970, with her brother, John Dobrocky, a University of Victoria graduate, she founded Dobrocky Seatech Oceanography. She sold the company in 1983 when John Dobrocky died, and she retired two years later. Margaret Garner is a great friend of the University of Victoria and a marvellous alumna.

It was another era, but it almost seems like another world. Old Victoria College yearbooks and copies of the student newspaper, the *Martlet*, reveal pictures and descriptions of life from simpler times. Canada was just a few years beyond the Second World War, and Victoria was still a quiet little town. It was so small that the phone numbers started with a single letter of the alphabet followed by four numbers. There were no area codes or postal codes. Mail took forever, it seemed, to go from coast to coast, and the cost of talking to someone on the East Coast for five minutes was prohibitive. Travel by airplane was slow and expensive. There was no jet travel as yet. Taking the train meant that one needed days to arrive at a destination, not hours. Everything took longer. There were no laptops, cell phones, Blackberries, or Nintendos. Today the speed of life has changed, but people remain the same. As dated as the photos and writings are in these old documents from the fifties, Victoria College students of that era had the same drive, goals, and desires as undergraduates today.

Reminiscing through the musty yearbooks filled with smiling faces and weird hairdos is not for the faint of heart. Were we ever that young? Did we really look like that, dressed in clothes that today's generation would hold in derision? We were just kids, barely out of high school and, for some of us, only by weeks. Yet here we were in the halls of academia, surrounded by books and peers with our brains at the mercy of our professors. These were the days of dead poets, beatniks, and coffee houses in other parts of the world, but in sleepy Victoria we were in awe of previous masters of the English language. We never saw a beatnik, except in movies, and the closest thing to a coffee house was the Goblin Coffee Shop, "Where the Knack of Snacks is our Specialty," or perhaps The Poodle Dog.

We did have fun with language (perhaps it was the influence of Professors Roger Bishop and Grant McOrmond). In a section called the "Scrapped Book of Poetry" in the February 1953 edition of the *Martlet* is a poem entitled "Liquor and Longevity," by an author who preferred to remain anonymous. In its lines the author describes all manner of animals who, though they drank only water throughout their lives, managed to live only a few years. "All animals," writes the poet, "are strictly dry. / They sinless live and swiftly die, / but sinful, ginful, rum-soaked men / survive for three score years and ten. / And some I'd say, but rightly few, / stay pickled, 'till they're ninety-two!" Indeed, whoever wrote those lines discovered that you didn't have to be dead to be a poet!

It seems liquor was also on the minds of the bowlers. The Bowling Club had twelve teams with such names as Walker's Woes, Rainers, Hi-Lifers, Mixers, Rubby Dubs, Lucky Lagers, Corby's Kids, Abstainers, and Seagram's Soakes.

The Student Council oversaw most aspects of campus life with its clubs and various activities, and some of its members took their responsibilities seriously – so seriously, in fact, that they wanted to make sure that the incoming freshman class, or frosh, quickly learned the routines of college life. In the first week of classes, unsuspecting, innocent young frosh were subjected to some outlandish indignities by their superiors, the sophomore class. All in fun, of course, but the experience was somewhat humiliating.

Frosh students had to dress for school that first week in ways that broke all the rules of typical dress. The Student Council set up the temporary dress code, the main principle being that the more ridiculous the better! So there were all of these new students running around campus dressed in ways that made them objects of derision and recipients of lots of guffaws.

Initiation into campus life was intended to be a publicly embarrassing experience, but it was all in fun. Frosh Week drew everyone's attention to the camaraderie and lively interaction among students and impressed on all of us that going to Victoria College was meant to be more than hard work and unrelenting professors! This was a time to make memories.

One freshman, a star rugby player, was told he was the lucky one and was ordered to wear something only for a very short time. He was to run down the main hall just as the students were coming out of the classrooms for lunch. His dress code was to be only one item, an athletic supporter. Nobody was more surprised than the sophomore on the Student Council who gave that order. He did not know that the star rugby player could run so fast. By the time he reached the end of the hall and disappeared, hardly anyone realized what had happened.

Other than trying to get through first year without too many scars, there was something of significance that took place that school year for the students. The UBC Invasion, an annual weekend of activities and sports events held in Vancouver, required stamina from approximately 160 students comprised of athletes and spectators. The Invasion would start with a dance at 8 p.m. in the Victoria College–Normal School auditorium, followed by students being transported to the CPR ferry terminal to catch the midnight ferry. From then on, well, "That's Vancouver's worry," boasted the author of the notice of the event.

However, this trip in 1952 turned out to be more than just Vancouver's worry. It seems that on the return trip back to Victoria on the midnight ferry the next day, a male student, who will remain unidentified, grew very creative when trying to find an easy way to open a bottle of beer. In a moment of lapsed judgment, he pried the cap off that bottle of beer with the help of an overhead sprinkler, which was actually designed to put out a fire in case there was one in the stateroom. What happened next sent a shock wave throughout the ferry. Water – rusty, of course – spewed everywhere, soaking everything and everyone in sight and causing a huge commotion, not to mention the damage. The news of this event did not take long to reach Victoria College, specifically the administration, and that one male student has since more than redeemed himself. Future Invasion trips were never so notorious.

As mentioned earlier, the Student Council oversaw our lives on campus. Sports and social activities abounded for the ones who had the time and inclination to get involved in college life. The 1953 commemorative edition of the *Tower* lists fourteen sports and twenty social activities. Some were more successful than others, it seems. The soccer team played six league games and lost all six. On the other hand, Bob Cross, Art Gamble, Geoff Conway, and Jim Sharp won twelve of their sixteen matches in table tennis and came home with the Pacific Northwest Championship. In rugby Sedge Richardson was the captain and a very fast runner, but it was Gary Webster and Malcolm Anderson who made the league's all-star team.

Then there was the Glee Club. That's a name we don't often see anymore for groups of people who want to get together and sing. However, at that time, glee clubs were common entities on many college campuses. Although the Glee Club's attendance faltered during the 1952–53 school year because "women outnumbered men 5 to 1" and it later folded "because of the lack of support during the second term," the club did manage to put on a presentation for the evening of the fiftieth anniversary celebrations in October. The Glee Club did not lie dormant for long. Revived and re-energized the next year by Roberto Wood, it included six very scarce tenors among the male recruits. Under Mr Wood's direction and leadership, the Glee Club had a very successful season in 1953–54.

An amusing write-up featured the College Chess Club, which, though small, managed to have its own tournament among ten players. Some even had their own favourite opening moves, such as the "Caro-Kann Defence," the "French Defence," the "Centre Counter," the "Alekhine's Defence," and the "Ruy Lopez." Those fierce openers must have kick-started some furious competitive bouts and struck fear and awe into opponents!

One of the largest clubs on campus was the Jazz Club, boasting fifty members. Remember, these were the heady days of intellectuals and far-out poetry readings held in smoky coffee houses in sophisticated places like New York City. There was the aura of live jazz in the background of these establishments, with a new brand of music that captured the imaginations of college students everywhere. Here in Victoria the campus Jazz Club was led by the spirited and well-respected Alan Pratt. Students would gather frequently to listen to records, and occasionally the membership was treated to the actual live talents of musicians such as Denny Boyd, Bruce Bennet, and Wally Grieve. This must have been heady stuff, indeed!

Notably, there was a clear distinction, it seems, between the Jazz Club's activities and those of the Music Appreciation Club, whose "highlight of the year" was an evening party held at the home of Mr Kriegel, the club's sponsor, where the members were treated to a recording of the Strauss operetta *The Gypsy Baron*. Considering there was no Victoria Symphony, Opera Victoria, or any music courses taught on campus, young people today will find it hard to grasp the limited opportunities available then for community members to enjoy live performances.

Those two years, 1952–53 and 1953–54, were eventful in ways other than just revelling and socializing. Dr Harry Hickman gained the principalship, confirmed earlier in the year on 12 May 1952, and began his first full year in that capacity in the fall. He was a gifted speaker in both French and English, and was dedicated to the arts and to high academic standards. He had risen from the ranks of the faculty and had earned their respect as a colleague and leader. In 1949 he had earlier been chosen as the founding president of the Victoria College Faculty and Staff Association. Dr Hickman continued the tradition of excellence in leadership when he later became president of the University of Victoria.

The Ewing Building was finished at a cost of $259,000 and opened on 15 October 1952. Included in the dedication ceremony was the presentation of a portrait of John Ewing, painted by Myfanwy Spencer Pavelic, whose aunt Sara Spencer had been a student in the first class of 1903. A huge fundraising effort got underway during the fall of 1952, benefiting the 50th Anniversary Library Fund, and enabling the library to add substantially to its collection. Bob Wallace became vice-principal on 1 January 1953, bringing considerable talent to the role that would benefit the campus as well as the community. He opened the campus to residents of the city through offerings of a variety of courses, both for credit and for leisure interests. Thus the Victoria College Evening Division established a precedent and a solid base on which to build the future adult education and extension programs at UVic.

Then in 1954 Judge Joseph Badenoch Clearihue, who had not only attended the college in the first year of its creation but also had been the Victoria College Council chairman since 1947, crafted legislation that was to pave the way for establishing the Victoria College Foundation, an entity for the administration of bequests and donations. This legislation, Bill 27, would lead the later Universities Act of 1963, which, incidentally, was largely drafted by Joseph Clearihue as well.

The members of the Student Council did such a tremendous job during these years of 1952–53 and 1953–54 that it would be remiss to omit their names. They were:

1952–53
President – Ray Frey
Secretary – Frances Appleton
Treasurer – Geoff Conway
Coordinator of Activities – George Metcalfe
Publications Director – Lyle Robertson
Sports Reps – Sally Pollard and Walt Young
WUGS President – Robin Maunsell
MUGS President – Ted Horsey (fall); Jack Ward (spring)
Frosh Reps – Anne Pomeroy and Art Anderson

1953–54
President – Bill O'Brien
Secretary – Kay Burnett
Coordinator of Activities – Bill Sturrock
Publications Director – Anne Skelton
Sports Reps – Marlene Vance and Brian Smith
WUGS President – Fran Fredette
MUGS President – Lee Branson
Frosh Reps – Myrtle Bratvold and Bill Gelling

Thus the two years from 1952 to 1954 were packed full of events and changes. They were years when the small college saw an abundance of talent go through its doors. The school produced more than its share of high achievers who went on to enhance the rep-

Ronald Lou-Poy, chancellor
of the University of Victoria.

utations of larger universities. The distinguished faculty helped to advance the school in scholarship, always demanding the best from its students. And students responded. They did so because they saw this time as an opportunity to create the kind of future that many of their parents could only dream about. They did so because they had faith that, with an education, they could make a difference. These were indeed years of excitement, of promise, and of visions of things to come. This little school had become their launching pad.

In addition to the yearbooks, Peter Smith's *A Multitude of the Wise: UVic Remembered*, the *Martlet*, and the *Tower*, edited by Bill Broadley and Gloria Molofy respectively, were immense sources of information for this reminiscence.

RONALD LOU-POY, CM, LLB, QC, LLD (hon.), is the senior partner at Crease Harman and Company, barristers and solicitors, in Victoria. He also serves as chancellor of the University of Victoria. Ronald Lou-Poy's community work is of long duration and exceptionally diverse, involving such areas as the arts, civic service, education, affordable housing, and cultural activities. In 1988 he was named an honorary citizen of the city of Victoria, a most distinguished recognition of his contributions to civic life. Ronald Lou-Poy has also been honoured with membership in the Order of Canada.

Such a difference a year makes. The school year 1952–53 was barely nine months long, but it was long enough to grow up a little, learn to challenge our world, and become excited about learning. It was also a year for making new friends through a variety of special-interest clubs, dates, parties, and dances – all wonderful memories from another era, over fifty years ago.

My Victoria College memories really start as a seven-year-old in the back of a car driven by my father on Sunday afternoon drives along Lansdowne Road past the college. Between 1942 and 1946 the campus was used as the Victoria Military Hospital. I remember seeing a long row of servicemen, and perhaps women, who had been wheeled outdoors to the front lawns to "take the sunshine." Wrapped in blankets and shawls, the soldiers reclined on wicker wheelchairs which looked about eight feet long! Standing by them were nursing sisters of the day, wearing navy and white uniforms and veils. The scene was fascinating to a child.

Before 1942 the campus had been the Provincial Normal School, but when it was needed as a facility for the wounded troops, the teachers' college was moved temporarily to Christ Church Cathedral in downtown Victoria. In 1946–47 the military hospital was converted again to become home once more for two educational institutions: the Normal School and Victoria College. Many of the first students were men and women veterans returned from the war.

When I graduated from high school in 1952, I needed to "put in a year doing something" until I was eighteen, old enough to enter nurses' training. My mother, who had gone to the Normal School, said that her year there had been "a lot of fun." She chose those words carefully, knowing they would appeal to me. They did! I became a student at Vic College.

Choosing what we would wear on "Opening Day" was particularly important. It was the beginning of Frosh Week, and impressions needed to be made – especially on the boys! As we rode our three-geared bikes with wicker baskets to school in our long skirts, blouses, sweaters, and saddle shoes, we were presentable and very much alike. In their jackets and ties, sweaters or vests, and slacks, the boys looked great. Our "uniforms" then were the hoodies and jeans of today.

Frosh Week offered a wonderful variety of clubs, but if we joined the Players' Club for theatre productions, swimming, tennis, and maybe the campus newspaper, the *Martlet*, how would there be time for classes? Classes began, however, and so did the delights of learning new subjects.

First-year students were required to take certain core courses; so I chose German, biology, math, English, and history. Our professors dressed in their own unique styles, reflecting their personalities and subjects: mathematics professor Phoebe Noble wore a black robe over her dress; historian Sydney Pettit wore his tweed jacket and vest; Gordon Field taught in the lab with his white shirt sleeves rolled up; Herr Frederick Kriegel taught German in a stylish, conservative suit and tie; English professor Lieutenant Commander Rodney Poisson was handsome in his navy blue blazer with crest on the pocket. Such are the memorable images of fifty-five years ago.

To our surprise, the classes were not like high school classes, where some of us had sat quietly listening, writing, and trying to remember information for exams. Our "profs" at college encouraged us to be involved, to ask questions, and even to express our opinions! One new friend, Alan Pratt, took advantage of the new attitude: he loved to ask provocative questions in history class. Mr Pettit seemed to thoroughly enjoy the resulting exchange, which included all of us and made even history refreshing! This was an early lesson for me on how rewarding it could be for a teacher to encourage a quiet or reticent student.

Alan was one of the first disabled students to attend college in Victoria. Although polio had confined him to a motorized wheelchair, he couldn't be stopped. He organized the Jazz Society, was a disc jockey for commercial CJVI, operated a ham radio, and tended wall-to-wall tanks of exotic fish in his home. More importantly, Alan enjoyed a circle of good friends who greatly appreciated his company. Sadly, he died a young man in 1955.

Some of us were very young and definitely naive. When Professor Rodney Poisson returned my paper on D.H. Lawrence's *Sons and Lovers*, he asked me to see him in his office. He kindly suggested that I reread the story and try again. I don't remember the point of the essay, but I do remember his sensitivity as a teacher. Giving a second chance to a beginning, and perhaps even a struggling, student was a lesson in understanding that I tried to practise later in life.

Herr Kreigel, a charming man who spoke with an intriguing accent, introduced us to the wonders of the world outside Victoria. I was fascinated! He taught us not only the sounds and grammatical structures of German but how to act out meanings by using body language and facial expressions. That we actually understood each other in a foreign language was remarkable. The world he represented was just waiting for me!

Professor Field drew our attention to the wonders of anatomy through the dissection of frogs. He taught us that they had once had life and so deserved our mindful attention and care. Finding and identifying specific parts of their anatomy was like a treasure hunt! Cries of "I've found his liver!" brought a curious and peering crowd. In that lab I began to realize how wonderful the human body is and knew to always treat it with respect.

Professor Phoebe Noble tried to coach me up the gentle slopes toward higher mathematics, but I got lost in trigonometry. Her efforts were not lost on others, however. Talking with friends today, I know that she was much admired and an inspiration in their lives as future teachers.

As enlightening as these classes were, we managed to fit in lots of fun through club activities and dances. In the spring, the Players' Club put on *The Curious Savage*. We were fortunate to borrow Katherine Youdall, a wonderful drama and English teacher at Oak Bay High School, to be director of the play. She was assisted by Professor Roger Bishop and Major Evans. John Sandys-Wunch and Walter Young, who later became Rhodes scholars, were both involved in the play.

Walter Young and Patricia Jones in Victoria, c. early 1950s.

The program, costing 10 cents, was sponsored by Ian's Coffee Shop on Richmond Road. Ian lent a friendly ear and made great milkshakes not only for college and Normal School students but also for student nurses from the Royal Jubilee Hospital, who lived in residence just across the street. But that's another story.

When we weren't involved in the clubs or delighting in learning, we were socializing; however, dating in those years was different from today. When a boy invited a girl to go somewhere in particular at a certain time, he probably took the bus to call on his "date." After arriving at the front door, he would shake hands with the parents and then wait in the living room until his date was ready. Waiting often included being entertained by his date's brothers and sisters. Some waits were incredibly trying.

Favourite places to go – by bus, most often, but by family car when someone was lucky enough to borrow one – were movies, bowling, cheering for the Shamrocks Lacrosse at Memorial Arena, and parties at Willows Beach around a bonfire. We didn't drink much, but surprise bottles of beer, rye, and ginger ale turned up at times hidden in small, brown paper bags.

How we dressed up for the dances! The boys wore suits, and the girls were in pretty, full-skirted dresses in taffeta or net. Emceed by the Men's Undergraduate Society at the Sirocco, the Crystal Gardens, and the Empress for the Christmas Ball, the dance lineup always included Spot Dances, Ladies' Choice, and a Conga line! Live bands played the fox trot, energetic jives, and slow dances. Sometimes the highlight of the evening was the crowning of the campus queen and king. Once we chose the queen of the cafeteria, or "queen of the caf."

For many, 1952–53 was a year of transition. Some stayed for a second and final year before going on to UBC or another university to complete their degrees; some transferred to Normal School or Nursing School; some left for other careers; and some to "settle down" in a marriage and raise a family. Although I stayed for only one year, I am very aware of the profound effect that Victoria College has had on my life: the gift of enthusiasm for learning that my professors gave me, the examples of tolerance and understanding set by the faculty, the activities that we shared outside the classroom, the exciting social life, and the very strong friendships that have lasted to this day. Through all of these experiences, Victoria College lives on in my heart fifty-five years later.

PATRICIA JONES, RN, BED, graduated as a registered nurse from the Royal Jubilee Hospital in Victoria. She subsequently pursued her profession in many parts of the world, including South Africa, Zimbabwe, New York, Montreal, and Vancouver. In 1974 she graduated from the University of British Columbia with a BED and then taught primary school in Vancouver. On retirement, she studied Japanese and taught English in Japan before returning home to Saanichton, BC. She also holds a diploma in French from the University of Victoria and is a great contributor to the community.

AVIS RASMUSSEN
VIC '55

EDITOR'S NOTE
Avis Rasmussen is a well-known West Coast artist whose work is regularly exhibited in various venues, including the Winchester Gallery in Victoria and the Burnaby Art Gallery in Vancouver. Her watercolour *Lansdowne Oaks I* was specifically painted for this book; it appears on page 127. E.B.H.

The Garry oaks that crown the campus and the recently restored Young Building feature in my 2007 painting for *The Lansdowne Era*. They were also the site of my classes as a student at Victoria College between 1955 and 1957.

I began my studies to be a teacher at what was, in 1955, the Normal School. I registered with Miss Dorothy Cruickshank – who knew everyone – in the Ewing Building for the following courses: English 100 and 101 with Professor Roger J. Bishop, French 120 with Dr Harry Hickman, German 90 with Dr Gordon Tracy and Professor Frederick Kriegel, History 102 with Professor Sydney Pettit, and Psychology 100 with Dr William Gaddes.

In an army hut over which the Garry oaks hung, the initiation of first-year students took place. Second-year students lorded it over the frosh, who had been ordered to appear clothed in sacking. Timothy Williams and Bob Kymlicka checked me over carefully

Lansdowne Oaks – I (2007), by Avis Rasmussen.

for conformity with their rules. Bob Kymlicka was a recent escapee from Czechoslovakia who had made his way to Victoria College, where he had been accepted without written credentials and proceeded to win the Canadian History Prize and go on to be a distinguished professor in this country.

Studying and researching in the Ewing Library, I was impressed by the number of books but even more by the framed reproductions of works by artists such as Franz Marc, Jose Orosco, and van Gogh. I was carpooling that first year from Sidney, my hometown, in which there was no library and no art gallery. Indeed, the Victoria Art Gallery had only recently opened in the large Moss Street house that had once been home to the Spencers, a leading Victoria family.

I learned folk songs in the German Club, sang in the Glee Club, and ate lunch on Tuesdays listening to records at the Tuesday Noon Record Club. The records we heard were often from student collections, most notably that of John Gittins. In my second year I boarded in town with family and, without the constraints of carpooling, could join more college activities, balancing them with a heavy schedule of academic and education classes and practice teaching in Victoria schools.

By second year, we were no longer in the Normal School but in the Faculty of Education as a result of the merger of the Normal School with Victoria College. That year I studied English 200 with Professor Rodney Poisson, Education Psychology with Dr Geoffrey Mason, and at least six other education courses designed to generate a knowledge of teaching skills in science, social studies, English, physical education, music, and art. As I had been drawing and painting throughout my childhood, my major was in art with Professor Wilfrid Johns. He taught from Victor Lowenfeld's *Creative and Mental Growth*, a progressive book at the time. Professor Johns was a great mentor who influenced me to complete a BEd and an MEd, as well as a BFA. I am so pleased that the Faculty of Education Art Gallery is named in his honour.

As I think back on those days at the Lansdowne campus on its own hilltop in Victoria – one of those hills so important to the landscape of the city – I recall an April day looking over to another hilltop in shock as smoke billowed against the Olympic Mountains from a fire at Government House. I went on to further degrees at the university in Gordon Head and have achieved my goals as an artist to a great extent because of the encouragement of university mentors and friends. I owe gratitude to the university, but lovely as the Gordon Head campus is, the Garry oaks and hilltop view from the Lansdowne campus remain in my memory as the setting for exciting times.

AVIS RASMUSSEN, MED, BFA, is a well-known West Coast artist whose work is regularly exhibited at the Winchester Gallery in Victoria and the Burnaby Art Gallery in Vancouver. She is also represented in public collections, such as Wilfrid Laurier University and the University of Victoria's Maltwood Museum and Art Gallery. Her watercolour *Lansdowne Oaks I* (2007) was specifically painted for this book, for which we are grateful.

THE HON. DAVID ANDERSON
VIC '55

For high school students in Victoria in the fifties who wished to proceed to university, the only real choice was whether to stay at Victoria College for a year or two and then go on to UBC or else to go directly to UBC. It was rare, very rare, for other Canadian universities, American universities such as the University of Washington, or universities in the United Kingdom to attract a Victoria teenager. Some children of military personnel who had strong ties with Halifax or Ottawa or those whose parents had a particularly strong attachment to a university that they had attended elsewhere might buck the trend, but for the vast majority of us it was Vic College now and UBC later or else UBC right away.

UBC took just about everyone, of course, including Vic College students who entered in second and third year, and was a massive institution of fourteen thousand students. We Victoria students looked forward to getting there, as at Point Grey would gather young people from every part of the province. Few of us at that time contemplated leaving the province; so the UBC years were years in which we discovered our contemporaries in the rest of the province, particularly Vancouver, which few Victorian young people knew well or, in some cases, knew at all. The ambitious among us in particular wanted to connect with Vancouver and UBC. We had been told for years that Vancouver, not Victoria, was the place where things happened. Getting there and making the connections that UBC, with its size, would provide was an important goal. Of course, if you were tired of living at home under parental eyes, UBC had yet another attraction.

That said, for the rest of us, Vic College had plenty to recommend it. First and foremost was cost. Living at home was a lot cheaper than paying $60–65 board per month for a shared room on West Fourteenth in Vancouver. Further, most of my Vic High friends were going on to Vic College. And for those of us worried about passing university exams, the college had a better reputation as a teaching institution than the impersonal academic factory at Point Grey.

The first year of university in those days was essentially a sorting-out period, where students from high schools throughout British Columbia with enormously different records of academic achievement were put through a year that was largely designed as preparatory for the university degree program, which to all intents and purposes began in second year. The failure and dropout rate in first year, therefore, was very high. Academic statisticians will know exactly what the figure was, but my memory tells me our rule of thumb as students was that the failure rate would be one-third (and it was that high). This was drummed into the incoming students at virtually every introductory lecture and repeated throughout the term. The standard warning was "Look to your right, and now look to your left. One of the three of you sitting there is going to fail" (the year or the course, depending on the prof's message of the day). President of UBC Larry MacKenzie replied to criticism of the wastage of resources caused by this high failure rate by remarking that it didn't really matter if a large number failed; even students who failed probably benefited in some way from their time at university.

I think he was right. It was an egalitarian system. Fees for first year in 1955 were about $185, easily earned during the summer after high school, and it didn't really matter in first year whether you had done well in high school or whether your high school had prepared you well. First year was a fresh start, and if you survived, you would probably make it through to a degree.

I mentioned that Vic College had some real advantages over UBC and the reputation of a better teaching faculty. I don't think classes were particularly small, but there was no doubt it was a teaching college, and I can't remember much interest in the research work that our faculty might have done. At Vic College we got more individual attention, a genuine attempt to teach rather than lecture, and teachers who knew our names and our families and were genuinely concerned that we proceed on as well prepared for our undergraduate work as possible. They took great pride in the successes at UBC of former Vic College students and never failed to mention how well Vic College students did when at Point Grey.

Part of this teaching tradition may have been a consequence of the great wave of demobilized postwar ex-military students who were in the system in the late forties. Vic

College had expanded rapidly to find places for them, and some high school teachers had been recruited to teach at the college. There really wasn't time for research. Their teaching loads would give heart attacks to UVic faculty today, but when the pressure of numbers eased as the ex-military worked through the system, as it did by the mid-fifties, Vic College was left with some very dedicated teachers who genuinely enjoyed the opportunity of dealing with the younger and more campus-oriented student body that followed the postwar crush. Also, we had very few young professors intent on just getting by on the teaching side so as to concentrate on publications. That, to us, was a UBC phenomenon which we would experience later, not one we particularly appreciated.

One consequence of Vic College's small size was that the professors became tightly linked to the subject of the course. If you didn't like French, it might well be that you didn't particularly like Miss Gladys Downes. Professor Elliott was the only economics professor – if you found him boring (and sadly many, though not me, did), then you found economics boring. History was Professor Sidney Pettit, and geography was Charles Howitson. English was Roger Bishop or Grant McOrmand. There may have been other math teachers besides Phoebe Noble (in fact, now that I think of it, the other one was Vice-president Bob Wallace), but her personality was such that Mrs Noble was math.

One incident involving Phoebe Noble that I remember well over the more than fifty years since it happened took place when I was cutting her class (as I regret to say I frequently did, at least up to that day). I was coming down the steps between the two buildings. I got halfway down when Mrs Noble's head appeared at the classroom window. She asked me where I was going that was so important, as the class list said I should be in my place listening to her. Naturally, I hightailed it to the classroom, red with embarrassment, mouthing some abject apologies and excuses, to the great amusement of everyone else in the room. Mrs Noble welcomed me with a wide smile and said that she was so glad I had come, as the problem she was discussing was so important for a proper understanding of the course that she would have been distressed had I missed it. As you can well imagine, after that, I attended her classes (almost) faithfully.

That incident was the mirror image of an experience of my brother, Malcolm (Vic College, 1951–53), except that in his case he was late for class, and Mrs Noble noticed that he was parking the car that he had borrowed (in those more simple days, students were able to park in sight of classrooms) and held up the lecture until he arrived. Again with great delight, she politely told him how important that particular lecture was and how she didn't want to start without him. Neither of us can remember any other student getting caught that way.

I should also make special mention of Grant McOrmond. He did not teach me, but he was the campus commanding officer of the University Reserve Training Plan, the Air Force component of the three military organizations that recruited and trained university students as reserve officers in the armed services. Calling him the commanding officer is a little pretentious – he was the only officer, and there were no other ranks either, just three or four student cadets, who were technically part of the UBC squadron. We felt that the RCAF had a great advantage over the other two services because it alone recruited female cadets, although there were so few cadets in the URTP at Vic College that if memory serves me correctly during my time, it was men only.

We had a great deal of fun on the Tuesday night parades, for which we were paid. We were so few that Professor McOrmond had a little trouble working out a serious program. How do you teach cadets to march and drill if there are only three or four cadets? We were also paid during our summer training, which in my case was air crew as a pilot. The basic pay was $250 a month, but air crew got another $75 risk pay a month, all in all a very good summer income.

The risk pay was probably justified. In my first hour of training, at Moose Jaw, my instructor took me up and flew me twenty minutes south to circle the smoking wreckage of a plane in which his other student had been killed earlier in the day. Typically, our parents worried more about the risk than we did.

Summer training was on the Prairies or in Ontario, in the Harvard Trainer, a bright yellow machine that burned about 20 gallons of fuel an hour, had a top speed of about 220 knots, and was capable of aerobatics, which was part of our training. Our instructors were sometimes ex–Korean War or ex–Second World War – many of them regarded themselves as the last of the devil-may-care pilots. From the fifties on, the RCAF took a much more critical view of high jinks with aircraft, but our instructors were fun to be with. When flying out of Trenton, Ontario, I remember touch-and-go landings on the new 401 Highway, which was being built. It was of course strictly forbidden, but that made it more exciting. Low-flying training was in an area where there were two lakes, which had fishing boats on them. One afternoon my instructor and I undid the straps of our harnesses, put them outside the cockpit so they would flap and bang against the metal, and then crouched down below the glass in the cockpit so we could not be seen from below. With the straps flapping in the slipstream, it looked like a plane with no one in it. Navigating was by looking through a tiny air vent about four square inches in size at the height of our knees. We went looking for fishermen, and when a boat was in sight, we flew over it at about ten feet off the water. The first fishermen saw the empty plane coming and dove to the bottom of the boat, and in the next a fisherman jumped overboard. It was all great fun, and we were paid to do it.

Vic College's principal, Harry Hickman, was a fine gentleman. Dr Hickman's personality was not outgoing. In fact, I remember him as rather shy and reserved, but nevertheless we students found him a very kind individual. His doctorate and the robes that went with it, particularly the outlandish hat, were a bit of an embarrassment to him on the occasions that he had to wear them. Students found them strange. Dr Hickman seemed to know the name of every student, what they were studying, and how they were doing. His wife also deserves fond mention – far more outgoing and vivacious than her husband. She was also an academic in French, and I believe took over his teaching when he returned to study in France for his final year before his doctorate. The two of them would have students to tea at their home just off campus on the hill of Foul Bay Road. They worked their way through most, if not all, of the student body, inviting us to tea every Wednesday, and yet did it with such genuine interest in the students that we in no way got the impression that this was a duty they felt obliged to carry out.

Vic College was small. We shared the buildings – there were only two of them if you didn't count the haunt of Mrs Norris, the cafeteria, an old wooden building at the back – with the Normal School, and so there were plenty of students on the campus, but I think at Vic College we only had between three and four hundred in first year and eighty-five in second year. The sharp dropoff in numbers was also related to the preparatory nature of first year – students going into Engineering, Forestry, Commerce, and the other professional schools had to go over to UBC to begin their specialized courses. Those of us in Arts were able to stay on, but many didn't. UBC, at fourteen thousand students, was clearly going to be more exciting than the eighty-five of us in second year at Vic College.

I thought that there were real advantages to the small enrolment in second year. The individual student was able to take part in many more sports and other activities than would have been the case at UBC. Finding fifteen for a rugby team meant going so far down the talent list that even I was on the team once in a while. We got used to being recruited by our friends into activities that in the normal course of events at a larger institution we would probably not have experienced.

Each spring Vic College would go en masse over to UBC for a rugby game and probably a grass hockey game as well. En masse might mean between fifty and a hundred students. We called it "The Invasion," not that many at UBC ever learned that we had come and gone. Second-year students were the majority of the group, and we were generally housed and taken care of at the Point Grey end by those Vic College students who had gone over to UBC for the second year or by brothers and sisters or other former Vic College students in third or fourth year whom we knew.

The excursion started with the boat trip over to Vancouver. In those days the BC Ferries system was not yet in existence, and so the midnight CPR boat to Vancouver was the only way to go. These had been designed as mini ocean liners with staterooms, berths, and lounges. With fifty to a hundred students on board, not many other passengers got any sleep for the first couple of hours or so, and then almost without fail, the captain would appear to order us to be quiet on pain of having the Vancouver Police paddy wagons on the dock to meet us on arrival. Whether this threat ever materialized I do not know, but we took it seriously. On one trip I remember the automatic sprinkler system going off, activated by a careless student opening a bottle of mixer. The captain and the CPR were not pleased about that, and the student was ordered to pay an enormous bill, something we found rather unfair.

Talking of boats to Vancouver, the passenger fare for the first BC Ferries ships was $5 for a car and $2 for a passenger. I don't think there was a special rate for students. We felt that was exorbitant, and students generally didn't like the Bennett government that had put in the ferry system. So a student or two would sometimes get in the trunk of the car on the hill just out of sight of the ferry terminal, only to emerge later when the car was parked on board. No one that I know of died of asphyxiation, but the cars we drove in those days were certainly no better than student cars since that time, and many had faulty mufflers. It was probably a dumb thing to do, but no doubt it is still done. Incidentally, at that time airfare on the DC3s that connected the two airports was $8.40. Of course, these fares were of more concern to us when we were at UBC than at Vic College.

Looking back, I can't say that Vic College changed the direction of my life. No doubt had I gone straight to UBC, it would have been much as it did. But I am very glad I was there. It was a great experience, it formed great friendships, and it certainly gave me the confidence to take on the challenges of university that followed. Had I not had the confidence that Vic College gave me that I could handle the course work at UBC, I probably would not have turned out for rowing, which was for me the greatest experience of my UBC years. In fact, from the vantage point of my seventieth year, I am sure that rowing for Canada in international competition with the UBC crew was the equal of any experience I have had since that time.

The Honourable David Anderson, PC, QC, LLB, LLD (hon.), left Victoria College after 1957 to continue his studies at the University of British Columbia, where, as a member of the UBC crew, he rowed for Canada in international competitions. A lawyer by profession, he has answered the call of public service many times, in particular by serving from 1993 to 2005 as Liberal MP for the riding of Victoria. During his time in Parliament, he held numerous cabinet posts, including minister of National Revenue, minister of Transport, minister of Fisheries and Oceans, and minister of the Environment. He continues his lifelong advocacy for the environment in his current assignments.

THE HON. CHIEF JUSTICE LANCE S.G. FINCH
VIC '55

So much freedom, so little self-discipline. I think those words capture the essence of my experience as a seventeen-year-old from Mount View High School entering a period of major transition in my life. I did not enrol at Victoria College with any well-defined vocational goal, nor with an inspired vision of how to improve the world. Rather, I went to Victoria College because my sister Donna had done so the year before and because both of our parents believed in and supported post-secondary education for all their children.

Very few students from Mount View High School went on to study at college. From my graduating class of 1955, I believe the only classmates to join me were Marlene Hunt, Ken Dawson, and Doug Patterson. I still see these old friends on rare occasions. The talented Marlene has had a successful career as an artist and musician. Ken pursued engineering at UBC and became a very successful mining geologist and consultant. Doug, who was one of the most gifted athletes I ever knew, became an educator in Vancouver and has since retired to the Gulf Islands.

I attended most of my classes but did little work on my own. I was much more interested in playing basketball, coached by David McLay, and in coaching the girls' team. But to me, the most exhilarating aspect of the new world that college presented was a social life filled with students from other, and much larger, high schools in the Victoria area.

I cannot recall, at this distance of time, all the many wonderful young people I met and became friends with. Some names stand out, however. A.J. Stewart Smith and Robert McKee from Victoria High School were outstanding members of the rugby team. Rugby players apparently have a tradition of post-game celebrations. These were often held in the home of Stu Smith's parents. I didn't play rugby, but I did go to the parties.

Stewart Smith was the gold medalist in his graduating year at UBC. He studied physics and has spent a large part of his life since graduation in accelerating particles at Princeton and elsewhere. Bob McKee graduated from UBC in engineering. He then went on a trip around the world and tragically lost his life while swimming in the sea off the Japan coast.

I will mention one other student who graduated, I believe, from Oak Bay High School. John Sparks was not physically large, but he had a magnificent baritone voice, and he became an accomplished actor. Sadly, he also died far too young.

For my part, too much time was spent on the front lawn of the grand old Young Building on warm sunny days, but more often in the cafeteria housed in an old army hut behind it. Known to us affectionately as the "caf" and operated by the kindly and maternal Mrs Norris, it was where we discussed all the things that seemed important to young people, occasionally straying into matters of more serious concern such as the Cold War, nuclear threats, and the Soviet invasion of Hungary. Local politics were also interesting. I remember the late George Gregory, QC, a provincial MLA at the time (and later a justice of the BC Supreme Court), speaking in the auditorium one noon hour. He had a wonderful presence and was a compelling orator. I also remember the then chief justice of British Columbia, Gordon Sloan, announcing his retirement from the Court of Appeal to become chair of a provincial inquiry into BC forestry practices. Because it was convenient, we sometimes went down to the Legislature to listen in.

Then there was the Student Council, with weighty matters to discuss and important events to plan. College dances were sometimes held in the basement common room of what we called the Administration Building. But all the more formal events were traditionally held in the upstairs ballroom at the Crystal Gardens Pool in downtown Victoria. My recollection is that the orchestra was most often the Lou Myles group, which had a big band sound and played all the most danceable tunes of the time.

In 1957 the college and the old Normal School merged, and our student population doubled to about eight hundred. The Normal School became the Faculty of Education, and it offered the first two years towards an education degree. The head of that faculty was a very fine man, Henry Gilliland, who served most ably in that capacity for nine years.

It is evident that an agenda so full of extracurricular fun and excitement left little time for study. The results were, of course, inevitable. The immediate, and at the time devastating, consequence was that I completed only two of my five second-year courses. The further, and more positive, result was that I had a third year at college at a time when only the first two years of university were being offered.

I had the benefit of courses from a number of very able men and women. They included Greek from John Carson (there were only four of us in that class, if you include Mr Carson's German shepherd); psychology from Dr William Gaddes (about whom more later); first-year English from Grant McOrmand; second-year English from Rodney Poisson (a memorable experience, with his asking a female student with a beautiful Ayrshire brogue to read Robert Burns's poem "To a Mouse"); German from Gordon Tracy; and chemistry from Lewis Clark. I offer them all a belated apology for not having been a better student.

In these years of personal turmoil and growth, I recall with great affection and gratitude the interest, concern, support, and encouragement of four men in particular. Our principal, Dr Harry Hickman, was a gentle man, serious and firm but understanding. The vice-principal, Dr Bob Wallace, was an equally strong and guiding hand, a true father figure. Two other men deserve my special thanks: Dr Bill Gaddes taught us psychology, but he was a clinician as well as an academic, and he took a special interest in trying to keep me on the rails; and Dr Beattie MacLean, a professor of German, from whom I never had a class, but who was a counsellor of great insight. He proved to be a practical source of wisdom and assistance. Without the kindly, unobtrusive safety net provided by these men, the triumph of freedom over my lack of self-discipline might have been complete. With their help, however, I emerged from Victoria College with a better understanding of myself and an appreciation that there were more important goals in life than the pursuit of fun and games.

After one more year of general arts courses at UBC, I entered the law school there, and for the first time in my life, I became an engaged and serious student. I am sure that without the assistance of the college faculty who came to my aid in a time of need, I might well have dropped out of school altogether. Their support, and the friendship and encouragement of my classmates, enabled me to complete my education and to have a satisfying and rewarding life as a lawyer and judge.

One final note: The highlight of my last year at college was to be a member of the Vikings Basketball Team, coached by Bill Garner. We won the Canadian Junior Men's Championship in the spring of 1958.

THE HONOURABLE CHIEF JUSTICE LANCE S.G. FINCH, LLB, after twenty years in the private practice of law, became trial judge in the Supreme Court of British Columbia in 1983. He served in that position until 1993, when he was appointed to the Court of Appeal of British Columbia. In 2001 he was appointed chief justice of British Columbia, in which capacity he continues to act. He is one of the distinguished graduates of Victoria College who serve or have served on the highest court of the province and brought wisdom to justice.

GEOFFREY CASTLE
VIC '55

EDITOR'S NOTE
In 1948 Professor Bob Wallace introduced the Evening Program at Victoria College. This innovation permitted hundreds of students to pursue their studies despite being employed during the day or otherwise obligated. Geoffrey Castle completed his BA degree entirely as a part-time student.
E.B.H.

One morning during a coffee break a colleague announced that he was enrolling for a math course in the Evening Division at Victoria College. It was the end of an Indian summer, but outdoor activities would soon be shortened along with the days. So I registered too. Then we could both work on problems that might arise throughout the term. As it happened, my associate apparently had a change of heart, having unwittingly set me on a path that would eventually change my whole life.

At the time I was a draftsman in Forest Management at the Legislative Buildings in Victoria without any concept of how to shape my carer. Persistent thoughts included architecture, journalism, and land surveying. Achieving any of them certainly would benefit from further education. This was my view at age twenty-four.

Initial impressions were both interesting and lasting. Until the first night of classes at 7.30 p.m. on Thursday, 27 September 1955, there was very little that I knew about this institution, its building and grounds, or its facilities, except that it was conceived as a Normal School and had served as a military hospital during the Second World War. A healthy curiosity revealed more information. The Young Building (1914) was designed by Vancouver architect W.C.F. Gilliam, who won in a competition after competing with fifteen other architects. The highly visible clock tower originally housed a water tank for fire protection of this eclectic Beaux Arts–style building. The grounds derive part of their charm from beech and linden trees, Garry oaks, and cedar trees.

Dr Harry Hickman was principal of Victoria College when I started, and Bob Wallace, who established the Evening Division in 1948, was vice-principal as well as associate professor of mathematics. Mrs Phoebe Noble was my instructor for Math 101. This happy soul with an infectious smile was well organized. All sixteen students thought she was a good teacher who enjoyed her work. Classes were held every Tuesday and Thursday, and I soon made friends with another student, Stanley Perkins, who was teaching industrial arts (shop) at a local high school. We took several more courses together and had some good study sessions. On occasion, Violet, his wife, would serve refreshments when we lost track of time. Stanley eventually went on to take his doctorate, assuming a position at Bowling Green State University in Ohio. What an inspiration!

In October the following year a significant event happened on the international scene when an uprising against Communist control in Budapest caused many people to leave Hungary. Among these, many forestry students and staff came to Canada, and some joined the BC Forest Service. This was around the time Israel invaded the Sinai Peninsula and Britain and France entered Egypt after that country closed the Suez Canal. Since I had lived in London during the war, there was some comfort in feeling that Victoria was a safe and desirable place to live.

The Evening Division left little choice of courses from my point of view, but I was pleased to have selected Geography 101. The instructor was Charlie Howatson. While he appeared to have an easygoing manner, he proved to be quite a thorough taskmaster. The classes ran from 7.30 until 9.30 two nights a week. By spring it seemed that geography would be a good major, depending upon the courses offered.

The day after Canada Day in July 1957 was the start of an intensive evening course. This was German 90, a beginners' course. Frederick Kriegel, our instructor, was affable and patient. This charming gentleman had received his training at the University of Vienna. Our class consisted of seven men and twelve women, most of whom were teachers. I recall that the seats seemed somewhat hard, and so there was little chance of falling asleep during a lecture! The six weeks soon went by, and the exam results were eagerly anticipated.

While never having evinced any interest in sports, I was aware that at the college there were opportunities to play badminton, swim, and play soccer and rugby. Generally, competitive activity never really appealed to me. Dancing – whether ballroom, old-time, or square dancing – and the music (not to mention the social aspects) were my preference. Dances in connection with the college, such as the July Alumni Dance with Bert Zala's orchestra, were well attended. The cost was only $2 for the student activity fee, and there was never any shortage of young women who liked to dance. It was a time when parking meters would accept as little as 1 cent. We devised many parking meter pranks to keep our costs down. Much to the embarrassment of the date who would be my future wife, I would use my student pass at the movies to reduce the price of admission!

In September of 1957 students were concerned about news of student rioting at Little Rock in Arkansas, which raised the spectre that this kind of situation could occur almost anywhere. The world was changing. In some ways it was becoming smaller. This became apparent with the start of the Cold War space race, marked by the launching of the Sputnik satellite by the Soviet Union.

Another first-year course offered in the evenings was English 101. The instructor was John Gruber, who came from Princeton University. He appears to have been at Victoria College for only a few months. I have very pleasant memories of some of the faces in that class and the dances we enjoyed. Class parties led to new introductions.

In another vein and evoking great national pride, the new Canadian Avro Arrow aircraft easily broke the sound barrier on its first flight on 5 March 1958. The biggest nonnuclear explosion ever was set off to take out Ripple Rock in Seymour Narrows. (As a hazard to navigation, it had claimed 125 ships over the years.) That took place on Saturday, 5 April 1958, at 9:31 a.m.

For the 1958–59 session Geography 409 was offered on Saturday mornings. The instructor was Charles Howatson; so we knew what to expect. With my bent for history, it was appropriate for me to study British Columbia's Centennial celebrations, scheduled for 19 November 1958, an event that would highlight the role played by Sir James Douglas in the settlement and development of trade and industry on Vancouver Island and in British Columbia.

On 18 February a recently constructed addition to the Ewing Building was officially opened. While the main building (later named the Young Building) had served reasonably well to date, with its handsome auditorium and white tiled interior passage walls, the need to accommodate third-year students required more space. Premier W.A.C. Bennett officiated at the opening and pleased us when he announced that his government would match dollar for dollar any funds raised for a university up to $1.5 million (subsequently substantially increased).

The premier had been in office since 1952 and would remain until 1972, making him the longest-serving leader in the province. In that time, tremendous economic growth, based mostly on resources, new highways, power dams, and railways, was of great benefit to virtually everyone in British Columbia either directly or indirectly. Though Premier Bennett was a showman, his promises were generally not made unless they could be achieved. On Saturday, 1 August, $70 million in cancelled bonds were set alight and burned on Okanagan Lake, not far from his hometown of Kelowna.

Another geography course was going well. The professor, visiting for the season from the United States, lectured for six weeks in the summer. "Weather and Climate" was a lab course, and there was an assistant, Barbara Westinghouse (Mordaunt). Her father was Aubrey Westinghouse, who started Westinghouse Airways. The family home was near the Victoria Yacht Club in North Oak Bay. Barbara's master's thesis was on the wine industry in Michigan.

Having made an arrangement with my supervisor in the Forest Service, I was able to attend Geography 201, an urban geography course, for a one-hour lecture on Mondays, Wednesdays, and Fridays. Dr Charles Forward's lectures were significant in more than one way. Quite early in the course I decided that my future lay in urban planning. Dr Forward's enthusiasm encouraged me to join the Canadian Association of Geographers. This eventually led to my meeting Don South, who was in charge of the Regional Planning Division in the Department of Municipal Affairs of the BC government, where I was later to start as a planning technician and serve a ten-year stint.

It was in late October 1959 when a favourite actor, Errol Flynn, died in Vancouver. The screen idol was only fifty years old when he succumbed to a heart attack. This lively character, born in Tasmania, gave moviegoers much enjoyment and still does, thanks to classic movies on TV.

The Social Credit government had been returned in a landslide victory in the previous month. The government fortunately favoured post-secondary education; so prospects for students were excellent. For the 1960–61 winter session I was taking English 200, and Grant McOrmond, assistant professor of English, was the instructor. He will be remembered for his strong voice, humour, and diplomacy. Years later, we became next door neighbours. His charming wife, Phyllis, was an avid doll collector, while Grant was a philatelist.

The Student Council arranged a dance at the Crystal Garden on Tuesday, 20 December. Unlike the earlier Club Services dances with George Kraeling's orchestra, which for many years played at McMorron's on Cordova Bay, on this occasion Len Acres and his orchestra were engaged. First, my partner and I attended a reception at Bob Wallace's, after which we visited the Joker's Club. After the dance we went to The Scene. I doubt that many alumni will recall these places. A good New Year's resolution was to work hard and complete the BA degree.

It is worth noting that the BC Ferries system was becoming increasingly popular after more than six months of operation, with the *Queen of Sidney* and the *Queen of Tsawwassen* linking the island with the mainland.

On 18 January 1961 the new Paul Building was officially opened. E.B. Paul had been the college principal at Craigdarroch Castle until he retired in 1927. For this auspicious occasion, the platform of dignitaries included Premier W.A.C. Bennett, the Honourable W.N. Chant, minister of public works, and Professor Bob Wallace.

Victoria College's first graduation ceremony ever took place on a bright, sunny 29th of May in 1961 and consisted of some twenty-nine men and fifteen women. Since I was a part-time student, only two graduates had been fellow students. Brian Carr-Harris, from a geography class, went on to become a dentist. Kathleen Thornberry became a teacher. They, like so many others I met at the college, were wonderful people.

Once again distressing news on the world scene intruded on my relatively composed life. In July there was the Russian buildup around East Berlin. Soon barbed wire was strung to separate Communist East Berlin and the Western Sector, heralding the beginnings of the Berlin Wall.

With the passing of summer, my thoughts were in the direction of German 110. The professor was Dr J.B. MacLean. He was a very patient teacher because on one memorable occasion, he mimed the German word *rauchen* for the English translation. Unfortunately, being a non-smoker, I was slow to comprehend, but the meaning eventually became entrenched for all time! Classes were held on Tuesday and Thursday evenings throughout the entire course.

German 200 would complete my language requirement for the degree, and this was offered in September. Frederick Kriegel was again the instructor. There were nineteen men and eight women in the class, which was held on Monday, Wednesday, and Friday at 4.30 in the afternoon. Final exams for some courses were written in room 35 of the Ewing Building in the last days of the college at Lansdowne. One of my fellow students was Daphne Gage, Campus Queen for 1963.

There had been increasing development in Victoria, like so many other areas in the post –Second World War era. It began relatively slowly at first but increased greatly by the sixties. The Lansdowne slope was laid out and subdivided by 1952. Several large new hotels were constructed in downtown Victoria, yet new construction came at an immeasurable cost in the destruction of historic buildings and the elimination of venerable business names such as Rithet Consolidated and J.H. Todd and Sons. Cordova Bay, Cadboro Bay, and Gordon Head, hitherto largely undeveloped, were becoming prime targets for developers. Luckily, Victoria College purchased land in Gordon Head in 1959. Future land purchases included the wartime Canadian Army Officers' Training Centre, some of the buildings of which were refurbished and used by the University of Victoria in 1963.

The Clearihue Building was the first to be opened on the Gordon Head site. Again, ever-smiling Premier Bennett had some encouraging words to say which, in effect, amounted to paving the way for Judge Joseph Clearihue becoming Victoria University's first chancellor.

Already exams were being written in the Gordon Head gym, and some students who harboured fond memories of the Lansdowne days adjusted more slowly. In retrospect, it might have been a better idea for me to attend college full-time, but as a career public servant, I held onto my job tenaciously. Meanwhile, it was fairly certain that graduation would come one day. Certainly, my time at Victoria College was now shaping and benefiting the prospects for my future.

A word of gratitude should be accorded Dorothy Cruickshank, college registrar, who struck me as organized and unassailable yet helpful. When I attempted to register for a science course with a view to pursuing a bachelor's degree in science, Dorothy was forthright in saying that she knew it was none of her business, but she urged me to take a master's degree instead. I accepted her advice and some years later graduated from UVic's School of Public Administration with a master's.

In the interim the Victoria College faculty moved to new buildings as they were completed. Among those college-day professors I had were Rodney Poisson (English), Sydney Pettit (history), G. Reid Elliot (economics), and Dr Reg Roy (history).

During the fifteen years prior to 1966, Greater Victoria's population increased by 75 per cent. Many incomers were retirees, immigrants, or university students, some of whom had been born in the early postwar period. All combined to influence the changing times. I, like so many others, viewed higher education as necessary for pursuing employment opportunities in a competitive world.

In the 1955–56 annual publication of Victoria College, the *Tower*, Dr Harry Hickman, in a message to students, told them to "enjoy living the present day and prepare themselves with a broad philosophy for a satisfactory morrow."

GEOFFREY CASTLE, BA, MPA, completed his BA entirely as a part-time student at Victoria College. Subsequently, he was one of the first students in the University of Victoria's School of Public Administration. He is the author of two books – *Victoria Landmarks* (1985) and *More Victoria Landmarks* (1988) – and has edited various other works, including *Saanich: An Illustrated History* (1989) and *Hatley Park: An Illustrated Anthology* (1995). Geoffrey Castle is a past-president of the Victoria Historical Society, a life fellow of the Royal Geographical Society, and a great citizen of the city of Victoria.

BARBARA L. CRAIGIE
VIC '56

I had always known I would attend Victoria College. My father and his three siblings had been students, as had my mother and her two sisters. It was written in the Book of Genesis that my brother and I would follow the family tradition. It wasn't until much later that I came to appreciate how fortunate we were to have such a fine institution right on our doorstep. While it was small and limited in course offerings when we attended, it provided a fine base on which to build.

In 1956–57, the first year of the merger of Victoria College and the former Victoria Normal School, there were about 550 students, of whom 220 were in the newly created teacher education department. While most of the Arts and Science students were from the Greater Victoria area, a large proportion of the Education students came from elsewhere in the province – from the rest of Vancouver Island and far-flung regions of the interior: the Okanagan, the Kootenays, and the North. This division of the province had been an accepted policy of the Vancouver and Victoria Normal Schools, continued by UBC and Victoria College. In fact, there was a long-standing lame joke that students from the lower Mainland and Vancouver area would go to school in Vancouver, while those from Victoria and elsewhere on Vancouver Island and those "beyond Hope" would go to Victoria.

The Victoria College experiences of these two groups differed substantially. Most of the Arts and Science students lived at home. Many regarded the first year of their college experience as a sort of senior matriculation year, an opportunity to decide what their futures might be. Those who opted to pursue such degrees as Engineering, Nursing, Home Economics, or Agriculture would head to UBC for their second year, while others would leave the campus to begin training, articling, and apprenticeships in nursing, land surveying, chartered accountancy, and lab and x-ray technology, for example.

Those of us left behind were taking basic second-year Arts and Science courses. Some of us lacked the initiative or financial resources to leave home, or maybe we just took longer to "find ourselves" – if there was a 1950s equivalent of that. The sophomore year enrolment in Arts and Science was significantly smaller than the first year. The upside was that we "felt as if we ran the place," as one classmate commented recently.

Major changes were coming. There was increasing pressure both on the campus and in the community to make Victoria College a degree-granting institution. In 1961, just three years after I left the campus, the first Victoria College (UBC) degrees were bestowed on thirty-seven graduates.

Education students tended to be goal and career oriented, many heading into classrooms after their second year. Several were older students, having already taught for a few years. The financial burden was greater for these out-of-town students, not only because of travel costs. Usually they boarded in private homes while they were in Victoria. According to the student handbook, the average cost for board and room was $55–60 a month. In a sign of the times, the handbook further advises: "Men and women students are not permitted to lodge in the same house, unless they are members of the same family, or receive special permission from the Faculty."

There were opportunities for the two groups of students to get together. Sports, social events, and a wide variety of clubs flourished during the two years I was a student at Victoria College. According to the *Tower*, in 1957 there were "twenty-seven clubs, fourteen athletic teams and organizations and twelve dances."

Each dance was sponsored by a different club or organization. Among these were the Radio Club's Blue Room dance and the Howdy Hop. Described as either "formal" or "semi-formal," these usually took place at the Crystal Gardens or in the Student Union Room in the Ewing Building, cost between $2 and $4 a couple, and sometimes included a buffet meal. Two of the most frequently featured orchestras were led by Bert Zala and Len Acres. We all remember the bottles in brown paper bags on the shelves conveniently located under the tables at the Crystal. Often the Student Council minutes following one of these affairs mentioned a need to enforce the prohibition of alcohol at college events. According to school lore, a hefty fine would be levied against anyone who fell, jumped, or was pushed into the pool at the Crystal Gardens during a college dance.

The Women's Undergraduate Society (WUGS) and its male counterpart (MUGS) each sponsored a dance during the year. Traditionally, they provided the entertainment at each other's event, usually in the form of a skit. Following the WUGS dance in February 1958, a letter of apology from the MUGS was read at the Student Council meeting concerning the entertainment presented at the event. It was accompanied by a bill of $2 for medical attention following an accident that occurred during that entertainment. A proposal presented at the same meeting recommended that from now on, each organization should provide the entertainment for its own dance. I wonder if anyone remembers what made the MUGS entertainment so offensive to our 1950s sensibilities.

We were typical of the times. Traditionally, the Men's Undergraduate Society hosted a "Smoker" and sponsored the Campus Queen contest. Candidates, nominated by various campus organizations, paraded across the stage in high heels, shorts, and tight sweaters to be "interviewed" by the emcee before the student population voted for the winner and runners-up. Innuendo was inescapable. "I see you have the support of the rugby team" brought down the house.

WUGS–sponsored activities featured a Freshette Tea with a fashion show in the fall, a Kristmas Kackle Koffee Party, and the Coed Dance in February, following TWIRP week. Does anyone remember what those initials stood for? (Answer: The Woman Is Requested to Pay). The WUGS had its own awards: Cafeteria Queen, Lovingest Couple, and the euphemistically titled International Good Head.

There was no shortage of activities through the lunch hour. If there wasn't already a club in your interest area, you could apply to start one. If it was approved, the Student Council would even supply an operating grant.

The Jive Club first appeared on campus in 1956 and soon had a membership of 250, an indication of the popularity of this new dance form. Once a week, over the noon hour, the club functioned in the Student Union Room, with the participants displaying a wide variety of skill levels. We danced to records – 78s, of course – the one most played, to my recollection, being *The Green Door*.

We were a well-balanced group. The chess club, another newly formed organization, could state that nearly a hundred students were taught the finer points of the game during the year. There was an active Radio Club, broadcasting to the cafeteria several hours each day. The staff of the *Martlet* struggled to publish within their budget, a challenge when the paper was sold for ten cents a copy. The Listening Club sponsored musical performances featuring several of the talented students at the college, as well as musicians from the Victoria musical community, some of them Victoria College alumni, such as Robin Wood.

From one of the student musicians: "A funny thing I remember was that (we), with, I assume, the janitor's and Boyce Gaddes's permission, moved an upright piano ourselves from the music room on the top floor, where we used to practise two-piano with two uprights, to the auditorium via the elevator. We may not have had permission, but a concert was coming up, and we were determined to practise in the auditorium, where there was already a grand! I can't imagine that happening these days."

Politics was in the air. Significant changes were occurring on the federal scene, if not on the provincial. A notable development during the 1957–58 year was the appearance on campus of four political clubs, one for each of the main political parties at the time. Each of these clubs presented speakers during the year, among them Robert Strachan, leader of the Opposition in the provincial legislature, and General George Pearkes, minister of defence in John Diefenbaker's newly elected Conservative government.

The year's activities featured a Model Parliament, after not just one but two general elections to determine the winning party (the Liberals). The session was opened with all due pomp and ceremony, complete with a speech from the throne, read by a faculty member in formal attire. The speaker was a law student from UBC, imported for the occasion. Ministers were appointed, and idealistic legislation passed, but nobody seems to remember the details.

Through the Lansdowne years, various banners and other objects appeared overnight atop the tower on the former Normal School building. Our years were no exception, although our antics did not approach the audacity of the teapot of 1959. A banner appeared on behalf of the Liberal party during the campaign for the Model Parliament election. Perhaps there was some collusion between the Liberal Club and the recently formed Outdoor Club.

Sputnik blazed across the skies in October of 1957, inspiring the Science Club of 1957–58 to embark on "The Norseman Rocket Project." According to the *Tower*, fourteen honours science students and seven professional advisers set out to build a fifteen-foot liquid fuel experimental rocket. The team claimed this was the first project of its kind in Canada. We could have had our own "Rocket Boys" (and one girl). The Student Council contributed $100 to the cause. At the semi-annual open Student Council meeting in February, there was a request from the floor to provide an accounting of this generous grant. At that time, it was reported, only $13 had been spent. The project was not off the drawing board at the end of the college year. Its eventual fate remains unknown, as does the fate of the remaining $87.

A major highlight of each year was the production by the Players' Club. The director during these years was Flora Nicholson, hired by the college from Victoria's active theatrical community. She produced several plays "in the round," creatively using the space in the Student Union room in the lower level of the Ewing Building. The 1956–57 production was *The Crucible* by Arthur Miller, noted on the program as a Victoria premiere. The choice for 1957–58 was *The Apple Cart* by George Bernard Shaw. Each of these ran for five nights, attracting not just the campus community but attendees from the community at large.

Various Vic College athletic teams attracted attention beyond the campus as well, especially rugby and basketball. The Vikings men's basketball team, in particular, distinguished itself, reaching the finals of the Canadian Junior Men's Championship both years and bringing home the title in 1958. This accomplishment was a first in the history of Victoria College. In 1957 the team left the campus for three weeks in March and played its way across Canada to reach the finals in Toronto. In an attempt to fill in the missing lectures, several students were assigned to make carbon copies of their notes to give to the team members on their return. In his "Principal's Message" in the *Tower* of 1956–57, Harry Hickman commented, "For many of us the two most tense and memorable happenings of the year were the overtime moments during which the Vikings became Provincial Champions, and the climax of *The Crucible*, when the screaming girls saw witches."

Besides basketball and rugby, there were numerous athletic teams for both men and women – men's soccer and women's grass hockey and volleyball, as well as coed activities such as bowling, curling, badminton, and ping pong. The level of participation was high and enthusiastic. The cheerleaders were an important asset, especially for those teams that attracted large numbers of spectators. In 1956 the Student Council authorized $2 for each of the seven cheerleaders for skirt material. To complete their outfits, each wore a white blouse, school sweater, plaid tie, white socks, and saddle shoes.

An Athletic Council, with representation for each team, was created for the first time in 1956 "to co-ordinate and control all athletic activities in the college." This included allotting money and selecting coaches. Practice facilities were often off-campus, and most teams competed against the local high schools or in community leagues.

As Victoria College was still affiliated with UBC, there was considerable interaction between the two campuses. On rare occasions one might fly to and from Vancouver, but most travel was by the legendary midnight boat, the BC ferry system not having been created yet. Each "major" sports team had an opportunity to travel to Vancouver to play against UBC, the Students Council sent a display to the UBC Open House of 1958, and speakers supplied by such organizations as World University Service appeared at Victoria College as well as at UBC.

Frosh Week, at the beginning of the term in September, mainly constituted the humiliation of the first-year students by those in second year in activities that came close to hazing, specifically prohibited in the student handbook. In 1956 we were paraded through downtown Victoria. One of us remembers: "We had to wear pants cut off in a ragged way to just above our knees with a sack for our top. Footwear was a pair of running shoes with one nylon stocking rolled to ankle length and the other to our knee. We had to paint on a black moustache and wear the blue and yellow cardboard hat with "Frosh" printed on it ... I think the Frosh Dance was held downtown, maybe at the Club Sirocco ... the Student Council president, Lance Finch, had to ask a frosh for the first dance, and I was the lucky girl!"

The Student Council had occasion to send its own letter of apology to a homeowner near the campus, after some exuberant frosh trampled his garden during the antics of Frosh Week. There was also the incident of debris that hit the suit of a downtown bystander during the Frosh Parade. The matter was settled with a donation of $1.25 in the gentleman's name to the Community Chest.

In the basement of the Normal School Building, there were separate women's and men's commons rooms, the former refurbished in 1957 at considerable expense and with major donations from Standard Furniture, among other sources. But these were dark and staid places, and besides, they segregated the sexes. As one of us said recently, "Why would we want to go there?"

Speaking of basements, does anyone remember the numerous basement alcoves, some with ancient typewriters, and the connecting tunnels between the main building and the Ewing Building? Rumour had it that some students went into them to (gasp!) drink and/or make out.

The favourite place for socializing was the cafeteria, housed in the old wooden army building at the rear of the campus. Faculty members could often be found there. This

Mrs Norris presides over her famous coffee at the Victoria College "caf" in 1951.

was the realm of Mrs Norris, campus icon. With coffee at less than ten cents a cup, food choices such as soup, hamburgers, and sandwiches, and the Student Council offices upstairs, it was for many of us the campus centre.

Another memory: I seem to recall, upstairs in that building, an enormous stuffed buffalo head, origins unknown.

The bulletin boards near the library and office were the main communication centre on campus. Important notices were posted there – lists of those whose library "caution money" had run out, for example. Pay up ($2) or lose your library borrowing privileges.

Most of us attended Victoria College because it was easy to do so. We took it for granted that we would go there for one or two years. It was affordable ($237 a year for fees). Graduation from high school on the University Entrance program virtually guaranteed admission. Even 8:30 a.m. lectures, including Saturdays, did not discourage us. The 7/8 attendance requirement permitted some selective skipping of classes. Unlike the 1940s and 1960s, the student numbers did not overwhelm the facility. We just accepted that science labs were adequately housed in army huts.

Transportation was not an issue. The city bus stopped at the door. If you were that rare student with a car, parking was not a problem. The student lot was large enough and free. The main complaint was the state of the path leading from the lot to the Ewing

Building. Letters were written to the college administration, and finally, a phone call from a member of the Student Council to the minister of the provincial Department of Public Works elicited a promise that the situation would be rectified during the summer. It was a simpler time.

Classes tended to be small, and the lecture style was somewhat formal. In class, women students were addressed as "Miss" and their surnames; men, by their surnames, with or without "Mr." However, most instructors were approachable. Some of Sid Pettit's history students even remember meeting him in The Snug, a favourite gathering place if you looked old enough to be admitted. It was said that the staff in that facility had a list of those students who were of legal drinking age – a unique "Dean's List." As each campus club and team required a faculty sponsor, there were opportunities for social interaction with teachers. The Camera Club, for example, could take advantage of Ed Savannah's expertise as a professional photographer. For many years, following Christmas exams, students travelled from house to house of various faculty members, singing Christmas carols. Many remember Lew and Lorraine Clark's welcome hot chocolate, served from the garage at their Fairfield Avenue home.

Second-year classes were usually small enough to be more like seminars. Tony Emery was the instructor for History 201, British History (from Saxon times to the present day). I think there were about a dozen students. As he covered this vast topic, Mr Emery suggested, as casual asides, book titles, both fiction and non-fiction, which were relevant to that day's lecture. These included such titles as *The Man on a Donkey* by Prescott. We ended the year with an impressive informal bibliography.

We could claim there was little time for casual reading during the term, but there was one novel many of us managed to read. *Peyton Place* was banned in Canada, but at least one smuggled copy made the rounds in 1958, in a plain brown wrapper. My own mother even stayed up all one night to read it. Who would have thought that fifty years later *Peyton Place* would be reconsidered as a classic of sorts. Even the classroom content was risqué by our standards: "Leda and the Swan," for example, introduced with delight by Grant McOrmond, who was also known to assign *Ulysses* for a first-year English essay. We weren't in English 91 any more!

We may have been self-absorbed, but we were not totally oblivious to the world beyond the campus. We were certainly aware of such world events as the launching of Sputnik and the Suez Crisis, when Lester Pearson made us proud to be Canadians. As we followed the development of the Hungarian Revolution in the fall of 1956, there was an almost impromptu fundraising drive on campus, which resulted in $130 donated to the Hungarian Students' Relief Fund. It is an interesting coincidence that those of us who proceeded to UBC met many students who had fled during that revolution. They were at UBC with us, part of the Sopron "university-in-exile," located there from 1957 to 1961.

We had the unique experience of having a sitting member of the provincial legislature as a student during our years. Tony Gargrave, the CCF member for the riding of Mackenzie on the Sunshine Coast, was an active participant in many campus activities. I clearly remember hearing him chuckling in the front row during a performance of *The Apple Cart*, probably appreciating the political satire more than the actors did. His photographs appear in the *Tower*, and he served as vice-president of the College Forum, an active club that presented speakers on various topics of current interest. He invited both the Student Council and the CCF Club to the legislature dining room and for an afternoon sitting of the House. Tony continued his studies at UBC. By the time he retired from the legislature, he had a law degree.

The 1956–58 classes at Victoria College produced many people who have made significant contributions to Canadian society and beyond. After leaving Victoria College, upon graduation from UBC, two were awarded the Governor-General's Gold Medal and one the University Medal for top marks in Arts and Science. Two Student Council members of those years went on to political successes on the federal and provincial stages. One of our future politicians was a member of the UBC rowing team that won the gold medal for Canada at the 1960 Olympics in Rome. Another was AMS president at UBC. Even with Google, it is impossible to produce a complete list of the class members' accomplishments. Among the best-known, one has received an honorary degree from UVic; another from UBC. Besides politicians, our distinguished classmates include a nationally recognized textile artist (who once produced publicity posters on campus) and a renowned jazz musician, composer, and UVic Music faculty member (who played at the Club Sirocco from age fourteen). We can count a number of published authors on various topics, including Canadian history, naval history, economics, opera, menopause, sports psychology, and at least one memoir. There are lawyers, including the current chief justice of British Columbia; a wide range of medical professionals; at least one clergyman; world-renowned scientific researchers in the fields of physics, chemistry, and geology; one university president; and several professors and administrators, including some at UVic as well as throughout North America.

The Victoria College of the mid-1950s had developed impressively from its beginning fifty years before. Fifty years later, although there are a few links to the past, the institution is unrecognizable. As this milestone anniversary of the University of Victoria approaches, it is fitting to note these connections from the Lansdowne campus of Victoria College to the current campus of UVic: the Farquhar Auditorium, the Hickman Building, the Climenhaga Observatory, and the Wallace Rugby Field. There are also countless awards, both academic and athletic, that bear the names of faculty and students from that era. I hope there are also some less tangible links in the spirit and nature of the current institution.

We were "green and golden," to echo Dylan Thomas. Lasting friendships were forged, enriching our lives for fifty years. Some of us arrived on campus with career choices and paths clearly defined. Most of us did not and were ready to be inspired by a class, a professor, or an extracurricular choice. We were encouraged to participate, to question, to stretch ourselves. The opportunity was there, and we embraced it.

BARBARA L. CRAIGIE, BA, was active on the Victoria College Student Council during the years 1956–57 and 1957–58. She then went on to the University of British Columbia, where she received her BA in English and history. This was followed by a year of teacher training. Over her career, Barbara Craigie taught or worked in school libraries in various places, including Vancouver, Prince George, Montreal, and Darien, Connecticut. She is part of the tradition of dedicated graduates of the Lansdowne years in the field of education.

Life is like a grinding wheel that can wear you down or polish you up, depending on what you are made of. As a typical teen, I needed a good deal of shaping and smoothing, and I believe that Victoria College accomplished some of that.

My father, Roy Melville, was an Anglican cleric who served in the army during both the First and Second World Wars in Europe and was posted to the Gordon Head Camp, the present location of the University of Victoria, in 1943. He was pleased to accept the parish of North Saanich at demobilization in 1945; so that is where most of my schooling occurred. I went to North Saanich High School, where the graduating class numbered twenty-three, as many classmates had gone fishing or logging or to work for the telephone company or had married long before the rest graduated.

After a year out to earn my grubstake working in the newly established Kitimat, I entered Victoria College at Lansdowne in the fall of 1956. That year saw the Provincial Normal School join Victoria College as its Faculty of Education. Many students started teaching in public schools at that time with only one or two years of training and continued their classes and degrees by summer school. This was the route taken by many of my classmates, such as Avis Bosher, Lloyd Gardner, Graham Rice, Dennis Holden, Dave Smethurst , and Anne Nimmo, but at the time I was more interested in biology and followed much later into teaching. So I spent only one year at Victoria College before going on to complete my BSc at UBC.

My parents saw me as a hormonal lad in need of purpose. My friends saw me as a laid-back, shy, but loyal guy with a flashy car. My high school teachers saw me as a "social animal with some potential" (meaning talks too much, studies too little), and I saw myself as a small-town James Dean, a rebel without a cause. In 1956, before I went to the "bigger school across the pond" (as UBC was commonly called), I carpooled with friends from Sidney, and it was the only time in my memory that Elk Lake froze solid enough for skating. We took advantage of it several times on our way home. The drive was less crowded then, and one was able to appreciate the changing seasons overlooking the Keating valley and the sometimes brilliant Olympic Mountains when approaching Royal Oak.

I do remember the valiant efforts of Professor Phoebe Noble to raise my interest in math, and the laboratory instructors in biology and chemistry making sense of the theory and developing in me an appetite for more. Professor Anne Saddlemyer taught classes in English that encouraged more reading and writing, even if the grammar continued to be a stumbling block for me. Even more exciting were lunch periods at Cattle Point watching the yacht races and playing bridge in the "caf" between many hours of swatting in the library. I found plenty of opportunity to continue my social ways in the Square Dance Club and Jive Club. Many classmates met their future mates in that melding of students from many high schools.

My two close friends, brothers John and George Cummings, spent two and three years respectively at the Lansdowne campus and went on to teach at the college and university level, while I eventually found my niche teaching in my old home district and

In *A Multitude of the Wise*, Peter Smith described this scene
as a "wild party in the Student Union Room, 1955."

even in my old high school. John and George found Vic College much smaller and more
personal than Victoria High School, where they had completed their secondary education. George talks about the intimacy of the college, where it was possible to know most
of the students and professors in the school, even those with whom one did not take
classes. He remembers that Dr Hickman, the principal, greeted him by name, although
George did not take a class with him. This was such a contrast from the vast and impersonal UBC, whose president one didn't meet until graduation. George has told me he
would always go to a Victoria College reunion but doesn't feel that way about UBC. He
also recalls Dr Lewis Clark, the chemistry professor, taking a trip to walk in the hills
around Sooke and saying that his proudest achievement was his book on plants and not
anything he'd done in chemistry.

Both brothers recall the Suez crisis vividly, students sitting in the caf listening to the
radio and believing that they would have to become soldiers and go to war after the
British bombing. But, as John remembers, "John Foster Dulles abundantly supplied
Egypt with American millions and we all went back to being college students." The
Cummings brothers were active in the college hijinks, such as freshmen pulling the seniors around in one of Victoria's fabled tallyhos or entering the coal chute off the college
driveway one night in order to access the old brick building, climb the clock tower, and
put a manikin head liberated from the Hudson's Bay Company store on the flagpole at
the top of the tower. They were also engaged in more serious pursuits such as the Players' Club, directed by Flora Nicholson. They both had a great social and academic time
at the college.

My one year at Victoria College was made very comfortable by my parents supplying room and board and much loving care at home, but in retrospect, living closer to campus would have allowed me to become more involved in these student pranks and the intense social life. Still, it was an important year, and my friends from college remain close even now.

TERENCE R. MELVILLE, BSC, entered Victoria College in 1956 and then went on to the University of British Columbia to complete his degree in biology. After ten years of military (RCAF) and private-sector employment, he returned to the University of Victoria to take a year of teacher training. For the next twenty-five years he taught general science, earth science, and biology in Victoria area secondary schools. He was also active in coaching sports. Terence Melville remains an enormously popular member of the community and an active citizen.

DAVID LEEMING
VIC '57

Entering Victoria College in September 1957 meant getting acquainted with many new students, mainly from Victoria schools but also from farther afield. It also meant engaging with a dedicated faculty who would bring us to the next level in our educational pursuits. During the first week, we "frosh," as we were called, were subjected to minor indignities, such as wearing a large conical dunce hat adorned with blue and gold crepe ribbons (these colours would later be adopted as the official UVic colours). The second-year students (they were never called sophomores) treated us frosh to a one-way bus ride to the Gordon Head army camp, where we were left – approximately where the Campus Security Services Building is today on the UVic campus (prophetic perhaps?).

Classes were small, and soon we knew almost every other student and most profs, even those who did not teach us. The cafeteria, run by Mrs Norris, was a gathering place for students and faculty alike. Registration was simple; a few volunteer students handled it under the watchful eyes of Registrar Dorothy Cruickshank and her assistant, Marjorie Hoey.

Student counselling was handled virtually solo by Professor of German Beattie MacLean. It was from conversations with Dr MacLean and some urging on his part – he went far beyond what would be considered appropriate today in offering his opinions about my potential – that I first considered the possibility of becoming a university professor. The thrust by Beattie MacLean plus the encouragement from my mentors in mathematics – Bob Wallace, Phoebe Noble, and Betty Kennedy – allowed my dream to eventually become a reality. I joined the faculty at UVic on 1 July 1963, which now afforded me the honour of having all four of these outstanding individuals as colleagues.

There was no assumption that we, as students entering Victoria College in 1957, would be able to complete all four years of our undergraduate education on the Lansdowne campus – two years at most and then on to UBC or elsewhere. Our second year,

1958–59, brought much talk and subsequent excitement, as we were told that a third year on the Lansdowne campus, with a limited selection of courses, was probable. Most of us chose to remain here for a third year, and those who stayed were able to complete their fourth year at the Victoria College campus. Convocation day in May 1961 included lunch at The Snug and an afternoon convocation in the Gordon Head army hall, which was presided over by UBC president N.A.M. McKenzie and Chancellor Dal Grauer. Thirty-three degrees in all, seven BSc's and twenty-six BAS, were awarded that day. Our parchments read, "University of British Columbia–Victoria College," and ours was one of only two convocations to hold that designation.

In the evening we enjoyed a dance in the same army hall. During the intermission, we were treated to piano selections by one of our grads, "Bud" White (now Dr J.P. White), who was and still is an accomplished pianist. Many of the members of the "first" grad class went on to successful careers, among them teachers, professors, writers, and medical doctors.

The vision of a university was well-established before the "class of 1961" convocated. That January saw the opening of the E.B. Paul Building, the first building erected to allow Victoria College to become a university. It turned out to be the last, as the vision now required some enhancement. This was first recognized by the College Board, led by its chair, Dick Wilson, and a handful of the faculty at Victoria College. Two things happened that together would ensure a large, permanent campus for UVic not far from the Lansdowne site. First, the board sought the advice of a San Francisco firm of eminent campus-planning architects. They saw the need for a larger area in order to properly develop a university campus. The potential of the Gordon Head campus site was presented to them, but that would require purchasing, among other parcels, the Hudson's Bay property, which was well over one hundred acres and had its south boundary along Cedar Hill Cross Road.

Second, since the campus architect, Don Emmons, was excited about that possibility, the Victoria College board set a course to acquire the necessary land components for the new campus, including the Hudson's Bay land, the Department of National Defence property, and several other smaller parcels that ensured the proper land size to develop a middle-sized university. We all owe a debt of gratitude to those individuals who worked tirelessly to make the vision of a proper UVic campus a reality. (Don Emmons's son now works for the same campus architectural firm and is today engaged as a UVic planning consultant.)

DAVID LEEMING, PHD, retired in 2004 after forty-one years as a member of the Department of Mathematics and Statistics at the University of Victoria. He served as department chair from 1989 to 1994. Dr Leeming is the author of over thirty papers in such areas as interpolation, rational approximation, and the Bernoulli polynomials. He has received much well-deserved recognition of his work, including the 2003–04 Faculty of Science Teaching Award from the University of Victoria.

CAROLE MACDONALD
VIC '57

EDITOR'S NOTE
Although 1958 was well before the organized student protests and activism that emerged on campuses in the 1960s, for students to give voice to their political views and dissent was not unknown in earlier times. As Carole MacDonald describes in her contribution, this was discovered by the then premier of British Columbia, W.A.C. Bennett, and the then attorney general, Robert Bonner, in the course of a visit to the Lansdowne campus. The fracas resulted in a number of outraged letters to the local newspapers and not a little commentary on "what young people are coming to." Nothing much to be concerned about was the conclusion of Professor Tony (C. Anthony) Emery, whose spirited defence of young people forms the second part of this contribution. I should mention that Tony Emery not only instructed me in the intricacies of Chaucer, Pope, Byron, and many other authors; he also made regular appearances at The Scene, a local jazz club run by myself and fellow undergraduate Garry Nixon, to read poetry to jazz. His "Christmas Present to the Students of Victoria College" is vintage Tony Emery. E.B.H.

It is the fall of 1958, almost a half-century ago. Imagine the Victoria College auditorium crammed full of noisy and boisterous undergraduates. Waving above their heads are cleverly worded posters and a floppy, colourful effigy. What could possibly persuade the students to forgo their beloved cafeteria during the lunch break to come to this stuffy auditorium? Would you be surprised to hear it is the then premier and attorney general who are paying a visit to speak to the students? I am among the students in the auditorium that day, and my recollections are vivid and strong.

The undergraduates anticipate a lively verbal engagement. They are fired up, excitedly waiting for the opportunity to question their political visitors and point out the flaws in their messages. It is to be a good-humoured political fray.

Unfortunately, as the meeting proceeds, the booing, hissing, and shouting prove to be distressing and disruptive to the politicians. Eventually, the premier, a big man with a big voice, abandons his attempts to shout over the noise of the crowd. He is a good sport, shrugging and smiling as he retreats to the rear of the stage. The attorney general, however, appears stunned by the raucous scene before him. Sputtering with anger, he runs forward to the front of the stage, red-faced, wildly waving his arms. The more he berates the crowd, the louder they heckle him. When the tomato from someone's lunch bag glances off his balding head, he bolts.

The meeting ends, but repercussions follow. The *Times* newspaper coverage of the event provokes many citizens on Vancouver Island to write letters to the editor, condemning the students as irresponsible, ill-mannered hooligans who will ultimately bring the country to ruin. It is all very disheartening.

Something remarkable happens at the end of the fall term – something that brings smiles to the faces of the undergraduates and lifts their spirits. As weary students exit the auditorium after completing their English 200 exam, Assistant Professor Tony (C. Anthony) Emery hands them a copy of an essay he has written, telling each student that it is a Christmas present from the English Department. It is entitled "They Filled Many an Older Heart with Admiration: Don't Sell Your Young People Short."

The Young Building auditorium on a less boisterous occasion than
the one described by Carole MacDonald. Bill Halkett photo.

Professor Emery's essay explains that it might help if he were to give his view of the
meeting, since he had actually been present, whereas the "moralizing correspondents"
had not. The professor describes intelligent, principled young people with strong ideals.
He sees them striving to identify abuses and eliminate them, objecting to any perceived
injustice or wrongdoing. He points out that undergraduates are not yet cynical or com-
placent like so many of their elders. Professor Emery knew that skullduggery is unac-
ceptable to undergraduates; they expect ideas to be expressed openly in an atmosphere
of trust.

Professor Emery's gift of support to the students on that day almost fifty years ago
has remained with me. Given life's experiences, it has taken on more meaning. I see it
reflected in my approach to helping post-graduate health-care students benefit from and
succeed in their clinical practicums. The demands of particular clinical placements can

cause the most promising students to falter. As a clinical coordinator, I enjoyed intervening and acting as the go-between with instructors and students. We identified problems and explored possible solutions that would create a good learning environment and an enriching successful clinical experience for both student clinicians and instructors.

Thank you, Professor Emery, for coming to our defence way back then. It made a difference in my life.

CAROLE MACDONALD, MA, studied at Victoria College between 1957 and 1959 and then went on to the University of British Columbia to complete her BA. She next proceeded to the University of Toronto, where she earned a diploma in speech pathology and audiology. While working as a speech pathologist and audiologist in Windsor, Ontario, she pursued her master's degree in this field at Wayne State University, Michigan. She then returned to Vancouver, where she worked in various capacities, including clinical instructor and, later, clinical coordinator in the University of British Columbia's School of Audiology and Speech Sciences, distinguished service in a vital field.

EDITOR'S NOTE
The following, faithfully transcribed from the original mimeographed material, is Professor Tony (C. Anthony) Emery's "A Christmas Present to the Students of Victoria College from the English Department." E.B.H.

They Filled Many an Older Heart with Admiration:
Don't Sell Your Young People Short

Tony (C. Anthony) Emery

What a very exciting world we live in. Until I read certain letters to the newspapers, I had no idea that a meeting I attended recently was such an orgy of bad manners and boorishness. My views on the matter are doubtless not to be relied upon, since, unlike our moralizing correspondents, I was present at the affair and so am obviously a prejudiced witness. If it will do any good, however, I will give you my opinion of the meeting.

It was a large assembly of Victoria College undergraduates, aggressively partisan in political sympathy, ebullient, noisy and good-humoured. Placards were flourished, effigies dangled, and loud remarks were made from time to time; but all the placards were witty; the effigy was just an effigy; and most of the remarks were "fair comment in a matter of public interest," as the lawyers say.

In short, it was a political meeting, composed almost entirely of young people for whom politics is not just a matter of roads and bridges, rebates on property tax, and the promises of great things the day after tomorrow.

Politics, for the intelligent young, is a matter of principle – of ideas – and they do not accept expediency or admit of compromise. They do not understand the cynicism or the complacency or the preoccupation with naked self-interest displayed by their elders.

They may be young; they may be "unrealistic"; but at least they have some positive political ideas which they are not afraid to express.

The premier was not paying a formal visit to the college. Had this been the case, the atmosphere would have been quite different. He came to address an audience which he must have known would be both hostile and outspoken, since he had a stormy passage with the student body of the University of British Columbia not long ago.

And it must be said at once that he earned a genuine, if grudging, respect from his audience before the meeting was over.

"You gotta hand it to him," said a student, whose diction betrayed excitement and a certain disregard for the niceties of spoken English. "He keeps coming back with an answer, even if it isn't the answer to the question."

The attorney general, alas, has clearly led a very sheltered political life. Not for him the hurly-burly of the hustings, the cut and thrust of the political arena. After a few ineffectual passes with the cape, his verbal veronicas failed to please the crowd, who evidently felt that the premier was better fitted to handle the bull. Luckily there were no manzanilla bottles at hand in this arena, though for a while it rained lunchbags.

As a temperamental anarchist with no party affiliations, I feel quite qualified to give a dispassionate judgment in this matter, and I have no hesitation in finding the accused "Not Guilty." In fact, after spending half a decade among people who would rather be caught in their underwear than reveal what party they vote for, I was delighted to discover a group who don't mind letting their right wing know what their left wing is doing.

Youth, on the whole, is much stricter in matters of honour than the more accommodating middle-aged. Young people boil over more easily at injustice, chicanery, corruption, and fraud, and the very suspicion, however unfounded, that these things exist in their society is quite enough to make them take steps to bring about reform.

Whether they are motivated by envy or malice, I know not, but some people there are who delight in seizing any stick wherewith they may belabour the young people of our community. I often wonder whether these indefatigable Mrs Partingtons and Mr Hurdstones know anybody under the age of twenty-five. I cannot believe that they do, or they would not take such a very gloomy and unflattering view of our young men and women.

I am very glad that I took the opportunity to grow up elsewhere, where the grown-ups were more interested in writing to the *Times* about the first cuckoo than about the latest manifestation of juvenile irresponsibility. The custom of the universities in the land where I was bred is to extend all the privileges of adult life to the undergraduate, insisting merely on these being exercised with discretion.

Their sense of proportion at these places may seem eccentric to you, but the authorities feel that a young person may come to more harm and cause more damage behind the wheel of a car than beneath the roof of a tavern. Undergraduates are expected to behave foolishly from time to time, and this is regarded, stupidly or not, as a valuable part of the learning process.

I for one cannot see the logic of a land where a youth may be trusted to control three hundred horsepower at 16, but has to wait until 21 before he can legally sip a quiet beer or a glass of sherry. That is the law, and of course I obey it; but I think it's a damn silly law, and I should like to see us change it.

Are our young folk so different from their British counterparts that they would immediately gallop towards cirrhosis and DTs if they were allowed to drink at 18? Does the law at present really stop any young person from getting a drink when he wants one?

If the law were changed do you think there would be any significant increase in the number of young people charged with "indulging to excess?" Of course not.

Old Dr Kettell, who was master of Trinity College, Oxford, in the early part of the seventeenth century (that is his lodging next to Blackwell's bookshop), held liberal views about youth, even in a day when most of his students came to him in their middle teens.

"He observed," says John Aubrey, who was up at Trinity in Kettell's time, "that the Houses that had the smallest beer had the most drunkards, for it forced them to goe into the towne to comfort their stomachs, wherefore Dr. Kettell alwayes had in his College excellent beere, not better to be had in Oxon, so that we could not goe to any other place but for the worse, and we had the fewest drunkards of any howse in Oxford."

In the comparatively short time I have been in Canada I don't suppose that I have come to know more than a thousand or two young Canadians at all well, but what I have learned of the character of this sample certainly does not fill me with gloom.

I think they compare more than favourably with their elders in many ways, and I think that the future of this province will be in hands at least as trustworthy as those that guide it now.

Don't sell your young people short. When the chips were down in Budapest, who took the load against tyranny and injustice? Your cozy clubman? Your maiden aunt? Your inveterate newspaper correspondent? Not on your life. It was the "irresponsible young student," who "treated his rulers with disrespect;" who behaved in a "rowdy and boisterous manner;" whose "hooliganism" filled many an older heart with admiration, envy and respect.

TIMOTHY R. PRICE
VIC '59

Looking back close to fifty years to my first year at Victoria College is to look at a world, and certainly a Canada, transformed. In 1959 we were still in the postwar recovery, although that was rapidly turning into industrial prosperity. The college students were still largely from the Victoria area and elsewhere in British Columbia, and they were studying arts or education. I was studying English and history and having a lively social life. In my extracurricular life on campus, I was a stagehand in the Victoria College Players' performance of George Bernard Shaw's *You Never Can Tell*, working with an interesting group of like-minded folks from among the students.

We may have thought we would eventually go into the business world, but we didn't see our undergraduate years as direct preparation for a business career. While there was a Commerce Club on campus, I was not part of it. The college, like most universities in that period, had no business school and inclined toward history, the classics, literature and languages, and sciences. We could not foretell how the future would unfold and change our lives.

Following my graduation in 1964 and my CA certification in 1969, I was fortunate enough to find a partner and mentor in Jack Cockwell, whom I joined in 1970. This connection has led to a long and successful career partnership through a number of businesses headquartered in Canada. These enterprises, predominantly financial, have given me broad exposure to boards of directors in a variety of fields. In the voluntary sector, I have worked on boards and committees in health, education, and the arts. With my wife, Frances, we have been active in supporting theatre – a long way from the Vic College Players' – as well as many other community ventures. In Toronto I have been deeply involved with York University for many years in several capacities, and I have seen each generation of students going through some of the same pleasures and sorrows that I experienced at Victoria College so many years ago.

In recent years I have had the opportunity to meet with the business school and alumni office of the University of Victoria and have come back into touch with my alma mater. What a changed institution it is! From a small liberal arts college to an important, full-scale university with many professional schools, including business, the University of Victoria is a great success.

As a supporter of the entrepreneurship program at the university, I reflect on the wide range of fields in which the skills and framework of entrepreneurial activity are important – in all areas of business, of course, but also in the not-for-profit sectors, the arts, and philanthropy. In all these endeavours, the ability to size up opportunities and risk and to determine an idea's fit or readiness within the market or environment is crucial. Also crucial is the ability to mobilize the resources of funding and people to turn the opportunity into a reality, keeping in mind the framework of law and regulation, and to recognize that our culture supports failure and resurrection. The business school has emphasized the entrepreneurial approach to its students, which should be of great value for them by providing exposure to more real-life experiences, the difficulties as well as the achievements that will season them for their careers.

Victoria College, small and restricted in programs though it was, provided much that was of value in building my own entrepreneurship. It may not have explicitly taught the ways and means of assessing risk and opportunity, but it did encourage creative risk and thinking "outside the box." I remember, for example, being part of a group of five individuals who put up a small grubstake to create a coffee house, The Secret, in an old hotel on Government Street. Who knows what the real risks were – we were young. We ran it ourselves with friends from the college, and two years later we sold out for a magnificent gain. I also played on a variety of soccer, field hockey, and rugby teams while at college. Interestingly, the most I learned from them was to try to operate as part of a team and avoid the risk of injury.

The college taught us a great deal about our own culture, Canadian and North American, both through the public talks by such important figures as Prime Minister Lester B. Pearson and Governor George Wallace of Alabama, who visited the campus, but also through the interest shown in the college and students by members of the provincial legislature and the business and cultural leaders of the town. I learned this first-hand through the coffee-house experience. Visitors from other parts of Canada and around the world were welcomed and treated with respect and interest by students and faculty alike.

There was a genuine interest among the faculty members in each student, and it was expected that each life would have its ups and downs without a sense of failure. Vic College students were notorious for parties and pranks. They were noticed and treated seriously, but not in a dismissive or punishing way. It was about responsible behaviour and civic life. We had to learn the skills to present ourselves well to those in authority, a perennially useful skill. In turn, when we did show responsibility and present ourselves well, we were treated with trust and respect. That gives confidence to young people, and it did to me. We learned how to build long-term friendships and partnerships based on those values. We learned that we were part of the wider community and had a role to play.

However, the current reality of the university is what is important now. As I see it, the university and its business school has kept many of those important values and added to them a wide range of contemporary knowledge in all areas. Furthermore, the openness to ideas from other sectors and from elsewhere remains as a strong and attractive feature of the university and in particular the business school. The current classes include people from a much wider range of cultures than we had the privilege of meeting, and this is important to budding business people and entrepreneurs. Building good relationships with people from a wide variety of backgrounds, understanding other ways of doing business, and equally, understanding fields other than business is crucial in today's world. Being part of the voluntary sector and participating in philanthropy are essential to understanding the wider community. All these values and skills build a strong country and a good life.

I met some good people at Vic College, and while we have not kept in touch, I still feel a commonality with the days of the early 1960s and the joys of the Lansdowne campus. It is gratifying to see the successful progress to the strong and meaningful university that it is today.

TIMOTHY R. PRICE, BA, CA, is chairman of Brookfield Funds in Toronto. Since leaving Victoria College, he has had a long and distinguished career in business. He serves as a director on the boards of several private corporations, including HSBC Bank Canada and the Morguard Corporation. He is also active in voluntary work, including serving as vice-chair of the Board of Governors of York University, chair of the Board of Directors of the York University Foundation, and a governor of Roy Thomson Hall/Massey Hall. Timothy Price is the deserving recipient of the University of Victoria Distinguished Alumni Award.

BRIAN R. LITTLE
VIC '59

Victoria College, our alma mater (from the Latin, "nourishing mother"), was a strange, delightful, needful, and compelling creature. Her nourishment and nurturing shaped our lives. The nature of this nurturing is fascinating to reconstruct, but also challenging; our memories are fallible, and some of our recollections may be self-serving or at least singular. But of one thing we can be sure – alma matters: being nourished during what developmental psychologists now call the critical period of "emerging adulthood" matters deeply. We were nourished by Vic College, in my case from 1959 to 1964, during a period that many would see as a very privileged time. Victoria was, well, Victoria – one of the places people visited before they died or, if they were lucky, where they took up permanent dotage. The Canadian economy allowed us to take the Black Ball Ferry to Port Angeles and get ten cents on the dollar to spend on exotic American things. The Second World War was long over, although the Cold War was heating up considerably; still the future seemed limitless.

Demographically, we were a small group of college students – just ahead of those who boomed after us. Many of us went to Vic College simply because that's what our class-mates did in 1959, in my case right out of Oak Bay High. Vic College was a reasonable alternative to driving a tallyho* for a living, although, in retrospect, that might have been a more salubrious and relaxing occupation than the one that eventually chose me – being a university professor of psychology.

The Mutual Nurturing of Strange Creatures

Vic College was strange in many respects, but primarily because it was in transition be-tween being a highly distinctive little college and becoming an excellent university. So in this respect, it was, like its students, en route from something small to something bigger. Whether that bigger was better was a matter of considerable debate for the city, the col-lege, and the emerging university. But to be there during the transition years was to witness the compelling maturation of an institution that was nurturing us even as it was flailing about trying to find and define itself. And, as we will see, the students were cre-ating some alma of their own, and it mattered in ways that I will contend were distinctive, perhaps unique.

Strange, too, was the juxtaposition of two very different academic lifestyles during those transition years. Vic College served both as a bastion of conventional Victorian (BC) sensibility and a magnet for a small but influential group of young lecturers and profes-sors who were cosmopolitan, sophisticated, and ambitious. I could almost detect the tremors of shifting tectonic plates as these strange creatures ambled on to the Lansdowne campus in the early sixties. Some of them changed my life's trajectory, so that I never had to cope with chronic tallyhosis. I will get to them in a moment.

What was delightful about Vic College? Okay, let's get this over with – it was definitely not Mrs Norris's coffee. But her cafeteria, "the caf," with its atmosphere and its charac-ters, was among the most memorable delights of Vic College. I actually worked for Mrs Norris, clearing tables and performing odd jobs. One of those jobs was not making the coffee. I say this because I'm not sure if there is a statute of limitations on class-action suits for the long-term effects of toxic agents, and I just want to protect my loved ones. When I was not busying myself with not making the coffee, I would be busing the dishes. But I always listened in on conversations, a habit my wife tells me I still possess. The caf buzzed

---

*For those unfamiliar with tallyhos, they are horse-drawn conveyances designed to show eager tourists the sights of Victoria. In high school I invented the term "tallyhosis" to describe the olfactory implications of getting stuck behind such conveyances.

with laughter, licentious intimations, rumours and revelations, yet more laughter, and a low-grade infection of high silliness.

Part of the pleasure of heading there rather than to the library was that it was where "characters" converged. By characters, I don't mean the standard array of strange people who could be found in Port Alberni or Port Angeles but, rather, a wild assortment of almost Dickensian characters. As I conjure up their image almost five decades on, a good number of these young students even then looked middle-aged or older. They were a multitude of the wizened. Many were thespians or poets or both. Although the conversations I would hear as I cleared tables were typically about the mundane delights of youth, there was no shortage of intellectual discussion, sometimes animated and heated. Many of the new faculty were from England, or pretended they were from England, and accented and accentuated opinions on everything from free love to false consciousness percolated alongside Mrs Norris's giant urns.

Depending on the time of year, another delight of Vic College was its landscaped grounds. Stretching out on the lawn that sloped down to Lansdowne Road was blissful, particularly when the daffodils and tulips were displaying themselves. We were young. Even the wizened lost their weary frowns and looked as if they might actually frolic.

Pauses and Passion: The Times and Timing of Our Lives
One step removed from the campus characters were the true eccentrics, and some of the faculty were walking embodiments of the term. It is not a total exaggeration to say that about 29 per cent of my professors were sufficiently eccentric to quality for serious treatment in an abnormal psychology text. Thank goodness they didn't receive treatment in a clinic, because it would have robbed us of some truly memorable mentors. They were the ones who, to invoke Leacock's depiction of Oxford tutorials, would smoke at us for a term.

One such smoker was John Carson, who taught me classical studies. I had been veering back and forth between the physical sciences and English before finding my home in psychology. I was deeply drawn to the joint course John (the Greeks) taught with one of the brightest young stars of the new faculty, Peter Smith (the Romans). John Carson chain-smoked, was deeply passionate about his field, and apparently also passionate about his lawn. He had a "Keep off the Lawn" sign written in ancient Greek, and to my knowledge no ancient Greeks dared to tread on that turf. There were about twelve students in his class, and I recall one lecture in which he waxed particularly passionate. It was on Peisistratus, "Tyrant of a Nation," and I happened to be sitting in the front row. As the lecture was winding down and the tales of tyranny had been told, he suddenly paused – just for a couple of seconds. I then saw tears welling up in his eyes. Immediately chills crawled up my spine. It was, I thought, my first exposure to genuine passion for teaching. He had not parked his emotions at the threshold but shared them with his class. He cared deeply about Peisistratus. A decade later, when I had the thrill of looking out at my own class of university students, I remembered John. I didn't hide my passion for my field then, and I have continued to not hide it throughout my career.

Lest I get too mawkish about contagious passion, I should raise another possibility. As I mentioned, John chain-smoked, and it is entirely possible that his tears that day may have had more to do with Player's than Peisistratus. But however distorted they may be, we get comfort from our core personal images, and that was one of mine. I prefer the "Peisistratus Blues" version of the presentation to "Smoke Gets in Your Eyes."

Technically, this involuntary chill-up-the-spine effect is called a piloerection, which John would have told us means "hair standing up," and my students and I have actually been starting to study the occasions when such effects occur. I think that one subtle component of chill-making is the pause which serves as a signal that something important or emotional is imminent and in itself amplifies the emotional impact. There were two other occasions (that I would feel appropriate to share) when I had piloerectory responses: one, as with Peisistratus, deeply pleasurable, the other a shudder of disbelief.

The positive chill, actually a set of them, occurred while I was a member of the choir at Vic College. We were a motley crew of varying degrees of talent. Our version of one of Kurt Weil's musical compositions was, in the memorable words of a favourite chemistry professor, "not totally awful." But our selections from the *Messiah* were actually pretty good. I was an enthusiastic singer, but clearly of the "not totally awful" rank. The magic chilling moment for me came not as a solo sound, however, but as a communal silence. In the exquisite concluding chorus of the *Messiah*, there is a point where the choir comes to a complete stop for two seconds' of rapturous silence, followed by the triumphant final "amen." Particularly when we sang in the college auditorium with full concert accompaniment, that two-second pause before the crashing, cascading conclusion always generated giant goose bumps. Just writing about it brings them on again.

The painful chill was one I shared with a generation. I was pulling out of the lower parking lot mid-morning on 22 November 1963 when there was an interruption of the regular radio broadcast. There was a brief pause and then the confirmation that President Kennedy had been shot. Unfortunately, that kind of chilling news would recur throughout the next decade. If we had been a residential college, I have no doubt we would have all converged at Lansdowne. But, in fact, most students I knew went home very quickly and were transfixed by the image of Walter Cronkite confirming the worst and pausing in disbelief for just a moment: Kennedy had been assassinated.

Chills are a key to the play of emotions in our daily lives, and I received my fair share of them at Vic College. The exquisite subtlety of pauses, passions, and their intricate orchestration reminds us that we are a strange little species attuned to the sounds and rhythms of the micro-moment as well as those of the times in which we live. The Kennedy assassination changed the way we listened. Something was blowing in the wind, and while it seemed to drift up from the south, it had a universal resonance that couldn't be ignored.

The Benefits of Barely Sufficient Bodies
In what sense was Vic College needful? I want to suggest a fairly technical answer to this one – an answer that derives from an area of social science known as ecological psychology. One of this field's core notions is, as it was called in the language of the day, "undermanned" behaviour settings. The caf was a behaviour setting; so were John Carson's classroom and the rugby games. A key question of behaviour setting theory was this: what are the consequences of having barely sufficient people to perform the roles

The *Victoria Daily Times* storefront, 22 November 1963. J.J. Philion photograph.

and tasks required for the maintenance of the setting? Vic College was a splendid example of a wide range of undermanned behaviour settings.

Research has shown that such conditions can actually be salutary, both for the students and for the institution. For example, studies of bigger versus smaller schools show, somewhat surprisingly, that they have roughly the same number of behaviour settings (e.g., drama club, rugby team, debating society, Frosh Week). But the smaller schools, of course, have fewer people to fulfill the various functions of acting, tackling, debating, and debasing. If the drama club has only thirteen members, you not only act in the play, but you build the props and sell the tickets as well, sometimes all on the same day.

The empirical evidence shows clearly that individuals working in such settings develop greater commitment, a stronger sense of group identity, and more detailed knowledge about the club's pursuits. And this was precisely what Vic College was like in the transition years. When I was elected director of clubs for the Alma Mater Society (AMS) in 1961, I was surprised to find there were almost as many clubs at Vic College as at UBC. And the commitment and passion to keep them going was palpable.

This was one way that Vic College was compelling. One simply stepped up; if a club or athletic event or social function required an extra pair of hands, they always seemed to be on deck. Shortly after I was elected director of clubs for the AMS, the president of the AMS resigned for personal reasons, and I found myself acting president. I also found myself becoming a bit more realistic about some of the deckhands on our tight little ship. Some of them were about to cause big problems, by which I mean problems that would hit the front page of both the *Victoria Times* and the *Victoria Colonist*.

Towns, Gowns, and Frowns: The Empress Was Not Amused

My first official duty as acting president of the AMS was to organize and oversee the annual Frosh Parade. It had a long tradition and essentially comprised the standard hijinks associated with similar rituals at any college. But the parade in downtown Victoria in 1962 went seriously awry. Of the hundreds marching, I suspect only about ten were actual participants in what ended up being a small riot on the lawn of the Empress Hotel. There was much heaving of fruit and other missiles, and I observed an elderly woman getting knocked over by a rambunctious and rather pie-eyed participant. The next day I held an emergency meeting of the AMS. The auditorium was full, and according to the *Martlet* of the day, I gave hell to the duly gathered. I am by nature a rather introverted person, but I had been singing on stage since a very early age and was not particularly daunted by having to address them. But I normally like to entertain, amuse, or uplift, and clearly my message was a very strong rebuke. My message was simply that "the town" had been appalled at the out-of-control behaviour. And intuitively pausing for a couple of seconds, I told them that I was appalled as well. In retrospect, it was an emotional speech, rather over the top. But what no one really knew was the personal symbolism of what had happened. At some point in their lives, all my family members had worked at the Empress Hotel. I had been a pageboy there at eleven years of age. Within an hour of the Frosh Parade dispersing, I received phone calls from the manager of the Empress and the mayor of Victoria. They were irate, and the possibility of legal action was raised. I didn't relate these details to the students at the meeting but simply said that we had to carry out an act of restitution. We needed the support of the city as we were going through a tricky and politically sensitive period of transition to university status. That evening I met with the Student Council members and told them we had to do something pretty audacious to salvage our reputation. Thus was born the first of many Log Saw events, in which Vic College students gathered at local beaches, hoisted chainsaws, and hewed logs. Victorians would drive by and open their car trunks, and we would fill them up with firewood and goodwill. Although I have been credited with initiating the Log Saw, it was the irrepressible Alf Pettersen who originally proposed the idea. But I will take credit for sounding an alarm that town-and-gown relations were getting beyond strained. In short order, the students had risen to the occasion and become exceptionally active in the town. They volunteered in local hospitals, sang Christmas carols at Government House and at the homes of favourite professors, and struck a workable balance between youthful rowdiness and adult responsibility. It was a time of exceptional student *activity* at Vic College. Student activism, a very different creature, was just a few years away.

In retrospect, I think I was a bit harsh on the students, even a bit sanctimonious. I was certain that I had ruined any chances of getting elected to the permanent presidency of the AMS the next month. But the students were surprisingly responsive. It was as though they realized that the city and its soon-to-be university really needed each other, but they needed to hear it from a student. Through a creative act of contrition, we as a student body had in a sense both lost our innocence and gained credibility with the city. A few weeks later I easily won the election for president of the AMS. Oh, and for the record, the old lady was not badly hurt; neither the Empress nor Mrs Whomever and the lawyers ever appeared.

The Convergence of Scale and Aspirations: Class Acts

The combination of several factors, but particularly the intimate scale and the arrival of faculty with large aspirations, created an atmosphere in which students and professors could do audacious things together. Drawing on the department I knew best, Psychology, I want to give some examples of how Vic College in the transition years was a class act.

When I arrived in 1959, I knew that at some point I would take Bill Gaddes's famous Psychology 206, a second- year course on "Human Adjustment" that had a reputation for being a "don't miss" course. Bill had an infectious enthusiasm, a true twinkle in the eye, a host of stories, and a genuine (and decades-lasting) concern for his students. Even today, in his nineties, Bill remembers personal details about his students (and now their children and grandchildren) from decades past. He certainly remembered my sister, Margaret, six years older than me, who was a medal-winning student at Vic College and had been a top student of Bill's. I was fortunate that Bill knew me as "Margaret's little brother," and he thus probably thought I was somewhat cleverer than I was. We know how a teacher's expectations can sometimes become self-fulfilling, and I may well have acquired a few extra brain cells as a result.

Bill Gaddes was the perfect model of the college professor during the transition years at Vic College: he was the inspiring and beloved teacher of the sort that the college famously created. We couldn't wait to get to his class. I remember him telling us how he used hypnosis to cure a man who had a chronic case of hiccups. Fascinating stuff. We all thought Bill Gaddes was "cool." (Isn't it interesting how "cool" has survived as a trans-generational term of approval, while "neato" or "groovy" have passed away?) Well, Bill Gaddes was – and is –cool, the embodiment of the ideal Vic College professor. But he was also a pre-UVic visionary. Research really mattered to Bill, and he was himself a highly respected pioneer in child clinical neuropsychology. He also had the vision and skill to recruit some truly exceptional research talent to the Department of Psychology.

The one with whom I had my greatest contact was G. Alexander (Lex) Milton, who arrived as the top-ranked doctoral graduate from Stanford, a rather extraordinary recruiting coup. Lex was truly brilliant. Some of his early studies, particularly on sex-role identification, were a decade ahead of their time, and I took each of the courses he offered over the two years we overlapped. Lex Milton was very much plugged into the San Francisco Bay area community of psychologists, then arguably the best in the world in the fields of personality, social, and developmental psychology. The network was co-anchored by Berkeley and Stanford and reinforced by the various Veterans Administration hospitals where clinical psychologists were trained. Lex's roommate at Stanford had been Dick Alpert, famous – or notorious, depending on one's sensitivities – for initiating with his then Berkeley colleague, Timothy Leary, research on magic mushrooms and other consciousness-altering agents. Lex wasn't that kind of psychologist. Rather, he was a very tough-nosed, rigorous researcher who taught us statistics at a level, I subsequently discovered, equivalent to many graduate courses in the field. He set extremely high standards, monitored progress on an individual level, and, in retrospect, was fundamental to a remarkable series of graduate school placements over the transition years.

One memorable example of the degree of intellectual intimacy and mutual trust that characterized those days was Milton's final examination in Research Methods. The first two-thirds was a standard, rigorous set of questions that we each had to answer. The final part was tailor-made to suit each student, based on Lex's awareness of our independent studies or our honours thesis research. I was working with a rather esoteric statistical technique known as non-parametric factor analysis, and Lex's question was simply: "Part II (For Brian Little). What the hell are you doing?"

I hasten to point out that he wasn't critical of what I was doing; he just hadn't come across it before, and he adopted the same informal tone that we had used in countless bull sessions with the honours students at his house. It was in these extraordinarily engaging and generous acts, class acts, that Vic College in transition left its mark on me. I felt entirely comfortable applying to Berkeley for graduate work, quite simply because Lex Milton had shown me how to think like a graduate student before I applied to graduate school. Had I been at a UBC or a Michigan or other large, outstanding university, I doubt I would have had the confidence to reach out to the best universities in the world upon graduation.

There was another side to the coin, of course. The new faculty in Psychology during this period were keen to do research, but there were no graduate students. This was another example of undermanned settings and how the timing was so right for those of us in our senior years as undergraduates. We were simply treated as graduate students. I helped Bill Gaddes build the equipment and testing instruments for the first neuropsychology laboratory in a room just down the hall from the auditorium. I was also entrusted with doing neuropsychological assessments with children that was both challenging and immensely rewarding. Bill and I trekked through the mud with testing equipment when we set up shop on the Gordon Head campus during my last term on campus.

There is a third example of the extraordinary interdependency between needful faculty and needful students. Norah Carlsen, who was finishing her doctoral dissertation at the University of Washington, needed assistance with the statistical aspects of her research, and so she recruited me as a keen student from Lex Milton's class in advanced stats. It was a giddy experience in many respects but also mildly terrifying. Churning out "split-plot analyses of covariance" on the mighty Monroematic calculator was challenging, but somehow things seemed to work. Mrs Carlsen became Dr Carlsen, and Mr Little realized that a possible self as a graduate student was not totally idiotic.

This possibility was nurtured by my closest friend at Vic College, Howard Lim. Howard was a luminously bright and complex man who headed off to Stanford for graduate work in psychology, a year ahead of my going to Berkeley. While still at Vic College, we spent two summers as customs officers, and given the infrequent arrival of large ships in the Inner Harbour, we were able to spend hours together reflecting on science, psychology, and life. I also allowed him to beat me at chess regularly. Howard was a model of the kind of student Vic College could turn out in the early sixties, and to say it was world-rank would not be at all a stretch.

The Immortal Profession: The Continuing Impact of Vic College
As I mentioned earlier, although tempted by tallyho driving, I ended up becoming a university professor. I received my honours BA in the first graduating class of UVic and believe I was the first man to get a UVic degree, preceded in convocation, thanks to the

strictures/conventions of the alphabet, by Sandra Came and Susan Dickenson. I went to graduate work at Berkeley in 1964, literally a week before the Free Speech Movement began and the student revolutions were catapulted into public consciousness. I identified with the student concerns in large part because much of what they were asking for was the kind of educational experience I had received at Vic College. True, I was not exposed to sixteen Nobel Prize winners at Vic College, but neither were most of the students at Berkeley. They were mainly taught by people like me! There was no doubt that I wanted to become part of the immortal profession, as Gilbert Highet called it; so being a professor was immensely attractive to me. I thought it would be daunting to be in the same graduate classes with undergraduates from Harvard and Princeton and Stanford, but I had been extremely well prepared and actually found graduate work, in one of the most notoriously difficult programs in the field, relatively easy. I credit this to the standards to which we were held during the transition years at Vic College, where being in intimate contact with faculty who cared meant that we came in with a real advantage.

A few years later I found myself teaching at Oxford University and smoking at the same students Leacock had told us about. At first I thought it might be a bit daunting to be a "don," but it was easy to engage these bright students in intellectual one-on-one exchanges because I had done it on a weekly basis at Vic College. I think of those students who literally end up getting their university degrees without ever having had to speak in class. At Vic College in the Psychology Department, it was often hard to get a word in, and one's tacit assumptions had better be dusted off and made explicit before someone challenged them – good-heartedly, searchingly, and in the best spirit of the immortal profession.

I have been fortunate, in my many years at Carleton University and more recently at Harvard, in getting some attention for my teaching. I trace that back to those strange creatures I have briefly portrayed in this fond essay. The passions of John Carson and Bill Gaddes, the standards and meticulous scholarship of Lex Milton and Norah Carlsen – each was assimilated into my style at the lectern. But as I think of it now, perhaps the most telling moment, the one where I knew that something was stirring in me that was incipiently professorial, was after the Empress Hotel fiasco. When I addressed the students, looked them in the eye, and told them they had to do better, they didn't boo. They were dead silent, and then they applauded. They would have no reason to know how profound an effect that affirmation would have. They, my fellow students at Vic College – and perhaps a very small dose of Mrs Norris's coffee – gave me the courage to profess with passion.

BRIAN R. LITTLE, PHD, is Distinguished Research Professor Emeritus at Carleton University and adjunct professor of psychology at McGill University. He received his honours BA from the first graduating class at the University of Victoria in 1964 and his doctorate from the University of California at Berkeley. Dr Little has taught at Oxford, Carleton, and Harvard universities and received numerous awards for both his research and his teaching. In 2000 he was one of the inaugural group of fellows at the Radcliffe Institute for Advanced Study at Harvard University. He stayed on to teach in Harvard's Department of Psychology, where he was recognized as a "favourite professor" for three years.

NELS GRANEWALL
VIC '59

Recollecting his brother, Swen Granewall, Vic '55

In the mid-1950s, Victoria College was viewed by rural Saanich residents as a temporary enclave for Oak Bay and Victoria High School graduates planning to ultimately go off-island to complete an undergraduate degree. Seen as a formidable bastion for the privileged, it was not intended for rough-hewn farm boys and girls whose dirt-poor parents did not have the funds to pay tuition and incidental costs. It was all the more remarkable, then, that the student who shattered these preconceived notions for me was an immigrant from Europe with a grade six education who did not learn to speak English until he was eighteen, lived as a member of a large family on a small unproductive farm in rural Saanich, and graduated from Royal Oak High School at age twenty-one with top grades and a government scholarship to pay three-quarters of his college tuition. Through sheer tenacity, he entered Victoria College in the fall of 1955 and subsequently graduated from UBC with a BSc in chemistry. During his two years at the Lansdowne campus, he was well-known as a BMOC, not because of his stint as the *Martlet*'s athletics reporter, but rather as the owner of a chopped and channelled 1949 Mercury Coupe. All the fellows wanted to be his friend on the odd chance that they might borrow the Merc when they had an especially important date!

It should now be clear that the object of my hero-worship was my older brother, Swen, who unfortunately is no longer with us. A large muscular man who had worked on the Great Lakes ships to buy his car and pay all other college costs that my parents could not afford, he was truly an inspiration to a typically gangly teenager like myself. I hung on every word when he came home from college to share with all of us what had happened that day. Names like Dr Elias and Dr Savannah, Roger Bishop and Syd Pettit, Bill Gaddes and Lewis Clark, all became familiar to me and my younger siblings, both of whom graduated from UVic. Copies of the *Martlet* would appear sporadically, and he would explain the gossip that appeared in "The Rovin' Reporter," as well as other campus rumours. He recounted that it was a sensational story when the *Martlet* printed a rumour to the effect that the price of coffee was about to shoot up to fifteen cents a paper cup!

During his final term at Victoria College in the spring of 1957, Swen was assigned by the *Martlet* editor to report on a public panel discussion entitled "Will Victoria College grant degrees?" Participating were Syd Pettit from the History Department, Carl Hare from the English Department, Bill Gaddes from the Psychology Department, and Tony Gargrave, who was both a student and an MLA representing the CCF party, now the NDP. Carl Hare and Bill Gaddes are able to ponder the wisdom of their comments from fifty years ago when they chose to participate in the graduation exercises and watch some 3,800 students annually obtain their degrees during UVic's Convocation week.

Although Swen had primed me for the dreaded Frosh Week, it was still with some anxiety that I joined the lineup of freshmen snaking its way down the Young Building's main corridor in the fall of 1959. We were in the process of being registered – scrutinized under the stark glances of Miss Cruickshank, Miss Sullivan, and Mrs Hoey, the triumvirate who formed the éminence grise behind Harry Hickman's rule of the Lansdowne campus. After what seemed an eternity, we were ushered into a large classroom to hear an inspirational address on how to succeed at college, delivered by Dr Reid Elliot. My mind wandered to the upcoming Frosh Dance, wondering if by any miracle the most beautiful girl I had ever seen might grace us with her presence. Elaine Ferguson, a second-year Education student, had been chosen as a princess in the Campus Queen contest at the Co-Ed Dance, but since she was a sophomore, she was clearly beyond the reach of a lowly frosh like myself.

The mind plays tricks on you when you are recollecting events from nearly fifty years ago, but the outrageous pranks masterminded by the Rugby Club are as vivid today as they were then. Who can forget the morning after Halloween Hellery, arriving at the Ewing Building to find that the front door had been completely bricked over? Or the infamous incident when the Queen's bust was abducted from Beacon Hill Park and ended up in the lobby of City Hall? And how did they ever manage to enter the well-guarded gates of the military college at Royal Roads to spirit away its massive cannon? Lesser incidents did not receive the same amount of publicity, but the same ingenuity was displayed when the silver ingot was spirited away from the Parliament Buildings and the door sign from Premier W.A.C. Bennett's office was made off with. No doubt there were others, but these stand out as the best examples of college pranks that had everybody chuckling but the victims.

Of the characters I met during my Lansdowne years – and there were many – "Mad" Mal Potts certainly stands out. Mal had hung the moniker "Mad" on himself to create a certain notoriety for him and for his budding career as a rock'n'roll disc jockey. The last I heard of him he was somewhere in the Australian outback still performing as a DJ. Somehow he had found out that I was a good speller, and he asked me if I would mind correcting the spelling in an atrociously badly written essay that he had to turn in for English 200 in order to pass. Besides correcting the spelling, I made enough other corrections for him to obtain the necessary grade. From then on, even though I did not relish the idea, I was his buddy for life. With his impishly infectious humour, he managed to convince enough of the student voters in the spring of 1961 that he would make a good VP of the AMS for the 1961–62 session. No sooner had he hoodwinked the student body than he announced that he would be stepping down to start the pirate rock'n'roll radio station KITN, transmitting to Victoria from Port Angeles in order to circumvent CRTC regulations. Before Mal's announcement had a chance to cool down, newly elected AMS president Karl Wylie, a handsome devil who went on to have a successful stage career across Canada, announced that he was resigning for business reasons, thereby throwing the AMS into a real crisis as some other council members also quit. Fortunately for the college, as future events would demonstrate, Brian Little stepped to the forefront and took over a badly bruised council. It is with good reason that Brian has been voted the most popular professor at Harvard on several occasions.

No sooner had the council chambers stopped reeling when another massive "bad publicity bomb" was lobbed in their direction. On 21 September 1961, a day of infamy in the history of Victoria College, the annual freshman march through downtown Victoria deteriorated into an uncontrollable riot, with eggs, tomatoes, flour bags, and water-filled balloons flying in every direction, particularly into numerous stores – this at a time when college officials were trying to convince the citizens of Victoria to open their pocket-books for the new campus at Gordon Head. The timing could not have been worse. Fortunately, the AMS rallied, and under the direction of Brian Little and Alf Petterson, perhaps better known as the proprietor of Wooded Wonderland at Beaver Lake Park, a gigantic log-saw operation took place soon after at Willows Beach where students bucked logs into fireplace-sized wood piles that were sold to the public and the profits donated to the United Appeal. The tradition continued for several years at Clover Point and definitely helped erase the black eye of September 1961.

NELS GRANEWALL, BA, commenced his post-secondary education at Victoria College and was a member of the University of Victoria's first graduating class. He directed UVic's student aid office for thirty-three years, and during that time, he served as president of the Canadian Association of Student Financial Aid Administrators on three separate occasions. His numerous honours include the 1984 graduating class gift of $20,000 to establish the Nels Granewall Bursary Fund. For forty years he also served as chief marshal for University of Victoria convocations.

THE HON. LORNA R. MARSDEN
VIC '60

After the Labour Day weekend in 1960, I walked up the hill to the Lansdowne campus of Victoria College. I was following in the footsteps of my older siblings, only one of whom had found an alternative path. I was ambivalent about starting college this way and had tried to persuade my father, to no avail, that McGill would be a better choice. Having twice seen *My Fur Lady* performed by the McGill University Players, I was fixated on their spirit of fun, political spoof, and sophistication.

My deepest fear was that I would be greeted in the Faculty of Education first-year program as I had been all through school – my talents and lack of same would be anticipated on the basis of my older siblings' excellent performances. Many of my high school friends were also at the college. The faculty members had been described to me in detail during all the family dinners, at which every aspect of the program and the people involved had been dissected. I had seen the textbooks, had heard how the professors greeted the new class, the timbre of their voices, and their expectations of papers and examinations. Already in the gender-segregated culture of the times, an invitation to the Freshette Tea had arrived. Freshette?

However, there were some very pleasant surprises at the college. The first pleasure was the mandatory English 101 course, taught by Joan Coldwell. She was a superb lecturer, was new to the college, and made the subject come alive. She had real depth of knowledge, and she built further on the work of a splendid English teacher at North Saanich High School, the late Gil Bunch. Second was the pleasure of meeting some of the other new students, among them the funny and delightful Kathy Butt from Saltspring Island,

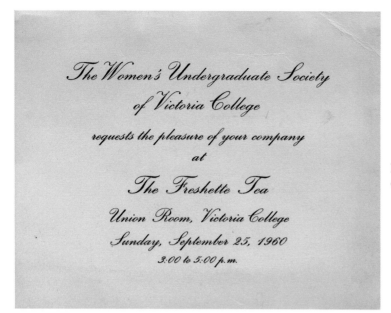

Invitation to the Victoria College Freshette Tea, 1960.

Sue Mearns, an athletic hero, and the two handsome M's – Michael Stephen and Martin Petter from Victoria. Third was the drama club directed by Tony Jenkins, also new to the college. Several of my friends, such as Chris Morley, were cast in *The Taming of the Shrew*, in which I played Bianca, and we had great parties led by Dale Irvine ("Mrs," as the *Tower* put behind her name). In fine art I wrote a paper on stained glass windows and found a new world of interesting history in doing so, and in history Tony Emery managed to convey his considerable boredom with the subject while remaining a lively and interesting person.

Apart from that, I recall little now except having to go into the classrooms to observe other teachers and a couple of highly enjoyable weeks staying with Kathy Butt's family on Saltspring Island, where we both worked in those schools. The highlight of that assignment was several cougar attacks on local sheep flocks. The island men killed the cougar and brought it into our classroom, where the very self-possessed young islanders had a good look at this enemy of sheep.

However, it was neither the courses nor the entertainment that I best remember looking back, but rather the atmosphere and values embedded in the college. It had been sponsored originally by McGill University; so the history and active understanding was that we were not just a provincial institution. By definition, the faculty members had studied elsewhere and saw themselves within the international context of their disciplines. They conveyed the sense that we were part of a much larger world of learning, scholarship, and public affairs – a world they knew about. There was a sort of "can do" message in their conversation and expectations for us: "You may be in Victoria now, but you can go anywhere in the world." It was truly the optimism of the early 1960s. Looking back, I see what a touchstone that message was for us all. We could get a job almost wherever we went; exciting things would happen to us all; Victoria College was much bigger in spirit than the city, the province, or even Canada. They exuded quiet confidence that gave many of us the grounding for our lives.

From the age of four in Sidney, I had known Michael Morris, and so at the Christmas break I went to Michael's party and met Edward (Ted) Harvey, a *coup de foudre*. They were part of a group determined to have interesting lives. Michael was already a recognized artist and knew the leading artists in the area. Katy Robertson was a budding actor, and I had known her in high school. The handsome Bob Howay was in film and, with the beautiful Val Byers, made a great couple. Ted organized jazz concerts at a downtown place called The Scene, and through him I met the bassist Charles Mingus and his manic drummer, Danny Richmond, and many other people in the arts. In the fall of 1961, Ted and I went to England, got jobs, and travelled in France and Spain.

Connected as I was to the experience of my older siblings, it took some time to realize what major changes were occurring in Canadian society at the time. It was truly quite discontinuous from the fifties in many ways and perhaps especially for women. The intimate memories of the war were diminishing. The baby boom was almost over. The women's movement was tuning up. The Quiet Revolution was emerging in Quebec. Postwar immigration was enriching the major cities and soon the entire culture. The music of dissent topped the sexuality of Elvis. We were challenged by the use of street drugs, the sexual revolution, and the independence we had won. Throughout our careers that "can do" attitude of Victoria College, that sense that change was welcome and that we had a solid footing in the world, helped many of us to cope with the challenges of our lives.

These early friends and acquaintances have turned up in many parts of my adult years in Toronto and in Ottawa, as well as in my visits home to British Columbia. Many of them, and many others I knew, became leaders in their fields – distinguished artists like Michael Morris, like Katy Robertson in New York and LA theatre, and like the late Jim Taylor in the judiciary – but all too many friendships disappeared as we got absorbed in our own careers and family lives. Some friends did not make it safely through the sixties and early seventies. My sisters and their friends, who have themselves led creative and fascinating lives but who at the time seemed much too old to be my friends, meld at reunions and family visits into the "Vic College crowd." Somehow we've all become the same age.

Now, forty-six years later, still married to Edward Harvey, and after a lifetime of work in universities, politics, and the women's movement, I can appreciate what Victoria College really gave us all: a taste of an expansive world and the confidence to explore it.

THE HONOURABLE LORNA R. MARSDEN, CM, OM, PHD, LLD (hon.), is a former senator of Canada. She has also held various senior university administration posts, including vice-provost at the University of Toronto, president and vice-chancellor of Wilfrid Laurier University, and president and vice-chancellor of York University. She serves as a director of a number of private-sector corporations, including Manulife Financial and SNC Lavalin. She is also a volunteer director of such public-sector corporations as Roy Thomson Hall/Massey Hall and the Gardiner Museum. Dr Marsden is currently president emerita and professor at York University, where she is active in research and writing. She is the author or co-author of numerous books and articles.

JOHN H. YOUSON
VIC '60

When I was asked to consider writing something about my memories of university life at the Lansdowne campus of Victoria College/UVic from 1960 to 1964, I had very positive thoughts of an experience that seemed like yesterday. I could not, however, focus on one aspect of the experience; rather, the words academic, atmosphere, social, and sports immediately came to mind. The following paragraphs are my recollection of these four features of university life at this campus during this period, with emphasis on their impact on my subsequent education and on my life as a university academic. To put things into perspective for the reader, I felt it was necessary to establish some sort of baseline in order to show development. The baseline was what I felt about education as I entered Vic College at the Lansdowne campus.

I came to Vic College in September of 1960 as one who had focused his prior educational experience on student politics and sports. While I was Student Council president at Oak Bay High School (OBHS) in 1959–60, a frustrated teacher of English summed me up as I was leaving the classroom (after my request to do so was denied) to make an announcement to the student body about the school dance that night as "160 pounds of useless meat." I was insulted because I was only a maximum 150 pounds at the time and believed that my muscles (i.e., meat) were useful on the soccer, rugby, and track teams. At any rate, I know now that she was probably making reference to my brain, and she still showed up to the dance that night with two detention slips in hand. I gather that the wind must have caught the door and made it slam on my way out of the classroom.

Given this background, the academic entrance standards could not have been too high at Vic College in the early 1960s. Many of us who entered the college in 1960 would likely not get into most universities today if we had only our high school credentials of that date. We did not think or worry much about not getting in, for it was a natural progression and the trend of the day. A glance at the first-year class of 1960–61 at Vic College looks like my graduating class of 1960 from OBHS. However, it was more like an amalgamation of graduates from several Victoria high schools to create a grade thirteen class at the Lansdowne campus. This gave me a sense of security and familiarity, for in the first-year class I was surrounded by friends from across the city whom I had known for years, primarily through my participation in sports and church activities. Small class sizes created kinship among classmates, and I made many new friends and discovered that not everyone was from Victoria. Throughout my four years, I never experienced a sense of competition but only a willingness to help others if the occasion arose. In 1969 I began my academic teaching career at Scarborough College in the University of Toronto with about the same student and faculty population as Vic College in 1960. I chose this place of employment over larger institutions because of my very positive experience as an undergraduate student at Vic College, but as one of the three campuses of a large university, my new college had an atmosphere of competition among students, particularly among those who had ambitions to enter health-related professions such as medicine and dentistry.

Despite our academic or study-habit deficiencies when we entered Vic College in 1960, many of us left as the first UVic graduating class (1964) with degrees of first- and second-class standing. Many of these graduates were not the "brainy ones" of high school years but the jocks and the loafers like myself who had found the right groove and the personal drive at Vic College. I attended the Convocation of the fortieth anniversary of UVic in 2003, when the class of 1964 was honoured and our degrees were reconfirmed. What an impressive group of successful individuals! The academic program at Vic College, Lansdowne campus, was doing something right in the early 1960s, and I have always believed that we early graduates of UVic were the positive product of good teachers and the freedom to explore different disciplines. Vic College was a wonderful liberal arts college, much like what we know today of Mount Allison University in Sackville, New Brunswick, with only approximately two thousand students but one of Canada's premier undergraduate institutions. However, Vic College was destined to grow into the highly respected, moderately large UVic of today, and I am extremely proud to say that I was in its first graduating class.

The bachelor of arts program that I encountered at Vic College in the fall of 1960 was one that had some structure, with mandatory courses, but also allowed some freedom of choice. The mandatory two years of English, the two years of a secondary language, mathematics, and a science course were a great influence on directing me into my future career but also were useful to this career. The modest structure in first year was an important directive for me, for I was still flying very high after my nearly two summer months in Europe with the BC Student Travel Association. I went into the college with the view of taking history, my favourite subject in high school. I started second year thinking I might be a United Church minister, but I graduated with a BA in zoology and biology, with two courses short of a sociology degree and a keen desire to enter graduate school in a biological discipline. My grandfather was a United Church minister, and he quoted me from the pulpit, when he asked me when I was quite young what I wanted to be when I grew up, as stating, "I would like to be a doctor but I don't think I have the brains, therefore, I will be a minister." The Vic College program and its educators did something well to help build my confidence and to guide me in a direction that led to my attainment of a doctorate, but a doctor of philosophy in zoology.

The academic program and the related experiences at Vic College were a major influence on me as a university educator and adviser. I forever supported the broad-based programs that permitted student freedom to explore, and during my duties as an adviser, I used myself as an example of how course diversity works in undergraduate years and can yield some big surprises. I had close to a failing grade in biology in December in grade twelve at OBHS, mainly because of my mistreatment of frog gonads with my friend Bob Turner. It was pleasurable to view the shocked look on the face of my OBHS biology teacher at the school's reunion in 1980 when she discovered that I was a university biology professor. The lasting effects of the Vic College academic freedom of choice, other than the mandatory courses referenced above and again below, was a bachelor of arts in biology and zoology sufficient to get me into graduate school in a medical department at McGill University, a lifelong passion to read history, an appreciation of the discipline of sociology, and a knowledge of Latin that was a boon to me as a biologist.

The mandatory courses were fun. It was a sort of status symbol to report how many times you had taken the second-year English course. The rumour at the time was that there was a sliding scale and they had to fail at least 50 per cent of the class; otherwise you would not be around to teach next year. I was given 48 per cent in both the regular final and then again in the summer supplemental (studied while I was surveying trees and insects for the Federal Forest Service in Prince George). When I went to see my new professor of English for the next year (Peter Smith) for advice on what was going wrong, he looked at my supplemental paper and said that he would have given me a minimum 65 per cent but he could do nothing at that point in time. The lesson here was that I never gave a 48 per cent in my thirty-six years of university teaching and never had to scale marks, although I never believed the story about the scaling of second-year English grades at Vic College. By the way, I enjoyed the second time around for second-year English mainly because of the teaching methods and enthusiasm of Peter Smith. I was so enthralled with his teaching that I took a course in Latin grammar from him and obtained the highest grade in my four-year stint at Vic College.

I got kicked out of one French class in each of my first two years at Vic College, both from classes in the Young Building. In first year it was by Mrs L. Travis, formerly Lorraine Brand, and we had grown up together in the same section of Richmond Avenue. Her father was George Brand, assistant to the director of Teaching Education. She lived next to Vice-Principal Bob Wallace, and the latter in turn lived next to Harry Gilliland, the director of Teaching Education – that is, three Vic College administrators in a row just several houses down the street from my home. I was sitting in the front row, and I made a perfect "swish shot" with a band-aid into the garbage can two feet in front of me and not near Mrs Travis. I had just given blood to the Red Cross during the noon hour, and according to the directives from the nurse who drew my blood, it was time to remove and discard the band-aid. In those days at Vic College, no favouritism was shown to neighbours, and my former neighbour asked me to leave her classroom. In my second-year French, we had a male professor whom I believe was Gerald Moreau. Every lecture he would come to class and yell, "Attention" (in French), and then slam his fist several times on the lectern. Like second-year English, a second year of a language was a prerequisite for a bachelor of arts at the time. So there were many like myself, and many jocks from the rugby and hockey teams, who were there for the credit only. On one particular day we had been discussing the ritual entrance of this professor to the classroom, and someone suggested that we should beat him to it someday. I did "it" that day, and he was not amused and I was asked to leave the room. The happy part of these stories for me is that I managed to pass both French courses, and they served me well in my years as a graduate student: first in my two years of an MSc in Montreal and secondly in my doctorate at the University of Western Ontario, where there is a secondary language requirement. Surprisingly, although I never learned to speak good French, those two years learning French grammar permitted me to read scientific French in preparing review articles for publication over my years as an academic. The second lesson I learned from these two experiences in French classes is that it is probably permissible to expel students from the university classroom if they are disruptive. In my first year as university professor, I expelled four students simultaneously from my first-year biology course for being inattentive. The four came to see me after class, and they all apologized and thanked me. They told me much later that this expulsion from class was a major turning point for them, for they were wasting their time. The four turned into a family dentist, an oral surgeon, and two MBAS (one also with chartered accountancy certification). They did their undergraduate theses in my research laboratory, I went to the weddings of two of them, and the oral surgeon extracted one of my teeth that had been fractured in an accident. Can we say that these success stories all began in my expulsion from French classes in the Young Building of the Lansdowne campus? Incidentally, I taught high school science to technical-stream students in Ontario for one year between my MSc and my PhD. Needless to say, flower parts (learned at Vic College in a botany course) were of little interest to these students, and discipline was my main focus. Perhaps a few lessons about classroom instruction were learned there too.

My memory of Vic College at Lansdowne was that, with few exceptions, I had excellent teachers. I had Peter Smith for two courses: my second time around for second-year English and for Latin. As noted above, Peter was everything you would wish for in a course instructor. His enthusiasm and energy were infectious, and he made you feel that he cared about your success. I also recall Roy Watson, who taught just about every course in sociology and left me with the impression that he knew everything about this discipline. However, Arthur Fontaine in biology became my unofficial mentor and had the greatest influence in directing me towards my future career. It impresses me to this day how the biology faculty, particularly Arthur, could teach so many different courses with such ease. Arthur was an instructor in Comparative Anatomy, Microscopic Anatomy and Embryology, Genetics, Ecology, Invertebrate Zoology, and the History of Biology. As a former department chair at the university level, I had to deal with pressure from faculty to reduce teaching assignments and wouldn't dare (for fear of reprisals from the Faculty Association) ask anyone to teach something even slightly different from their research field. I was particularly stimulated by the field of microscopic anatomy (histology), and Arthur directed me to apply to the Department of Anatomy at McGill University. A McGill graduate in biology himself, he was aware of the high profile of the chair of the anatomy department. The acceptance of Arthur's suggestion turned out to be very positive for me, for I found my confidence and my niche, and I met my wife of nearly forty-two years. I know of at least three other Vic College/UVic graduates of my era – Ernie Leenheer, Conrad Reifel, and Bruce Crawford (the latter is a professor in the Division of Medical Sciences, UVic, Island Medical Program) – who went to graduate school in a similar field and had successful teaching and/or research careers in Canada. The common element among us was instruction in histology by Arthur Fontaine, mostly in the cramped quarters of the biology laboratories in the annex section (wooden buildings) at the back of the Lansdowne campus. A research project Arthur assigned for ecology – to monitor and interpret data with my class partner, Ann Thompson (now Scarfe), the daily and hourly inflow and outflow of ducks and other waterfowl into the ponds and fields of Beacon Hill – was the first stimulus to my hidden talent of research curiosity. I still can identify most western waterfowl, and every morning when in Victoria on my morning walk in Beacon Hill Park, I think of that research project.

I recall having one poor teacher of first-year mathematics. There was no doubt that this instructor had a brilliant mind, but he had no gift or ability to explain principles. I got through that course, along with my long-time friend and neighbour Brian Wallace, only because his father was the chair of the Mathematics Department and graciously gave up some of his professional (not neighbourly or fatherly) time to teach Brian and me the basics. I don't believe that instructor was around for a second year.

A secondary form of education for me at Vic College at the time was the number of excellent lectures by invited speakers given in the auditorium of the Young Building. In particular, I remember hearing Lester Pearson, later to become prime minister of Canada, and how direct the questions were from the student listeners. In retrospect, this was an example of the way that university students and other young people around the globe in the 1960s would challenge the status quo.

Lansdowne campus was the home of a small college where everyone seemed to know one another. What other secondary education facility was small enough in 1961 to allow the picture of every student in their fine attire in the yearbook, the *Tower*? Throughout my four years, to be included in a photograph for the yearbook meant student members of clubs in only their finest: men in shirts, ties, and jackets; women in skirts with blouses or in dresses.

There was a feeling of change with the opening of the E.B. Paul Building in 1960 and designs for a science building. I liked the Lansdowne campus, and I don't recall great personal excitement with turning of the sod for the campus at Gordon Head. I had only a single biology course and a chemistry course in one of the first buildings at Gordon Head, the Elliott Building, and the library is a vague memory. After the cramped, antiquated quarters for science laboratories at the Lansdowne campus, it seemed at first as if I had finally arrived in the modern world. However, I missed the intimacy of the old facilities and the interaction with friends in other disciplines. Besides, we had to put up with the mud on our shoes when tramping around in the early days at Gordon Head, and then we brought it back with us to the seemingly pristine environment at Lansdowne.

The atmosphere of academic freedom in classroom attendance did not work well for everyone. Two of my first-year classmates were present mostly in name only, for they decided to run a new radio station, either KTEN or KTIN (also the acronym for "kitten"), that supposedly attracted "teenyboppers." Their office was in the front window of Woolworth's store at Yates and Douglas. We always knew when they were on campus because the dressed-up vehicle of one of them was distinguished by its lowered seats and bedroom atmosphere. Another OBHS classmate was purported to be trying to date his young geography professor. Not much went on without the knowledge and the comment of most of the students (and probably the faculty too) in this intimate campus atmosphere. As is the situation today, university life was not for everyone, and a degree did not guarantee success. What I do know is at least two of these individuals referenced above have been successful businessmen and committed participants in the life of their communities.

The majority of us at the Lansdowne campus were from Victoria, and in later years we have commented on how insulated we were from outside events. Then 22 November 1963 took the innocence and the isolation away, and we realized by our emotional reaction to the assassination of President J.F. Kennedy that we had entered into the real, new world. I still visualize myself in the front row of a classroom in the E.B. Paul Building when the professor made the announcement that, in respect and because he could not go on, that the class was cancelled because President Kennedy had been shot.

Other than the graduation dance at the Curling Club, where I first heard and danced to the Beatles, and the "Sock Hops" at the new Student Union Building in my final year, most of my memories of dances are of more formal events at the Crystal Gardens. To the smell of chlorine from the pool, we drank our rye and 7 Up or ginger ale. The mickey of rye (purchased at the only government liquor store that I remember in Victoria, on Humboldt Street) was under the table in a paper bag, for nobody was supposed to drink at these dances. I didn't like hard liquor and hated the breathalyzer test my mother gave me when I got home, but for many, it was the thing to do. Dancing at the Crystal was called semi-formal, but it was very formal by today's standards, with a corsage for the women and sometimes a boutonniere for the guys. We danced to some rock and roll but usually with bands such as the Acres, made up of members the age of my parents. There was much "big band" music, but. I remember this band particularly because the drummer, Bert Acres, was a junior partner in my father's business.

The "caf" was the place to be, and particularly in my first two years, I spent far too much time there. A lot of crib and other card games were played, particularly "Hearts." In the first year one of my former OBHS classmates had his "office" there, where he bought all old quarters that you could bring to him at sometimes twice the value. I think I made more that way than I did working part-time on the weekends in the Hardware Department of the T. Eaton store on Douglas Street. I recollect a very stern, at times, but fun-loving manager of the café, Mrs Norris. She had her favourites; so it was important to be nice to her. In retrospect, I believe that she put up with a lot of poor student behaviour in very antiquated, smoky quarters.

Frosh Week and TWIRP week were the highlights for me in my first year. The treatment of the frosh was harsh but fair. I particularly remember lining up on the Gordon Head field with frosh in one line and others, more senior, facing them in another line. Eggs, tomatoes, and other items were thrown. I felt uncomfortable wandering in long lines through various stores in downtown Victoria, especially when the police arrived. In later years I was part of the group of seniors who made the frosh endure the same pain and embarrassment that I had suffered. My views of the Frosh Weeks in my years as an academic were that they were very calm compared to those four years that I had observed at Lansdowne. The TWIRP week, when the women held the upper hand, was a fun time, as long as you were not selected to be centred out by a group of vengeful women.

You certainly had no excuse to be idle, for there were clubs for everyone and everything. Included were different language and discipline clubs, groups for each political party and every hobby or activity (jive, jazz, band, and choirs), and even a Listening Club. The WUGS and the MUGS were the most prominent clubs on campus and had most of the highly active students as members. Having been very active in student life in high school, I had the highest respect for students who devoted their time to governance.

Because of the absence of sports facilities at the Lansdowne campus in my years at Vic College, anyone who played a sport was introduced earlier than the non-participant to more aspects of the Gordon Head campus. Even then, the playing fields, the primitive change rooms, and the gymnasium (the hanger) were no more than just adequate.

Throughout most of my high school years, Victoria High School dominated in basketball. Vic High graduates made up the nucleus of the successful basketball teams of my period at Vic College (with smaller contributions from OBHS and Esquimalt High). In my first year the upstart men Vikings beat the UBC Jayvees. The women's team was second in the BC finals. These earlier successes may have marked the beginning of the trademark excellence of Vic College/UVic basketball that has lasted to the present day.

My specialty was soccer, and many members of our team in my first year also played for the senior team, Victoria West, in the Victoria District League. The college made the decision that members of its soccer team could play for only one team, and so Victoria West was my choice for years two and three and for year four for UVic. The teams were strong from 1960 to 1964, but good competition was hard to find, and the team was rather low-profile on campus in these early years. Speaking of difficulty in finding teams to play against, one of my close friends, Ron McMicking, recalls the game against the William Head "Steelers." The 1962–63 Vic College team was a powerful squad that topped their local league and also beat the UBC Thunderbirds. The soccer Vikings had entered the Victoria District League competition by the time I graduated. The influence on me was that after graduation from UVic, I went on to play on the McGill University team that won the Ontario-Quebec Athletic Association championship over my future employer, the University of Toronto.

The team sport with the highest profile was rugby. There was sufficient interest and talent to field a first and a second team. The *Tower* of 1961 describes Vic College rugby teams as "warlike," and I can vouch for the fact that this was the truth, both on and off the field. Members were party-loving and hard-drinking animals who usually were the instigators and "accomplishers" of most of the pranks on and off the campus. There was a particular dislike of the "rodents" of Royal Roads Military College in Colwood, for they played rough in rugby and they stole our women for their sophisticated formal dances. One day their cannon appeared at the meeting place between the Young and Ewing Buildings. It is surprising that this rugby team yielded so many high-quality alumni who had successful careers in law, medicine, academia, and business.

The men's hockey team had its inaugural season in 1960–61, and by the time I graduated from UVic in 1964, it was the team that had the largest following and generated the most enthusiasm among the student population. Like the "ruggah" players, the "hockey jocks" were a rough-and-tumble group who made their mark off the ice on the Lansdowne campus. Their successes and failures on the ice were a common topic of the campus.

There were strong teams in women's grass hockey (sufficient interest for a first and second team) and in men's water polo and volleyball. The situation in the women's grass hockey team, the first team called the Valkyries, may be partially explained by the early training of many members in the girls' private schools in the Victoria area. In my days at Vic College, they were consistently on top of the Victoria Ladies League, where they won the Bridgman Cup several years. Men's grass hockey teams (the Goths and the Vandals) appeared during my tenure at Vic College and were an instant success story in a men's league in Victoria. The men's water polo team in the early years had many members of the strong high school swim teams of Victoria, particularly OBHS, including the Olympian Bob Wheaton.

In retrospect, I am very happy to have experienced the familiarity and collegiality of Vic College at the Lansdowne campus but also to have been in the first graduating class of a new university that developed its base at the Gordon Head campus during my years at the institution. As indicated above, some of the events of my education at Lansdowne, although they seemed problematic at the time, ended up contributing the most to the direction and execution of my career. I feel particularly grateful for the well-balanced, educational program and the excellent teachers who put up with my antics, stimulated my interest, and brought out of me, for the first time, a hidden curiosity for biological research.

JOHN H. YOUSON, PHD, is a distinguished comparative endocrinologist who spent most of his career at the University of Toronto until his recent retirement. While continuing his research – he is the author of over three hundred publications – he also served as an administrator at the university in such capacities as chair of the Department of Life Sciences, associate principal for Research and Graduate Studies, interim vice-president, and interim principal of the University of Toronto at Scarborough. He is the recipient of many important awards, including the J.C.B. Grant Award from the Canadian Association of Anatomy, Neurobiology, and Cell Biology in 2003 and the F.E.J. Fry Medal from the Canadian Society of Zoologists in 2005.

JOHN SARGENT
VIC '60

Since I have only a very limited supply of entertaining stories or profound reflections from the one year I spent at Vic College, I shall pad my recollections with some statistics intended to help put the college in 1960–61, especially that year's entering class, in context. I would have preferred to be able to provide the scoop on how many students majored in bridge, to the exclusion of virtually any classroom attendance, and how they fared at year-end, or on how far the administration went in insisting that women students wear skirts rather than slacks. (I owe these two examples to Jane Gilliland Patterson.) Hopefully, other contributors from the same era will fill these and other gaps.

While my impression was that I was attending an institution not that different from the Vic College of the mid-1950s (Peter Smith's "golden age"), the transition from a two-year college to – at least – a four-year college still under the UBC umbrella was in fact well underway by my entering year. Third-year courses had been introduced in 1959–60, and fourth year courses in 1960–61. The student body, however, was still heavily weighted to first and second year. In Arts and Science, first-year students accounted for 61 per cent, and second-year students 22 per cent of the total 816 registered. In Education, first-year students accounted for 36 per cent, and second-year students – whose number was influenced by a substantial inflow of "transfer" students from elsewhere in British Columbia – accounted for 54 per cent of the 576 total. Including 21 students in first-year Commerce and Business Administration, first- and second-year students in all faculties accounted for 85 per cent of the total student body of 1,413. The Arts and Science student body was predominantly (72 per cent) male, while Education was 70 per cent female. Men accounted for 56 per cent of the entire student body.

I do not recall Vic College being exceptionally crowded, though several labs and the cafeteria were housed in old army huts. My recollection is that the courses I was in ranged in size from around twenty to around eighty. I have no impression, however, of the office space situation for professors. The opening of the Paul Building part way through 1960–61 did ease any strain.

It was the case, nevertheless, that the student body had been growing at a substantial pace starting after 1956–57. The number of first- and second-year Arts and Science students receiving credit for at least some courses in the 1960–61 final exams was more than twice the corresponding number in 1956–57. Including the newly added third and fourth year and all faculties, the student body in 1960–61 was two and one-half times its size in 1956–57. This rapid growth, which was the pattern across Canadian universities in this period, reflected both a considerable increase in the student-age population, resulting from the progressive recovery of births from the Depression low in 1937 plus immigration, and an increased participation in university education. Rapid growth continued in the immediately following years and then received a further boost as the leading edge of the baby boom reached university age in 1964–65.

The decision to construct a new campus at Gordon Head was announced a few weeks after the end of the 1960–61 academic year. I can't recall being aware that something along these lines was brewing or that the change in status to an autonomous degree-granting institution, announced in January 1963, was also in the wind. From a rereading of Peter Smith's *A Multitude of the Wise: UVic Remembered,* it seems a reasonable guess that those more aware of internal discussions may well have seen that these fundamental changes were coming. But a substantial number of other frosh persons may have shared my ignorance.

I had presumed through high school that I would follow the old model and attend Vic College for two years and then transfer to UBC. (Engineering students had to transfer after first year.) With very few exceptions, my acquaintances who went on to college entered Vic College rather than choosing to go somewhere further afield, at least for their initial year. Most or all lived at home during their time at Vic. I didn't even consider other possible options; nor did high school teachers or my parents raise the possibility of other options. This probably reflected a mix of Victoria tradition, cost considerations, some preference for a gradual transition from high school to life away from home at large institutions, and implicit confidence in Victoria College's reputation for providing a very solid academic base from which to go elsewhere at a later stage.

In first year I decided, on rather slim grounds, that I wanted to do an honours degree in economics and political science and began studying the UBC calendar. I found that the honours degree course requirements would leave little opportunity to take courses outside these fields, started looking at other universities, found that McGill and Queen's had somewhat less constraining honours economics and political science programs, and ended up at McGill in second year. But until I began preparing this reminiscence, I had presumed that the majority of my classmates who went on to complete an undergraduate degree had continued the pattern of transferring to UBC for their last two years. In fact, registration statistics for 1960–61 through 1963–64, in the UVic Archives suggest that a majority of my Arts and Science classmates who made it to second year appear to have completed their degree at UVic.

One aspect of Vic College in 1960–61 that was likely little changed from several years earlier was the heavily Greater Victoria–weighted origin of the student body in Arts and Science. On the basis of the published final exam results, which conveniently list each student's hometown, 80 per cent of the first-year Arts and Science students came from Greater Victoria (including Sidney), 13 per cent from elsewhere on Vancouver Island, 6 per cent from the BC mainland, and a handful from elsewhere in Canada and from the United States. In Education, however, Greater Victoria accounted for only 46 per cent of first-year students, elsewhere on Vancouver Island for 19 per cent, and the BC mainland for 35 per cent.

Another feature that I believe had prevailed over several years was the rather high dropout and failure rate of first-year students, especially in Arts and Science. Of those registered in first-year Arts and Science in 1960–61, 44 per cent received a clear pass or better on the final exams; another 32 per cent received a pass with one or more supplemental exams or received credit in certain subjects. The fact that admission was open to any student who satisfactorily completed the high school University Entrance program likely resulted in less stringent admission standards than those that apply today.

My final context point relates to fees: they were $340 for the full 1960–61 academic year. This figure would correspond to $2,400 in 2007 dollars, taking account of the more than sevenfold increase in the Consumer Price Index since 1960. Current UVic fees are $5,154 – thus slightly more than double the 1960–61 level in real terms. It may be that, if we were to take account of growth in incomes over the last forty-seven years, there would not have been a major change in fees relative to average family income. It is worth noting that in 1960–61 the BC government provided a 50 per cent fee reduction to all students with a first-class average and a 33 per cent reduction to students with an upper-second-class average.

When I turn to the first-year experience itself, my recollections are favourable. I enjoyed the substantial increase in freedom relative to high school – freedom for the students in organizing their work; freedom for the profs, perhaps especially in English courses, in choosing literature selections and in their commentary; freedom for the student newspaper; and so on. All this is no doubt to be expected as one moved from high school to university, but it was nonetheless welcome. I found the professors for the courses I took to be generally good and in some cases outstanding. The library was quite adequate for first-year students, and the provincial Legislative Library was available as a supplement if desired in certain areas – for example, the first-year Canadian history course.

Perhaps my most memorable course was English 100, taken by all first-year students. The course had relatively small classes (under thirty, I believe) and, among other things, was intended to challenge students to improve their writing style. I was fortunate to have Professor Grant McOrmond, a talented and hard-working teacher who gave stimulating lectures in the literature component of the course and was determined to whip our writing style into better shape. We received short (two- to five-page) essay assignments every two or three weeks. McOrmond marked these with care and rigour; the version one received back was often colourful both in terms of red ink and the nature of the comments. His practice was to return the papers in class starting with the one that received the lowest mark. He would toss it to the unhappy recipient – often halfway across the room. For the first few essay assignments in the course, virtually everyone's paper warranted a "toss back." After a while, he was willing to hand-deliver a few of the better papers or at least toss them only a short distance.

The demanding standards and individual attention in this course made a real difference to me, both in subsequent years in university and in my career as a government economist. The course provided one of the most valuable and lasting benefits I received from attending Vic College. More generally, I found that first year at Vic College left me well prepared for second-year honours courses at McGill. The only qualification would be my guess that, in those years, first-year pre-honours math at Vic College may not have been as demanding as first-year pre-honours math at McGill.

One need only glance at the *Tower* for 1961 to see that Vic College offered a wide range of athletic, theatrical, musical, academic, and social extracurricular activities. My casual impression is that participation was widespread. Not included in the *Tower* but a significant activity for a fair number of the male students was participation in the reserve officer training programs: the UNTD for the navy, the COTC for the army, and the URTP for the air force. Training was generally one evening a week during the university term and full-time during the summer vacation. For me, on the basis of my experience in the UNTD, one of the benefits of these programs – especially the four-month summer training period, generally located at a single base for officer cadets from all Canadian universities – was contact and friendships with contemporaries from across the country.

Overall, my impression – admittedly not at all original – is that the Victoria College of this period provided a very solid first-year academic program in a congenial environment. As mentioned, I'm not in a position to comment on the upper years. Vic College also furnished lots of opportunity for other activities. I have always viewed the college with respect and affection.

JOHN SARGENT, BA, entered Victoria College in 1960 and, after a year there, went on to McGill University, where he received the gold medal on graduating in economics and political science in 1964. After three years of graduate studies in economics at the Massachusetts Institute of Technology, he taught economics for three years at Queen's University. In 1971 John Sargent joined the federal Department of Finance, where he held senior positions in such areas as fiscal policy, financial sector policy, and tax policy. He was seconded to the Macdonald Royal Commission in the early 1980s and later served on the Royal Commission on National Passenger Transportation. He retired from the public service in 2003.

My freshman year at UVic was in 1962–63, the year before the university moved to Gordon Head and started granting its own four-year degrees. Many of my classmates from Oak Bay High School went right on to UBC or transferred there after two years, but I never even considered doing either one. I was only sixteen as a freshman, not ready to leave home yet. I planned to major in English, and the UVic department had a good reputation. I could live at home for four years, and my tuition would be covered by scholarships; my parents and I would not be out of pocket for any of my college expenses. At Bryn Mawr College, where I did my graduate work and where I now teach in the English department, my students pay somewhere in the neighbourhood of $30,000 for each year's room and board; it's an enormous financial investment. Not only did I graduate from college with no loans to pay off; by the time I was a junior, I had enough money left over from scholarships and a summer job in the Registrar's Office to buy a used Volkswagen. I loved that little car; it cost me $500.00, if memory serves.

The year before I enrolled as a freshman, my parents took me to a production of Shakespeare's *Othello* in the Young Building. I had acted in plays as often as I could since the third grade, but I hadn't seen much grown-up theatre at that point in my life. What was especially exciting about this production was that the cast was largely made up of UVic faculty members: Anthony Jenkins played Iago with a full measure of delight in his own capacity for evil; Peter Smith was lovably buffoonish in the role of Roderigo. These would be my teachers in a few years' time: how exciting was that! – as my teenage granddaughter might have said. They would also be involved in faculty-student theatre productions throughout my time at the university. Tony Jenkins, whose honours seminar whetted my appetite for the study of poetry, also directed a production of Harold Pinter's *A Slight Ache*, in which I was lucky enough to be cast. Peter Smith taught a classics-in-translation course that I took in my junior year, but by then he had already adapted Aristophanes' *The Birds* for Carl Hare's 1963 production, giving the play's satiric spirit a purchase on current political events. *The Birds* was an ambitious undertaking in every way, with an enormous cast. I spent many happy hours waiting to rehearse my scenes as a member of the Chorus in the army hut that became a transitional theatre space while the university relocated to Gordon Head.

Carl Hare's first year at UVic was also my freshman year. The following year he was joined by Robert Hedley, and from that point on, a first-rate theatre program began to take shape on the Gordon Head campus. But Hare and Hedley were members of the English department at first; while I was an undergraduate, the Theatre department as such was still a long way off. In retrospect, however, I feel fortunate to have arrived on campus before you could major in theatre. Those of us who were stage-struck may have spent more time producing plays than was good for our academic work, but the plays we worked on had been chosen with a view to giving us an education in European and American drama. During my four years at UVic we did Shakespeare, Jonson, Ibsen, Yeats, Christopher Frye, Arthur Miller, Edward Albee, Harold Pinter, and Eugene Ionesco – a rich diet of classical and contemporary plays. *The Death of a Salesman* was required reading in my freshman English class, but I learned more about modern tragedy by working as assistant director on another play of Arthur Miller's, *A View from the Bridge*. Bill West, a local artist who taught for many years at Oak Bay High, was our set designer for many of these productions; Biddy Gaddes, whose husband chaired the Psychology Department, designed the costumes and supervised their construction. These adults shared their time and expertise and also, to some extent, their lives with us; we got to know them "in the round."

One or two of the plays we performed every year included faculty members in the cast, and it was a great privilege to work alongside these older actors, watching them find their way into the material as the rehearsal period unfolded. Harry Hill, a wonderful comic actor, always stuttered quite badly to begin with – so much so that he would change the text as needed to avoid certain combinations of letters. And yet by the time the play opened, the lines would all be there as written and Harry's stutter would be gone. "Who is it, Fool, who is shaking the bench?" my fellow student Walter Bell would say to Harry every night at the climax of W.B. Yeats's *Riders to the Sea*, playing the Blind Man to Harry's Fool. And every night would come the tragic answer, with its special, unforgettable music: "It is Cuchulain who is shaking the bench; it is his own son he has killed." Wow! I wasn't in the cast, but I would sneak into rehearsals to watch that scene in the more intimate of the Phoenix Theatre's two performance spaces. A number of careers in the theatre got started during those years. I think especially of Paul Bettis, who played Cuchulain in *Riders to the Sea*; Bettis had become a "towering presence" in Toronto's experimental theatre scene, his obituary notice said, by the time of his death in 2005. My fellow undergraduate Michael Whitfield became the resident lighting designer at the Stratford Shakespeare Festival, where he is still working, as far as I know.

As a young woman, I was getting mixed messages at the beginning of the 1960s about what to do with my life. Should I be preparing to have a career other than marriage? If I insisted on having a career, was I condemning myself to spinsterhood? My mother could not have been prouder of my academic achievements, but she also wanted me to be happy. One day she came home from a social gathering to report on her conversation with a twenty-something woman who had grown up in Victoria, studied for a master's degree in England, and was teaching at Vic College. "Tell Janey," this woman had purportedly said to my mother, "that a master's degree is okay, but if you go on for the PhD, then no one will want to marry you." My parents and my friends' parents had married "for life"; none of our mothers worked outside the home (except one, whom I pitied for having to come home after school "to an empty house"). My lawyer uncle had explained, when I told him I might like to be a lawyer, that as a woman I would never get to try any cases in court; I'd end up working behind the scenes for trial lawyers who were men. I never wanted to be a doctor, but one of my friends did; at our twenty-fifth high school reunion she told me she had become a hospital social worker instead of going to medical school, "because we didn't want to take a man's place." I remember that whole way of thinking very clearly: the problem with encouraging women to go to medical school was that it was an expensive course of training, and a woman could be expected to quit working as soon as she began to have children.

After graduating from high school with the highest marks in the province on the provincial matriculation exams, I was interviewed by the *Victoria Daily Times* in the summer of 1962. My parents kept the clipping; many years later I found it stashed away in a trunk full of keepsakes and came disconcertingly face to face with a sixteen-year-old whose bravado was equalled by her ambivalence. "I hate barging women," I am reported to have said; could I really have uttered those words? Six years later I would be in graduate school at Bryn Mawr, reading *The Second Sex* and barging off to Washington, DC, to demonstrate against the Vietnam War. I wanted to be a teacher, I told the *Times* reporter, because it was a career I could combine with marriage and children. Over the summer, I planned to read the novels of Tolstoy and Dostoevsky. That was pure bluff: I still haven't read *War and Peace*, and I was bluffing in other ways as well. The real reason I wanted to be a teacher was so that I could go on being a student for the rest of my life; that was what I did best and what made me happy. But not to be married was truly unthinkable. And, indeed, I would marry right out of college and then immerse myself so fully in my work that there didn't seem to be any time to start a family. By the time I had tenure, I was divorced; by the time I married again, it was too late for me to have children. Would I have made a good mother? Perhaps not. I am a good teacher, but the skill set is different. I am, however, fortunate to have grandchildren by way of my second marriage, and at this point, being a teacher does make it easier to spend time with them. *Carpe diem*, I say to myself as I arrange to take my granddaughter to the dentist and then drop her at school before heading over to teach my afternoon class.

Bryn Mawr, where I have been teaching Renaissance literature and poetry of all periods for over thirty years, is a women's college. "Only our failures marry," its first woman president is reported to have said – or perhaps what she said was "Our failures only marry." And sure enough, nowadays most of our undergraduates are headed for professional careers as well as for marriage and parenthood. In this, however, they are no different from women students in coeducational settings. Even at a women's college these young women do not want to call themselves feminists, but they do feel entitled to the fullest possible range of professional opportunities and life choices. Most of them marry later than I did; some of them don't marry men but enter into committed lesbian partnerships; some never marry; and some raise children as single parents. They become teachers and social workers, but they also go to law school and medical school in large numbers. Many of them work from home while their children are small or put their careers on hold with the expectation of picking up where they left off once their children are in school or in college. I worry that today's young women take too much for granted; we still have not figured out as a society how to structure our work to accommodate family life. But it's good to have been able to retire certain stereotypes during my lifetime: the "barging woman," the over-educated woman who has taken a man's place, the unhappy spinster with a PhD and no husband.

In spite of the mixed messages I was getting from the larger society in the early 1960s about what to do with my life after college, my teachers at UVic were as demanding and supportive of the women in their classes as of the men. And just as I was fortunate to have attended UVic before there was a major in theatre, so I feel fortunate to have been there as an undergraduate before there were graduate programs. Especially in the honours program, our classes were small; our professors gave us their full attention; we did a lot of writing. We took our fellow students seriously as readers and thinkers; our teachers did as well. Our extracurricular activities also had real substance. My friend Nan Elliott played on the basketball team; one year she had to take her final exams on the road, while the team was playing in the national championships back east. The Alma Mater Society was first incorporated in 1964, but there was a history of student government at Victoria College that extended further back. In the early sixties, university students were just beginning to flex their collective political muscle; we may not have had Hillary Clinton among us, but we did have strong political views.

On Lansdowne campus, my favourite place was the coffee shop behind the Young Building, where we gathered between classes for coffee, cigarettes, and conversation. Upper-classmen from the Players' Club seemed to spend entire days there – didn't they go to classes at all? As a freshman, while my status was still that of an "extra," I listened hungrily to the conversation, soaked up the atmosphere, and learned how to smoke. Meanwhile, I was also learning how to do college-level work from teachers whose classes I didn't cut as often as I was willing to have my friends think I did. My freshman English teacher, Margaret Doody, was herself fresh from Oxford, in her first year of teaching, with a distinguished career ahead of her as a scholar of the English novel. Miss Doody didn't just "correct" my essays; she would use her comments to get into conversation with me about the books I had written about and recommend further reading. At the time I wasn't ready to have my work taken quite so seriously; I probably did very little of the extra reading Miss Doody recommended. As I look back now, though, I see an implied lesson in her comments about the difference between high school and college that I want my students to learn as early as possible. Tony Jenkins, in my sophomore year, went out of his way to give me another lesson for which I was grateful, when an essay of mine was submitted to an essay competition he was judging. Professor Jenkins summoned me to his office, told me I had a lot to learn about how to write a good essay, and showed me the essay that had won the competition so that I could see for myself what was lacking in my own. Up to that point I had been a straight A student; I hadn't supposed that there *was* anything lacking, especially in my English papers. But I knew he was right: there was another level I could get to, an essay that would be more interesting both to read and to write than the one I had written.

Why did I not take even one philosophy course while I had the chance? Don't make that mistake, I say to my student advisees. I never took a course in art history either; whenever I go to an art museum, I buy the audio guide and wish I had more knowledge of the history of painting. That said, I know that the education I received at UVic was all of a piece: if I had made room for philosophy and art history, I might never have read Kafka's *Metamorphosis* in German or studied enough French to puzzle over the novels of Robbe-Grillet. The best kind of undergraduate education is formative rather than informative; a particular set of courses and extracurricular experiences induces a multifaceted process of intellectual growth. The University of Victoria gave me that kind of education. In recalling some of my crucially formative experiences for this little memoir, I have been freshly struck by how exciting it was to be there as a student during a time of such enormous change. I and my contemporaries attended UVic while the university's educational mission was itself under formation; we were luckier than we could possibly know at the time to be part of that process.

E. JANE HEDLEY, PHD, is Laurence Stapleton Professor of English at Bryn Mawr College, where she did her graduate work and has been a member of the faculty for over thirty years. She has directed the freshman English program, chaired the English Department, and recently served a three-year term as associate provost. Her scholarly work includes widely recognized publications on Renaissance lyric poetry, William Shakespeare, and American women's poetry since 1950.

IN MEMORIAM

EDITOR'S NOTE
Sadly, a number of members of the Lansdowne generation have died in the intervening years. Each of them has been mourned by family and friends and each of them has contributed to their communities and countries. Five of these alumni were mentioned several times by those interviewed for this book and so we memorialize them here while mourning the loss of all those who have died over the years. E.B.H.

WALTER D. YOUNG, 1933–1984
Victoria College '51

Walter Young entered Victoria College in 1951, but like so many others in his time at Lansdowne, he soon went "across the water" to UBC, where in 1955 he received his honours BA in English and history. He was awarded a Rhodes Scholarship and went on to Oxford; he obtained his MA there in 1957. After various teaching jobs back in Canada, he continued his graduate studies at the University of Toronto, receiving his doctorate in 1965.

Walter was a member of the Department of Political Science at UBC between 1962 and 1973, serving as head of the department for the last four years. He then moved to the University of Victoria to assume the chair of the Department of Political Science. He was also active in the New Democratic Party but resisted the temptation to run for public office. Scholarship was his true vocation, a calling reflected in his extensive writings. His 1969 book, *The Anatomy of a Party: The National CCF, 1932–1961*, published by University of Toronto Press, is widely considered a defining work on that period of Canadian socialism. Walter's talents and accomplishments were recognized in many ways, including his 1978 election to the presidency of the Canadian Political Science Association.

I first met Walter Young in 1969 when I was at the University of British Columbia for the summer. As good fortune would have it, he and his wife were planning a long trip co-incident with my time on the West Coast, and they kindly sublet their house to me. Located close to the university and enjoying fine views, it was a perfect venue for entertaining many of my old friends from my own UBC days. I recall a number of interesting conversations with Walter from that time.

Tragically, Walter Young died of a brain tumour at the age of fifty-one. His untimely death was a great loss to family, friends, and Canadian intellectual life.

E.B.H

HOWARD LIM, 1940–1995
Victoria College '58

Howard Lim entered Victoria College in 1958, and four years later he received an honours degree in psychology. He was an outstanding student with personal characteristics that matched his academic capabilities. His achievements were reflected in the numerous scholarships he received over his student career, the culmination of which was his being awarded a Woodrow Wilson Fellowship in 1962 to pursue graduate studies in psychology.

Howard had an easy, engaging manner that belied his driven nature. He would frequently get up at 5:00 a.m. to study, not typical behaviour in college students! He enjoyed the friendship and admiration of his peers and was active in college life. Among other things, he served as president of the Psychology Club and brought great energy and innovation to that organization.

Howard decided to pursue his advanced studies in psychology at Stanford University. I suppose we all expected him to enter university professorship; certainly, he had the requisite intellectual capabilities and communication skills. Instead, he took his expertise in psychology to the private sector, working with companies such as General Foods and JCPenney. Later in life, he increasingly devoted his energies to the study of Zen Confucianism and became involved in helping underprivileged people in Yonkers, New York, the area in which he lived.

As Dr Brian Little, a close friend of Howard's and one if his Lansdowne-era student colleagues, comments in his contribution to this book, "Howard was a luminously bright and complex man ... (He) was a model of the kind of student Vic College could turn out in the early sixties, and to say it was world-rank would not be at all a stretch." Tragically, Howard Lim died in 1995 at the hand of one of those people he was trying to help. He was fifty-five years of age.

E.B.H.

ROBERT HOWAY, 1938–1994
Victoria College '59

I never met anyone who didn't like Robert "Bob" Howay. Bob was a remarkable person. He was consistently genial and kind in his relationships with others. Beyond this, he was always loyal. I was fortunate to count him as a friend during my own time at the Lansdowne campus.

Bob was an exceptionally good-looking fellow, and this feature, combined with other talents, led him to a career in acting. His films included *Sweet Substitute* (1964) *Deadline for Murder* (1964), and *Waiting for Caroline* (1967). He was also active in television. His stage work included a late 1960s production of *Fortune and Men's Eyes*. Bob then decided to leave his acting career and go to law school. After completing his studies and being called to the bar, he established a successful entertainment law practice in Vancouver.

I last saw Bob in 1990 – after a hiatus of several years – when I was in Vancouver on business. We had a pleasant dinner, but more importantly, we took up the conversation with the ease of people who had last seen each other a week earlier.

Bob Howay kept himself fit and, among other things, was an enthusiastic mountain climber. Tragically, in June 1994, while climbing Border Peak near Chilliwack, BC, he slipped off a ledge and fell six hundred feet to his death. He is greatly missed by all of us who had the good fortune to know him.

E.B.H.

THE HON. JUSTICE JAMES D. TAYLOR, 1942–2006
Victoria College '60

The Honourable Mr Justice James D. Taylor was serving on the Supreme Court of British Columbia at the time of his sudden death of heart failure in January 2006. He had had a most distinguished career in legal practice, as a Crown prosecutor, and on the bench. While his law degree was from UBC, his undergraduate arts degree was from the University of Victoria, where he carried on from his first years at Victoria College.

For many of us, Jim was a great and admired friend. He had moved to Sidney as a schoolchild and graduated from North Saanich High School. With several of us from the school, he went on to Victoria College. Jim was always a serious student and stood at the top of the class in school and in the law as a careful scholar. But it was his personal character and his gentle, thoughtful ways that endeared him to so many of us. He was always wise in his judgments and responsive to the concerns of others, even as a teenager. There were many tributes to him from his legal colleagues when he died, but those of us who knew him before he was a lawyer shared affection and respect for an exceptional person, one we will not forget.

Whether Victoria College was important to him one can only guess, but he reflected many of the best qualities of the college and contributed to them in turn. He left a great legacy, not only to his four children and his wife but also to the province and the country.

LORNA R. MARSDEN (classmate)

JANICE (HICKMAN) SARGENT, 1943–2006
Victoria College '61

Janice Hickman was born in Victoria in 1943 and died there of cancer in 2006. She was the daughter of Grace and Harry Hickman; her father was the last principal of Victoria College before it became the University of Victoria, and both her parents were French specialists. She attended public schools in Victoria, Neuchâtel Junior College, Victoria College, and UBC (BA, honours French and English '64). She then continued French studies at Harvard (MA '65 plus completion of doctoral course work).

In second-year Arts and Science, Janice particularly valued and enjoyed her courses in English with Roger Bishop, in French with her father, and in Greek with Peter Smith.

She was an outstanding student, placing first in second-year Arts and Science at Victoria College and receiving the French government medal on graduating with first-class honours from UBC. Through her natural talent (perfect pitch likely helped), her family background, her studies, her year at Neuchâtel, and summers in France when in her early twenties, she became fluently bilingual.

Janice married John Sargent, also from Victoria, in 1966. After teaching briefly at Queen's University (she taught French and John, economics), they moved to Ottawa in 1971 when John joined the Department of Finance. Their daughter, Laurie, was born that year and son, Ted, in 1973. Laurie is now a lawyer with the federal Department of Justice in Ottawa, and Ted is a professor of electrical engineering at the University of Toronto.

In Ottawa, Janice led a productive and busy life as a mother and as a volunteer in her children's activities and at her church, often in leadership roles. In a message received by the family after her death, a friend and neighbour from that period wrote: "We remember Janice as a smiling, caring and vigorous member of our community. Her infectious enthusiasm in her quest for the best education in all fields: academic, sports and the arts, made our community a much richer environment in which to raise our children. What a joy it was to have been a part of her book fair team." And a friend from her church observed: "Janice made things happen."

During almost all of her thirty-three years in Ottawa, Janice was also employed: at first part-time as a freelance translator and later full-time as a school board policy officer. The director of the Ottawa-Carleton District School Board wrote of her: "Likely only you and I, John, know just how much Janice put into her work with me in Ottawa. Believe me, the students, staff and senior staff at the board had a treasure in Janice."

After retiring, Janice and John Sargent returned to Victoria in 2004. Although already suffering from cancer, she participated actively in St Aidan's United Church in committees and choirs, in the PEO sisterhood, and in the UVic Alumni. She bore the news of the initial diagnosis of breast cancer and of the subsequent metastases with little complaint, though she would dearly have loved to participate for much longer in her family's life. Until her last few weeks, when asked how she was feeling, she would usually respond, "Fine." In the last weeks, she might sometimes allow, "I've felt better." Until the end, Janice gave her time, energy, and love to her family and in the community.

JOHN SARGENT

PART THREE

CONCLUSION

THE LANSDOWNE ERA:

AN ENDURING TRADITION

EDWARD B. HARVEY

Such a difference a year makes. The school year 1952–53 was barely nine months long, but it was long enough to grow up a little, learn to challenge our world, and become excited about learning. It was also a year for making new friends through a variety of special-interest clubs, dates, parties, and dances – all wonderful memories from another era, over fifty years ago.
PATRICIA JONES, Vic '52

For most of us, Victoria College was a place we attended for a year or two before going on to other institutions to complete our post-secondary education. And yet – and the contributions from the former Lansdowne-era students certainly reflect this – the relatively short time was highly formative for many of us. It was so influential for many reasons, both personal and much larger. The largest reason was the atmosphere, the spirit, the *essence* of the era – it was a period in Canadian history of considerable optimism. It corresponded with what were probably the only couple of decades in our history when the ideal of the nuclear family was actually put into practice. For more women and men than ever before, a decent job, marriage, family, a house, children, good health, and education were available not only for the well-to-do but for the majority. As we recovered from the separations and privations of the war years, this was an incredible opportunity for our generation and especially for our parents. They had lived – most of them – through war and depression and then more war. Many had had their lives shortened and their dreams destroyed. They now lived through their children. We were those children and we were lucky.

The optimism I refer to above was a national phenomenon. But in Victoria, a smallish city where we met our student colleagues all over town, the mayor and other civic officials knew many members of the college community by name. We didn't live in residences at Victoria College for the simple reason that there weren't any. So we lived with our own or other families, and we were definitely part of civic life. Our pranks, our speakers on campus, our athletic triumphs, our successes, and our failures were in the local papers.

Of course, not everyone shared the optimism. As the Cold War advanced, some thought our future looked more dangerous, not less so. Racism, prejudice, and discrimination were still very much alive, and many students and would-be students were excluded and marginalized. Pursuing higher education was still a privilege and, as today, depended heavily on the values and assets of one's family. As students of the college, we did behave as an elite in the city. Our pranks had consequences for the work of others, and our apparently free time must have caused rancour in those school leavers who had to get a job right away. All of this was evident to some of us and had effects at the time, and more importantly, it defined the future lives of many of those who went into fields such as law and justice, social work and health care, education and public life. It can also be seen in the donation activity of many Lansdowne alumni, fostering opportunity through scholarships and bursaries, and through other forms of service to the university that started as a college.

In the college itself the sense of privilege was palpable: we could get to know our professors, and they took a real interest in us and our futures. The classes were quite small, and faculty members knew our names. As the stories in this volume show, they kept in touch with us throughout our lives, and we felt a bond to those who had been our first mentors. They cared about their teaching; they were conscious that we would leave for other places, and they hoped to prepare us.

Among ourselves, friendships and factions grew up quickly. Where one sat in "the caf" or in the classroom mattered and led to joining certain clubs, walking home with particular students, taking other students to dances or games. We had interesting debates across campus, and we learned a lot from one another – notwithstanding the brain cell–destroying properties of Mrs Norris's coffee in the notorious caf. Often we knew one another's families quite well as siblings followed each other to the college.

And we met people with a far wider range of interests and experiences than we had known at high school. There were people from the interior of British Columbia and from other parts of Vancouver Island. One of the Cold War consequences that actually affected us was the arrival in Canada of refugees from Eastern Europe. Some came to Victoria, and some of these became members of the college community.

One was Bohuslav Bohnmil Kymlicka, a twenty-five-year-old refugee from Czechoslovakia known as Bob to his friends. Kymlicka entered Victoria College in 1954 with no certificates of his prior education. As he explained in a talk he gave at Victoria College in March of 1956, "Dr Hickman was very kind. He took me by my face value." (For details of this talk, I am indebted to Avis Rasmussen, who attended the talk and knew Kymlicka personally.) Like so many of Harry Hickman's decisions, this was a good one. Kymlicka went on to be a distinguished academic, ultimately settling at the University of Western Ontario, where, in addition to his research, writing, and teaching, he held important administrative positions, including chair of the Department of Political Science, acting dean of Education, and dean of Social Science.

Students acquiring the beginnings of knowledge in the Ewing Building library, c. mid-1950s.

I did not know Bob Kymlicka at Victoria College (I attended rather later), but we met when we were both involved with the Commission on Post-secondary Education in Ontario. In one of our conversations, he mentioned the kindness and tolerance he had experienced from the people of Canada and, in particular, the exceptional openness, trust, and support he had encountered at Victoria College.

When I was in my second year at the college, I met another refugee from Czechoslovakia: Ambios Prechtel. Ambios was a compact, muscular, and invariably well-dressed man with an easy and engaging manner. He had two characteristics that differentiated him from most male students at Victoria College at that time. He was about ten years older than the rest of us, and he had a neatly trimmed, red-hued beard. (In that era, beards were not frequently seen.) Along with some of my friends and some of his, we would periodically gather at a new coffee house in Victoria which, with its checked tablecloths and Chianti-bottle candle holders, was set on emulating the beat generation culture that had taken root with the publication in 1957 of Jack Kerouac's *On the Road*. Ambios talked lucidly about his many experiences and adventures in Eastern Europe, including a stint of providing "close protection" to a prominent Czech family. But he also talked about the openness, tolerance, and support he had encountered in Canada and, closer to home, at Victoria College.

For the most part, we Victoria College undergraduates were young and did not have much experience of life. The opportunity to meet and dialogue with a wide range of people was an eye-opening experience, something that contributed to our maturation in a significant way. But this did not happen by chance. The college, apart from its commitment to scholarship and quality teaching, actively encouraged social exchange and expansion. This worked, at least in part, because of the optimistic spirit of the times, growing prosperity, and the fact that there were so few threats in our immediate environment. All of these factors re-enforced a certain openness and generosity of spirit, both institutionally and individually. It was a time when the middle class of the postwar era truly took root.

Victoria College was successful in fostering two qualities that are fundamental in shaping one's life. It gave us the opportunity to acquire the beginnings of knowledge that would enable us to go forward successfully in our education and our ultimate careers. For many, it fostered a lifelong love of learning. With its many social clubs, athletic events, and small size, the college also gave us the chance to develop and broaden our social skills – to learn from the different experiences of new friends, to develop an aptitude for teamwork, and to gain a better understanding of the diversity and complexity of life.

The words of former Lansdowne students express it well:

The distinguished faculty helped to advance the school in scholarship, always demanding the best from its students. And students responded. They did so because they saw this time as an opportunity to create the kind of future that many of their parents could only dream about. They did so because they had faith that, with an education, they could make a difference. These indeed were years of excitement, of promise, and of visions of things to come. This little school had become their launching pad.
RONALD LOU-POY, Vic '52

I am sure that without the assistance of the college faculty who came to my aid in a time of need, I might well have dropped out of school altogether. Their support, and the friendship and encouragement of my classmates, enabled me to complete my education and to have a satisfying and rewarding life as a lawyer and judge.
LANCE S.G. FINCH, Vic '55

Vic College ... was a class act.
BRIAN R. LITTLE, Vic '59

... after a lifetime of work in universities, politics, and the women's movement, I can appreciate what Victoria College really gave us all: a taste of an expansive world and the confidence to explore it.
LORNA R. MARSDEN, Vic '60

In recalling some of my crucially formative experiences for this little memoir, I have been freshly struck by how exciting it was to be there as a student during a time of such enormous change. I and my contemporaries attended UVic while the university's educational mission was itself under formation; we were luckier than we could possibly know at the time to be part of that process.

E. JANE HEDLEY, Vic '62

At the University of Victoria today, if you talk to the students, the faculty, the president – even the chancellor – you come away with a clear vision of how the values and qualities that shaped the Lansdowne era have prevailed over time. It is an enduring tradition.